KINDERGARTEN
Fours and Fives Go to School

Carol Seefeldt
Professor Emeritus
University of Maryland, College Park

Barbara A. Wasik
Principal Research Scientist
Center for Social Organization of Schools
Johns Hopkins University

Merrill
Prentice Hall

Upper Saddle River, New Jersey
Columbus, Ohio

Library of Congress Cataloging-in-Publication Data
Seefeldt, Carol.
    The kindergarten : fours and fives go to school / Carol Seefeldt, Barbara Wasik.
      p. cm.
    Includes bibliographical references and index.
    ISBN 0-13-014835-0
      1. Kindergarten. 2. Education, Preschool. 3. Early childhood education—Curricula. I.
Wasik, Barbara A. II. Title

    LB1169.S39 2002
    372.21'8—dc21   2001044493

Vice President and Publisher: Jeffery W. Johnston
Executive Editor: Ann Castel Davis
Editorial Assistant: Keli Gemrich
Production Coordination: Lea Baranowski, Carlisle Publishers Services
Production Editor: Sheryl Glicker Langner
Design Coordinator: Diane C. Lorenzo
Photo Coordinator: Valerie Schultz
Cover Designer: Ceri Fitzgerald
Cover Photo: Corbis/The Stock Market
Production Manager: Laura Messerly
Director of Marketing: Kevin Flanagan
Marketing Manager: Amy June
Marketing Coordinator: Barbara Koontz

This book was set in Palatino by Carlisle Communications, Ltd. It was printed and bound by R.R. Donnelley & Sons Company. The cover was printed by the Lehigh Press, Inc.

Photo Credits: Scott Cunningham/Merrill, pp. 9, 21, 41, 67, 70, 112, 154, 175, 245, 248, 251; Laima Druskis/PH College, pp. 61, 127, 148, 235; Jo Hall/Merrill, p. 88; Ken Karp/PH College, pp. 49, 101, 166; Teri Leigh Stratford/PH College, p. 171; Anthony Magnacca/Merrill, pp. 3, 33, 91, 131, 143, 233, 259, 265; Merrill, p. 81; Barbara Schwartz/Merrill, pp. 23, 64, 267; Seattle Post-Intelligencer Collection, Museum of History and Industry/CORBIS, p. 5; Julie Peters/Merrill, pp. 123,150; Anne Vega/Merrill, pp. 15, 27, 84, 136, 161, 192, 196, 201, 205, 209, 210, 221, 226, 241, 264; Todd Yarrington/Merrill, pp. 47, 107, 183, 187; Shirley Zieberg/PH College, pp. 44, 105.

Pearson Education Ltd., *London*
Pearson Education Australia Pty. Limited, *Sydney*
Pearson Education Singapore Pte. Ltd.
Pearson Education North Asia Ltd., *Hong Kong*
Pearson Education Canada, Ltd., *Toronto*
Pearson Educación de Mexico., S. A. de C.V.
Pearson Education—Japan, *Tokyo*
Pearson Education Malaysia Pte. Ltd.
Pearson Education, *Upper Saddle River, New Jersey*

10 9 8 7 6 5 4 3 2 1
ISBN: 0-13-014835-0

This book is dedicated to our families. Carol Seefeldt dedicates this text to the memory of her husband, Eugene Seefeldt. Barbara A. Wasik dedicates this book to the family that made her: Dad, Mom, Maryann, and Christine, and to the family she made: Jim, Julia, and Tommy.

PREFACE

chools for four- and five-year-olds are nearly universal today. These may be called kindergartens, pre-kindergarten, preschool, early enrichment programs, or some other name. Regardless of the name, more than 90 percent of all five-year-olds and more than 60 percent of four-year-olds in our nation attend kindergarten. Kindergarten is found not just in America but throughout the world, including England, Europe, the Far East, South and Central America, and some African nations.

Kindergarten programs may be half day or full day and everything in between. Full-day programs are popular because they offer children more learning time and respond to parents' needs for full-time schooling for their children. Today more than 56 percent of five-year-olds attend a full-day program, and about a fourth of all four-year-olds attend full day.

A new kind of teacher, one who is highly skilled and knowledgeable of four- and five-year-olds, their families, and the community in which they live and of the process of teaching curriculum content, is called for. This book, *Kindergarten: Fours and Fives Go to School,* was written to enable students to become effective teachers of four- and five-year-old children, whether they will teach in preschool, pre-kindergarten programs, or kindergarten for four- and five-year-olds. Because the text offers current, up-to-date views of readiness and deals with continuing issues in kindergarten education, in-service teachers will find the text a valuable resource as well.

FEATURES

Comprehensive

Kindergarten: Fours and Fives Go to School is a comprehensive guide to teaching in today's kindergartens or preschool programs for four- and five-year-olds. Part I places the kindergarten in historic perspective and presents current issues surrounding today's preschools and kindergartens. Part II includes chapters on the growth, development, and learning of four- and five-year-olds, and how to prepare classrooms, schools, and teachers to work with four- and five-year-olds. Part III presents chapters on planning and assessment and the integrated content areas of art, music, literacy, mathematics, and the life, physical, and earth sciences.

Focus on Child Growth and Development

Based on theories and principles of child growth, development, and learning, *Kindergarten* offers teachers a solid foundation on which to develop teaching skills. A separate chapter illustrates the growth and development of four- and five-year-olds and children with special needs. Throughout the text the principles of growth and learning, which guide the curriculum and teaching, are made clear. Specific experiences or ways of including children with special needs are found throughout the text as well. Special attention is given to children just learning English.

Integrated

Kindergarten: Fours and Fives Go to School views learning as an integrated whole that involves schools, families, and the community. Thus, there is a focus on working with administrators, aides, supervisors, resource persons, and others within the school as well as with families.

Likewise, the curriculum is presented as a whole entity. How to plan for thematic, project learning is the focus of one chapter. The curriculum areas of art; music; the language arts; the life, physical, and earth sciences; and mathematics, although appearing as separate chapters, are presented in a way that forms an integrated, whole curriculum. Assessment and evaluation are not separate from the curriculum. Authentic evaluation techniques, which are integral to learning experiences, are advocated. Standardized testing and its merits, as well as its detriments, are explained.

Active Children, Active Experiences

Four- and five-year-olds, as all humans, learn through their physical, mental, and social activity. Thus, this text presents experiences that require children to be active. Specific suggestions for teaching content through play are given in each of the chapters.

Reality Based.   Both of the authors bring an extensive background of educational experiences that are reflected in this text. The first author has taught both four- and five-year-old kindergarten in a number of settings. The second works with preschools for both four- and five-year-olds in the Baltimore City Public Schools.

The vast educational experiences of both authors bring reality to *Kindergarten: Fours and Fives Go to School.* All the suggested experiences in the text are based not only on theory and research but also on the real, firsthand experiences of the authors. This gives the text a practicality that will be of great use to the beginning kindergarten teacher as well as the expert.

ACKNOWLEDGMENTS

We wish to acknowledge the support and expertise of our editor, Ann Davis; the production editors, Sheryl Langner and Lea Baranowski; and the dedicated work of the reviewers, Richard P. Ambrose, Kent State University; Ann Harsh, Hattiesburg Public Schools, Mississippi; and Steven F. Reuter, Minnesota State University, Mankato.

DISCOVER THE COMPANION WEBSITE
ACCOMPANYING THIS BOOK

THE PRENTICE HALL COMPANION WEBSITE:
A VIRTUAL LEARNING ENVIRONMENT

Technology is a constantly growing and changing aspect of our field that is creating a need for content and resources. To address this emerging need, Prentice Hall has developed an online learning environment for students and professors alike—Companion Websites—to support our textbooks.

In creating a Companion Website, our goal is to build on and enhance what the textbook already offers. For this reason, the content for each user-friendly website is organized by topic and provides the professor and student with a variety of meaningful resources. Common features of a Companion Website include:

FOR THE PROFESSOR—

Every Companion Website integrates **Syllabus Manager**™**,** an online syllabus creation and management utility.

- ◆ **Syllabus Manager**™ provides you, the instructor, with an easy, step-by-step process to create and revise syllabi, with direct links into the Companion Website and other online content without having to learn HTML.
- ◆ Students may log on to your syllabus during any study session. All they need to know is the web address for the Companion Website and the password you've assigned to your syllabus.
- ◆ After you have created a syllabus using **Syllabus Manager**™, students may enter the syllabus for their course section from any point in the Companion Website.
- ◆ Clicking on a date, the student is shown the list of activities for the assignment. The activities for each assignment are linked directly to actual content, saving time for students.
- ◆ Adding assignments consists of clicking on the desired due date, then filling in the details of the assignment—name of the assignment, instructions, and whether it is a one-time or repeating assignment.
- ◆ In addition, links to other activities can be created easily. If the activity is online, a URL can be entered in the space provided, and it will be linked automatically in the final syllabus.
- ◆ Your completed syllabus is hosted on our servers, allowing convenient updates from any computer on the Internet. Changes you make to your syllabus are immediately available to your students at their next logon.

FOR THE STUDENT—

◆ **Topic Overviews**—outline key concepts in topic areas
◆ **Web Links**—general websites related to topic areas as well as associations and professional organizations
◆ **Read About It**—timely articles that enable you to become more aware of important issues in early childhood education
◆ **Learn by Doing**—put concepts into action, participate in activities, complete lesson plans, examine strategies, and more
◆ **For Teachers**—access information that you will need to know as an in-service teacher, including information on materials, activities, lessons, curriculum, and state standards
◆ **Visit a School**—visit a school's website to see concepts, theories, and strategies in action
◆ **Electronic Bluebook**—send homework or essays directly to your instructor's e-mail with this paperless form
◆ **Message Board**—serves as a virtual bulletin board to post—or respond to—questions or comments to/from a national audience
◆ **Chat**—real-time chat with anyone who is using the text anywhere in the country—ideal for discussion and study groups, class projects, etc.

To take advantage of these and other resources, please visit the *Kindergarten: Fours and Fives Go to School* Companion Website at

www.prenhall.com/seefeldt

CONTENTS

PART 1 Today's Kindergarten

Today's Kindergarten:
The Past Is Present

*Y*ou step inside a classroom like no other you've seen before. There are no desks. And instead of children sitting quietly listening to a teacher, they are scattered throughout the room. At first glance it seems a bit noisy, perhaps even disorganized, but you soon realize that the noise is the busy hum of happy children whose minds and bodies are actively engaged in learning.

You begin to observe, and you see children working with others in small groups or by themselves. Some are building with blocks, others are playing board games, reading books, using the computer, completing puzzles, or working intently on art projects. Two children are deeply engaged in conversation as they splash brightly colored paints on paper on a large easel. A group is playing a game at a table, counting seashells and placing them in different containers.

Three children are playing house. They are having a problem getting the "baby" to sleep. One says, "I know what to do," and walking to the library area picks out a book of nursery rhymes. She takes the baby doll from the others and, sitting in the rocking chair, opens the book and starts to sing nursery songs to the baby. "There," she says, putting the doll in bed, "now you can sleep."

There must be a teacher; after all, this is a school. But where is she? Then you see her in the block area discussing balance and the use of an incline plane with a group of children. She leaves the block builders and moves to join the children playing with the seashells. She finds a clipboard, paper, and markers for them and shows them how they can record their findings in the form of a graph.

At another table a group is randomly playing with dominoes. The teacher sits with this group and demonstrates how to count the dots and play the game. Next she sits with a child working alone on an art project and, asking several questions, engages her in conversation. It seems that each encounter between teacher and children is taken as an opportunity to teach, to challenge children, and to expand and extend their knowledge and thinking.

You think you are in an ideal place for four- and five-year-olds. And you are. You are observing in a kindergarten, a school for four- and five-year-old children.

The purpose of this book is to describe appropriate education for four- and five-year-old children, whether they are enrolled in a kindergarten program or another program for four- and five-year-olds, such as pre-kindergarten, preschool, a child care setting, or nursery school.

Part I of this book defines schools for four- and five-year-olds within the context of the history of the kindergarten. The issues surrounding the concept of readiness and other current kindergarten issues are discussed. Part II presents the characteristics of four- and five-year-old children and addresses how schools and classrooms respond to the needs of young children. The final section of the book describes an appropriate kindergarten for four- and five-year-old children.

Throughout the book, the term "kindergarten" represents schooling that takes place prior to the age of six. This schooling is usually for four- or five-year-old children and takes place in a public or private elementary school. It is recognized, however, that many school systems sponsor kindergarten programs that enroll children as young as two or that may be titled preschool, pre-kindergarten, early learning program, or some form of an early enrichment program.

THE PAST

Kindergarten and other schools for four- and five-year-old children in our nation are not new. Friedrick Froebel (1782–1852) opened the first kindergarten in Germany in 1837. He conceived of the kindergarten literally as a garden in which two- to six-year-old children could grow as naturally as flowers and trees grow, bud, and bloom in a garden. Right from the start the kindergarten was recognized as a very different type of school for young children. So lovely and special were the first kindergartens that they were once called a paradise of childhood (Wiebe, 1869).

When Froebel formalized his ideas of the kindergarten, it was a time of absolute idealism in Germany. Influenced by the times and by the writings of Jean Jacques Rousseau (1712–1778), Froebel, a romantic, was sometimes labeled a mystic. Certainly his writings were mystical and obscure. Froebel's major concern was for unity. He wrote, "All is unity, all rests in unity, all springs from unity, strives for and leads up to unity, and returns to unity at last" (Froebel, 1889, p. 69).

For Froebel, the source of all unity was the all-pervading unity, God. The goal of his kindergarten was to bring children to unity with God. Play and self-activity were the means by which children's development could be enhanced, and through creative self-expression, sense perception, and harmonious living with one another, children would achieve unity.

Games and songs were included in Froebel's gifts.

To ensure that children would learn through play and self-activity, Froebel designed a series of *gifts* and *occupations.* The gifts consisted of knitted balls, wooden balls, cylinders, cubes, brick-shaped blocks, surfaces, lines, points (beans, lentils, seeds, and pebbles), and softened peas or wax pellets and sharpened sticks or straws. The occupations were solids (plastic clay, cardboard work, and woodcarving), surfaces (paper folding, cutting, parquetry, and painting), and lines (stringing seeds, beans, and perforating paper). In addition, songs, games, finger plays, and movement and dance were included as gifts and occupations.

Each gift and occupation held significance. The blocks, which were one inch square, would give children the feeling and perception of oneness. The knitted balls gave children something to grasp and promote free activity. Froebel's mysticism and romantic ideals, as well as the obscurity of his thinking, are seen in the belief that through repetitive play with the balls and blocks, children would be grounded in the importance of the whole life of man—of disjunction and separateness of present and past possession.

The circle itself held great significance for Froebel. It, too, represented unity. By arranging children in circles for songs and stories, they would become infused with the idea of unity and become one with God.

Because each of the gifts and occupations held significance, children could not select the ones they would work or play with, nor were these just handed to children randomly. Rather, teachers were given explicit and thorough directions for the use and sequencing of each of the gifts and occupations. Each gift was "to be used alone until all possible meanings were pursued, then they were to be employed in combinations with other gifts for expansion of ideas. The manipulation of each gift, and the study of its meaning might require weeks for completion" (Weber, 1969, p. 13).

It seems strange, looking at today's busy, active kindergarten filled with all kinds of objects, games, and toys, that when Froebel's rigidly prescribed gifts and occupations were first introduced they were considered very radical. Remember, though, that this was during the 1800s, when children's play and activity were thought of as a form of depravity. The very idea of children playing was deplored as the pathway to evil. Salvation would be found in exact obedience and only when the playful impulses of children were controlled. Thus, Froebel's ideas were, as Vandewalker (1908) wrote, "a new gospel—that of man as a creative being and education as a process of self-expression. They substituted activity for the prevailing repression, and insisted upon the child's right to himself and to happiness during the educational process" (p. 2).

Perhaps it was this idea of freedom of thought and self-expression that was responsible for the wholehearted acceptance of Froebel's kindergarten in America. Americans saw the ideals of the kindergarten as "the educative expression of the principles upon which American institutions are based" (Vandewalker, 1908, p. 1).

Whatever the reason, when German immigrants brought the kindergarten with them to America, both the idea and the ideals of the kindergarten were eagerly embraced. Mrs. Margarethe Meyer Schurz, one of these German immigrants, was credited with opening the first German kindergarten in America in 1856. Having been educated in kindergarten methods by Froebel, she began a kindergarten in her home in Watertown, Wisconsin, for the purpose of preserving the German language and culture for her children (Newell & Putman, 1924).

It was a small program, never enrolling more than six children under the age of six and lasting for only a few years, yet it had a great and lasting impact on American education.

A chance meeting between Elizabeth Peabody and Mrs. Schurz led to the Americanization of the kindergarten. Impressed with the precocity of Mrs. Schurz's daughter, Peabody, who was interested in metaphysics and philosophy and was a member of the New England Transcendentalists, asked to read some of Froebel's writings. Reading Froebel's *The Education of Man* (1889), Peabody found Froebel's ideas fascinating and decided that every child in America should have the benefits of the kindergarten. She began by opening the first American kindergarten in Boston in 1860 (Weber, 1969). By all accounts she was a charismatic teacher. An anonymous former student wrote in *The American Magazine* (Pilgrim's Scrip, 1911) that he remembered Peabody with fondness: "What she said and how she did it filled every crack and cranny of our minds. I do not remember to have ever heard a word said about not whispering or 'keeping' still. She created an appetite for knowledge and then satisfied that appetite" (p. 123).

Peabody continued with her mission of spreading the kindergarten throughout America by traveling throughout the country lecturing on the kindergarten. With her nightdress under her day dress and toothbrush in her purse, she was ready to go everywhere to bring the kindergarten to every child in our nation (Weber, 1969).

Social Forces

Social forces also led to the ready acceptance of Peabody's ideas. During the late 1880s and early 1900s, there was a new wave of immigration to America. The German idealism and methods of the kindergarten appealed to those whose goals were to prepare these most recent immigrants for citizenship in their new country. Churches and missionary leagues founded kindergartens because of their religious overtones of bringing children in unity with God. Those wishing to bring a better life to those living in poverty found the kindergarten as a way to reach children and their families: "So akin are the social settlement and the kindergarten in spirit that several head residents of settlements were originally kindergarteners, and several well-known settlements began as mission kindergartens and became settlements by the natural expansion of their work" (Vandewalker, 1908, p. 107).

The kindergarten was popular. It was so popular that it was not long before it was adopted as a part of the elementary public school. In 1873, Susan Blow, along with W. T. Harris, the superintendent of St. Louis Public Schools, opened the first public school kindergarten.

This move was pivotal to the maturation of the kindergarten. Almost immediately, kindergarten practices and methods were challenged. Some complained that German educational methods were not appropriate in American schools; others argued over the cost of the kindergarten (Beatty, 1995). The age of the children was another issue. Froebel and Blow wanted to enroll three- to five-year-old children, but legal action challenging the school's right to use public monies to operate programs for children under the age of six led them to change the entrance age to five and charge a quarterly fee (Beatty, 1995).

CHALLENGES

Once in the public school, the purpose of the kindergarten was questioned. Rather than bringing children to unity with God and others, educators recommended that the program ready children for "real" school by preparing them to read (Weber, 1969). Conflict between the kindergarten and primary teachers ensued. In an attempt to bring unity between the kindergarten and early primary grades, S. C. Parker and Alice Temple wrote *Unified Kindergarten and First Grade Teaching* (1925), thinking the book would help promote "continuous and delightful" educational experiences for children.

Change was inevitable. Not only were pressures from public schools affecting kindergarten practices, but as the kindergarten spread across the country, the kindergarteners (the name for the teachers, not the children) found it challenging to match Froebel's rigid practices to the needs of the diversity of children they were teaching.

Changing ideas of children and how they learn brought more changes in the curriculum and methods of the kindergarten. Stanley Hall's (1844–1924) observations of children, the way teachers charted their growth and development, were of interest to the "kindergarteners," the name for kindergarten teachers and administrators. Edward Lee Thorndike's (1874–1949) work on animal learning, which led to the idea that learning occurred by connecting a stimulus with a response, was also being considered.

Perhaps most influential of all were the writings and philosophy of John Dewey (1859–1952). Dewey did endorse Froebel's belief in self-expression and creative play, but he showed the kindergarteners how involving children in their here-and-now world, solving real problems, and asking them to make choices and initiate, would develop in children the ability to think as well as the skills and knowledge necessary to become citizens in a democracy. Picking up on these ideas, Anna E. Bryan, returning home to a small town in Kentucky after training in Froebelian methods, found it feasible to give children practical problems, like asking them to weave a blanket for a doll bed, instead of weaving paper. And Alice Putnam, teaching in Jane Adam's Hull House, said it was not necessary to rely on Froebel's gifts and occupations because she could have a kindergarten anywhere, even in a meadow with only flowers and grasses as materials for learning (Weber, 1969).

For Dewey, learning was a social activity. He believed that when educational experiences are arranged to sustain children's individuality on the one hand and a broader sense of community on the other, children would be prepared for their future roles of citizen. In the democracy of the classroom, Dewey expected children to interact freely with one another, argue, and reach consensus. If children are to get along at all, they must consider the ideas, thinking, and wishes of others (Dyson, 1988). Through the type of informal give-and-take that occurs in a democratic classroom, children are forced to consider the perspectives of others and, in the process, are building the foundation for future participation in a democracy.

Change is never easy, and the changing ideas of the kindergarten curriculum caused a great deal of conflict among the kindergarteners. Records of the meetings of the Kindergarten Union, a professional association, document the hurt feelings and bitterness between those supporting strict adherence to Froebelian methods

For Dewey, learning was a social activity.

and those who wanted to bring new ideas and thinking to the kindergarten (Newell & Putman, 1924).

By the 1920s the kindergarten was firmly entrenched in America. Private nursery schools and a few public schools for younger children, those under the ages of four and five, were developing at the same time. The nursery schools, which were firmly based on theories of child growth and development or Freudian theories, paralleled the growth of the kindergarten.

In Europe, the Montessori method was receiving a great deal of attention. Maria Montessori, the first female physician in Italy, designed a set of didactic materials that were to serve two purposes: promoting learning through the senses and developing the skills of reading and writing. William H. Kilpratick, as well as many kindergarteners, went to Italy to observe the Montessori program; however, believing that Froebel had greater insight into the educative process, they found little of interest to them (Weber, 1969). Other than the initial flurry of interest, the Montessori method had little effect on the kindergarten.

CONTINUAL CHANGE

Social forces and new theories of child growth development and learning brought still more expansion to the kindergarten along with more change. During the Great Depression of the 1930s, the Works Progress Administration funded nursery schools. The purpose of these schools was to provide employment for unemployed teachers, give economically deprived children an educational boost, and help families in need. Kindergarteners wrote curriculum and taught in these schools. The experience broadened their ideas of both the curriculum and the practices of the kindergarten.

The next social force influencing kindergarten education was World War II. The Lanham Act, passed and funded by the federal government, provided care for children under the age of six so their mothers could work in factories for the war effort. Although these were preschool programs, kindergarten teachers were influential in developing and teaching in Lanham Act centers.

Throughout the 1950s the kindergarten was a peaceful, if unnoticed, place for four- and five-year-old children. The 1960s changed that. This was a time of social unrest. Inequalities between rich and poor and the African American and white populations were made clear. President Lyndon Johnson, responding to the need to bring equity across our nation, declared a War on Poverty, including a program named Head Start.

Research was demonstrating that intelligence was malleable and could be influenced by environment (Bloom, 1964; Hunt, 1961). Children reared in enriched environments scored higher on intelligence tests than those reared in poverty. Head Start, a comprehensive early educational program of health, social services, and community and parent involvement, was created as a means of offering all children early and enriching educational experiences.

The War on Poverty and Head Start dramatically changed the field of early childhood education. First, after the inception of Head Start, the field expanded rapidly. If the early educational experiences of Head Start were beneficial to children and their families living in poverty, then why should all children in our nation not have the benefit of early education? Public schools, which had sponsored kindergartens for three- and four-year-olds in the past, reinstated these programs. Other states made kindergarten attendance mandatory.

Head Start's focus on parent and community involvement prodded kindergarten teachers to reconsider the role of parents and the community in their programs. Parents were asked to volunteer in their children's classrooms and serve on advisory boards. Cooperative efforts with community agencies were initiated to help meet the needs of all children and their families.

Head Start was, and continues to be, grounded in theories of child development. It views children, their families, and the communities in which they live as a dynamic whole. The natural unfolding of children's growth, within the context of the community, was seen as the basis for curriculum development. The work of Jean Piaget (1896–1980), a Swiss philosopher, was being translated into English about the time Head Start was being designed and buttressed Head Start's maturational philosophy. Piaget, who spent a lifetime studying and interpreting the growth of children, was influenced by Rousseau but extended the idea of natural unfolding by maintaining that knowledge is created as children interact with their social and physical environments.

Early on, however, the developmentally appropriate, whole-child practices of Head Start were challenged. Parents and communities advocated for more discipline and wanted their children to learn, not play, when in Head Start and kindergarten (Greenberg, 1969). The purpose of early education, many argued, was to prepare children to succeed when in school, not to play.

Differing curriculum approaches based on differing philosophies and ideas of children's learning were explored, such as direct instruction, a responsive environment model, the cognitively oriented curriculum (High Scope), and others. Follow Through, a program designed to follow Head Start children from kindergarten through the first three grades with one of these new approaches, was funded by the federal government. Although not directly involving kindergarten programs with the exception of those participating in Follow Through, new ideas, methods, and practices found their way into the kindergarten.

THE PRESENT

Today kindergarten is nearly universal for four- and five-year-olds, and not just in America. Kindergartens are popular all over the world, throughout England and Europe, including eastern Europe, the Far East, South and Central America, and some African nations. In America all 50 states offer four- and five-year-old kindergarten programs (National Center for Education Statistics [NCES], 1997). Over 90% of all five-year-olds and more than 60% of all four-year-olds are enrolled in some sort of public or private preschool or kindergarten program (NCES, 1997). In Georgia more than 70% of the state's four-year-olds were enrolled in a public school preschool. Some school systems also sponsor kindergarten programs for three-year-old children as a means of providing early enriching educational experiences to all children. Kindergarten for four-year-olds may be called prekindergarten, preschool, an early enrichment program, or some other name (U.S. Government Printing Office, 1999).

Kindergarten programs in the United States are usually sponsored by the school system and are designed primarily for four- or five-year-olds. Although most kindergarten programs are sponsored by the public school, some children attend kindergarten in private schools or as a part of a full-day child care program.

Kindergarten programs may be half day or full day and everything in between. Full-day programs are popular because they offer children more learning time and respond to parents' needs for full-time schooling for their children. Today more than 56% of five-year-olds attend a full-day program, and about a fourth of all four-year-olds attend full day (Graue, 2001).

In areas where transportation is a problem, some four- and five-year-olds attend full or half day kindergarten on alternate days. Some half-day programs are followed by some type of in-school child care program or extended half-day program. Full-day programs as well may be extended and followed by some type of in-school child care program. About 30 states sponsor year-round kindergartens in some districts, and many others offer mixed-age kindergartens enrolling children from three to five years of age.

The goals of kindergarten programs differ by state and locality. Your state or local school system may have developed a policy statement outlining the goals and specific purposes of the kindergarten. Regardless, the overriding goal of kindergartens today is that of offering children under the age of six opportunities for academic, intellectual, social, emotional, and physical growth through a well-rounded program of activities and experiences (Willer & Bredekamp, 1992).

THE PAST IS PRESENT

Look at a picture of one of the early kindergartens in the United States, and you will immediately know that today's kindergartens have changed dramatically from those of the past. One photograph taken in Susan Blow's kindergarten in St. Louis, Missouri, shows children sitting at tables, their hands folded waiting for the teacher to show them how to fold, weave, or perforate the paper in front of them. Compare these passive children to the physically, socially, and intellectually active children observed in today's kindergarten classroom, and it is clear that kindergarten curriculum and practices have evolved and changed.

Even though very different from the past, today's kindergartens echo those of the past. Many of the philosophical underpinnings and ideals of the original kindergartens, as well as their methods and practices, are present in today's kindergartens.

Philosophical Similarities

Philosophically, today's kindergartens share some of the same philosophical views as those of the past. Today's kindergartens, as those of the past,

◆ view child development as the foundation for the curriculum,
◆ support teacher training, and
◆ perceive the kindergarten as a means of providing early educational experiences and social services for those children and their families in need.

Child Development.   Froebel, like the early kindergarteners, took seriously Rousseau's command that all education must be based on knowledge and understanding of children's development. Froebel gave prominence to the developmental needs and status of children's development.

Despite his reliance on the religious and his mystical philosophy, Froebel based much of the kindergarten program on his observations of children. "Come, let us live with our children," he invited (1889). Only by living with children, observing them, and studying them could a teacher know, understand, and appreciate the child's nature.

Today Froebel's beliefs that all education is built on a foundation of understanding each child's development continues (NCES, 2000). *Developmentally Appropriate Practice in Early Childhood Programs* (Bredekamp & Copple, 1997) delineates how all early childhood teachers need to understand the developmental changes that typically occur in the years from birth through age eight and beyond, variations in development that may occur, and how best to support children's learning and development during these years. The National Association for the Education of Young Children states the following:

Developmentally appropriate practices result from the process of professionals making decisions about the well-being and education of children based on at least three important kinds of information and knowledge:

1. what is known about child development and learning-knowledge of age-related human characteristics that permits general predictions within an age range about what activities, materials, interactions, or experiences will be safe, healthy, interesting, achievable, and also challenging to children;

2. what is known about the strengths, interests, and needs of each individual child in the group to be able to adapt for and be responsive to inevitable individual variation; and

3. knowledge of the social and cultural contexts in which children live to ensure that learning experiences are meaningful, relevant, and respectful of children and their families.

(Bredekamp & Copple, 1997, pp. 8–9)

Teacher Training. Only teachers trained in the Froebelian method were permitted to teach in the early kindergartens. As the kindergarten spread throughout the nation and the ideas of Hall, Thorndike, and Dewey were adopted, a new and different type of teacher was called for. Kindergarten teachers were asked to create the curriculum instead of depending on Froebel's prescriptions. A greater knowledge and understanding of children gained through research on the way children grew and learned was necessary.

Kindergarten teachers today are required to have a great deal of knowledge and understanding, not just of children and how they grow and learn but also of how to fulfill the potential of children with special needs. They must have knowledge of the effects of culture, working with parents and the community, as well as of every content area (NCES, 2000; Yelland, 2000). As Piaget pointed out, the younger the child, the more "difficult it is to teach him, and the more pregnant that teaching is with future consequences" (Piaget, 1969, p. 127). Thus, teachers of young children needed more, not less, training than those of elementary and secondary children.

State departments of education concur with Piaget's beliefs. An estimated 30 states now have policies and detailed guidelines for the preparation of kindergarten teachers (Ripple, Gilliam, Chanana, & Zigler, 1999). Professional associations also concur with Piaget's beliefs (Hyson, 2000, West, Denton, Germino-Hausken, 2000). The National Association for the Education of Young Children, the largest early childhood professional association in the world, maintains that in order to "make valid decisions about how to teach young children, teachers must know how children develop and learn" (Bredekamp & Copple, 1997, p. 36).

Early childhood teachers should have college-level specialized preparation in early education/child development. Teachers should be encouraged and supported to obtain and maintain current knowledge of child development and its application to early childhood education and practice.

(Bredekamp, 1987, p. 1)

Most states require that kindergarten teachers hold a baccalaureate degree, and approximately 20% of kindergarten teachers in the United States hold a master's degree (NCES, 1997). Calling for teachers to be adequately prepared to demonstrate the knowledge, performance, and disposition specific to their teacher specialization (National Association for the Education of Young Children [NAEYC], 1996), professional associations also offer kindergarten teachers opportunities for continual training and professional development (Myers, Griffin, Telekei, Taylor, & Wheeler, 1998).

Serving Children in Need.   Many of the first kindergartens were driven by the mission of serving children and families in need. Today the belief that kindergarten is beneficial for children whose families live in poverty not only continues; it continues to lead to the expansion of kindergarten programs. Some of this expansion is related to federal mandates. Twenty-eight states now fund pre-kindergarten programs for children believed at risk. These programs vary by size and program. Three-, four-, and five-year-old children can be enrolled. Most focus heavily on family involvement and support in addition to compensatory kindergarten experiences for children.

Federal laws, like the Individuals with Disabilities Education Act (IDEA) and the Americans with Disabilities Act (ADA), ensure that every state offers early educational experiences for children with disabilities and developmental delays as well as children at risk for developmental delays.

Similarities in Practices

The past is also present in today's kindergarten curriculum and practices. Similarities include the continuation of

◆ circle time—language and community,
◆ play as a mode of learning,
◆ focus on equipment, materials, and supplies, and
◆ the involvement of parents.

Circle Time.   "Here's the church, and here's the steeple. Open the door and see all the people," recite kindergarten children as they sit in a circle. The circle, the finger plays, and the songs of today's kindergarten are all reminiscent of those of the original kindergartens. Probably no one today believes that sitting in a circle will bring children to unity with God. But children still are taught songs and rhymes as they sit in a circle or, as in the case in some kindergartens, on circles painted on the floor.

Mutter and *Kose-Lieder,* Froebel's collections of finger plays, rhymes, and songs for children, are no longer used. And today the idea is unacceptable that, "What a child imitates, he begins to understand. Let him represent the flying of birds and he enters partially into the life of birds" (Poulsson, 1893, p. 5).

Today, group meetings are conducted in different forms and for very different purposes. For example, in Reggio Emilia, a town in northern Italy known for its quality child care centers, five-year-olds sit on a riser, like the seats in a sports stadium or movie theater, for their group meetings. Other kindergartens hold group meetings on small benches in a corner of the room or sitting together on a gathering rug.

News and information are shared. Problems are discussed and possible solutions presented. Children may tell about something they did or listen to a visitor. Yes, children still do recite finger plays, but now group meetings are more likely

Froebel's belief in the power of play continues today.

to be held to introduce children to the life-lifting language found in poetry and literature.

These thoughtfully planned group meetings give children practice in following a common idea, arguing a point, listening to others' viewpoints, and forming their own opinions (Seefeldt, 1993). More important, they build a sense of community. By singing together; listening to stories, poems, and rhymes together; and sharing news and information, children feel a oneness with others, which is so critical to becoming a member of a democratic society (Dewey, 1944).

Play and Activity as Modes of Learning.   Froebel's belief in the power of play and activity continues. Today it is well documented that children's play is the vehicle for their social, emotional, and cognitive development as well as a reflection of their development. Piaget's (1952) theories and the research supporting his ideas demonstrated that play is a cognitive process (Christie, 1998; Jarrell, 1998). To Piaget, play was the way children come to develop the ability to use symbols and understand their world. As children play with objects and things in their environment, they are gaining knowledge of the physical properties of the world in which they live. Experimenting with a wide variety of objects and materials, they learn that some things are heavy, others light, and that some are rough or smooth, sharp or rounded. These are concepts that cannot be taught through direct instruction but can be learned only through firsthand, direct experiences and play.

When children play, they observe things in their world and begin to compare these. They classify and sequence objects and things and relate new information to their existing ideas of how the world works, fitting it into their schemes or ideas. When information they take in does not fit their existing ideas, they change their ideas or create new ones. As they do so, they are constructing their own knowledge and storing it as concepts, rules, or principles (Piaget & Inhelder, 1969).

Vygotsky (1986) believed that play led development. He hypothesized that written language grows out of the oral through symbolic play. To Vygotsky, play was also the way that children could practice new skills, try out new social roles, and solve complex problems. Through play, children have the opportunity to explore deeply and attend in great detail to things of interest to them. Play gives children the needed opportunity to function independently and challenge themselves physically and intellectually.

Familiar Equipment, Toys, and Materials.   A number of the original kindergarten classrooms in St. Louis are still in use. These are spacious, beautiful rooms. Fireplaces are at each end of the room. The hardwood floors gleam, as do the lovely wooden cabinets for equipment and supplies. So large are these original kindergarten rooms that one has a swing set, slide, and large sandbox at one end.

Most of today's kindergartens are much less spacious (Sussman, 1998). Many have not been specifically designed for young children. Yet all contain the small tables and chairs, toilets, and sinks and many of the same materials found in the original kindergartens. Equipment unfamiliar to the kindergartens of the past is present as well. Computers, CD players, and other technology is found in today's classrooms (Wilson, 1998).

Instead of selecting and designing equipment and materials for children on the basis of bringing children to unity, today's teachers select materials and equipment that will do the following:

◆ Help children recognize their own potential and power. Open-ended materials such as wood, water, or sand can be controlled by children. Children must act on these.
◆ Offer children novelty and challenge while reflecting the familiar and experienced life of the children.
◆ Invite exploration of the world beyond the classroom and family. Dramatic play materials invite children to enlarge their perspective and expand their understanding of relationships in the world beyond their classroom.
◆ Necessitate the involvement of others and provide for the involvement of children with special needs. Materials should be sufficiently flexible to involve a number of children, including those with special needs. For example, large boxes, blocks, and boards require more than one person (or child) to move around and create constructions (Cuffaro, 1995).

Involvement of Parents.   Early kindergarteners thought of parent involvement as parent education. Susan Blow gave lectures to mothers on Froebelianism as well as Greek philosophy, and early nursery schools offered practical information to parents. Two associations, the Parent Teacher Association and the Child Study Association of America, grew out of the kindergarten movement. The goal of these as well was to fulfill the "immensity of the need for parent education" (Beatty, 1995, p. 152).

A more active, integral role for parents is found in today's kindergartens than in those of the past (NCES, 2000). Kindergarten teachers today continue to offer parents practical information, but parents are expected to be involved in the kindergarten as equal partners in their children's education. Parents are asked to make decisions about their children's educational experiences as well as serve on advisory boards and participate in their children's education. Parents of children with special needs have a unique role. They must be involved in creating an Individual Educational Plan with their children's teachers and are asked to participate in other ways in their children's education.

IN SUMMARY

From the small beginning of six children working with Froebelian materials and reciting finger plays in the Watertown home of Mrs. Margarete Schurz in 1856, the kindergarten grew and expanded in America. Sponsored by all 50 states, kindergarten is now universal for nearly all five-year-olds and over 60% of four-year-olds in our nation. Kindergarten programs, sometimes called preschool or enrichment programs, for three- and four-year-olds considered at risk, as well as for children with special needs to ensure that every child in our nation will receive the benefits of early education, are supported by the federal government.

Built on the firm foundation of the best of the past and current research and theory, today's kindergarten continues to be a special and unique place for children under the age of six. Today's kindergarten places emphasis on the natural instincts of children—their love of companionship, desire for activity, love for the beautiful, and love of learning (Vandewalker, 1908). The philosophy of valuing, treasuring, and protecting young children's right to their childhood makes today's kindergartens, like those of the past, a paradise of childhood (Wiebe, 1869).

In the kindergarten, highly educated teachers guide and challenge young children to new learning by implementing a program based on principles of developmental appropriateness. A small democratic community of learners is built as children share ideas, sing together, and listen to poems and stories.

Research and theory on the power of play and activity in children's learning supports a curriculum based on children's play. Understanding that children learn through their own activity and play, kindergarten teachers provide children with equipment and materials that at the same time are familiar yet challenging.

Effective kindergarten teachers involve parents as partners in their children's education. Parents are asked to make decisions about their children's education and to participate fully. In today's kindergarten the past is present, and the present is the preamble to the future.

EXTEND YOUR IDEAS

1. What is your personal history of kindergarten? What do you recall about the experience? What things did you enjoy, and which did you find unpleasant? Do you have records of your kindergarten work? Reviewing your personal kindergarten history, can you determine what aspects of your kindergarten experience had roots in the Froebelian kindergartens of old? In class discuss your different personal kindergarten histories.

2. Survey the kindergarten programs in your state. Use the Web or call or write your state department of education to find out: When did kindergartens first begin in your state? How many four- and five-year-olds are in kindergarten? Are there programs for three-year-olds? What state and federal regulations govern kindergarten practices? In class discuss the differences in programs and how these affect today's children.

3. Visit several kindergarten classrooms. Observe the equipment, materials, and supplies. Which of these do you think have their roots in Froebel's gifts and occupations? Why?

4. Interview several kindergarten teachers. Ask them why they chose to teach kindergarten? What kindergarten practices and methods do they implement and why? Share your discussions in class. 🖐

RESOURCES

Associations

Associations have many resources for teachers. E-mail, use the Web, write a postcard, or call the following associations and ask for their free or inexpensive resources for teachers of young children.

Association for Childhood Education International
17904 Georgia Ave., Suite 215
Olney, MD 20832
1-800-423-3563
e-mail: *ACEIED@aol.com*
http://www.udel.edu/bateman/acei

National Association for the Education of Young Children
1509 16th St. NW
Washington, DC 20036-1426
1-800-424-2460
e-mail: *membership@naeyc.org*
http://www.naeyc.org

Publications

America's Kindergartens (2000), by the National Center for Educational Statistics, 555 New Jersey Avenue NW, Washington, DC 20208, offers a complete overview of the statistics of today's kindergartens.

Historic Foundations

The Carondelet Historical Society
6303 Michigan Ave.
St. Louis, MO 63111
314-481-6303

The Carondelet Historical Society is located in the old Des Peres school, site of Susan Blow's first public school kindergarten. Here you can see the original Frobelian gifts and occupations and other early kindergarten work and writings.

REFERENCES

Beatty, B. (1995). *Preschool education in America: The culture of young children from the colonial era to the present.* New Haven, CT: Yale University Press.

Bloom, B. (1964). *Stability and change in human characteristics.* New York: John Wiley & Sons.

Bredekamp, S. (1987). *Developmentally appropriate practice in early childhood programs serving children from birth through age 8.* Washington, DC: National Association for the Education of Young Children.

Bredekamp, S., & Copple, C. (1997). *Developmentally appropriate practice in early childhood programs* (Rev. ed.). Washington, DC: National Association for the Education of Young Children.

Christie, J. F. (1998). Play: A medium for literacy development. In D. P. Fromberg & D. Bergen (Eds.), *Play from birth to twelve and beyond* (pp. 50–56). New York: Garland Publishing.

Cuffaro, H. K. (1995). *Experimenting with the world: John Dewey and the early childhood classroom.* New York: Teachers College Press.

Dewey, J. (1944). *Democracy and education.* New York: The Free Press.

Dyson, A. H. (1988). The value of time off task: Young children's spontaneous talk and deliberate text. *Harvard Educational Review, 57,* 396–420.

Froebel, F. (1889). *The education of man.* New York: D. Appleton (Original work published 1826).

Graue, E. (2001). What's going on in the children's garden? Kindergarten today. *Young Children, 56* (1), 67–73.

Greenberg, P. (1969). *The devil has slippery shoes.* New York: Macmillan.

Hunt, J. M. (1961). *Intelligence and experience.* New York: Ronald.

Hyson, M. (2000). Growing teachers for a growing profession: NAEYC revises its guidelines for early childhood professional preparation. *Young Children, 55*(3), 60–63.

Jarrell, R. H. (1998). Play and its influence on the development of young children's mathematical thinking. In D. P. Fromberg & D. Bergen (Eds.), *Play from birth to twelve and beyond* (pp. 56–68). New York: Garland Publishing.

Myers, V. L., Griffin, H. D., Telekei, J., Taylor, J., & Wheeler, L. (1998). Birth through kindergarten teacher training. *Childhood Education,74,* 154–159.

National Center for Educational Statistics. (1995). *The condition of education: Indicator 2.* Washington, DC. U.S. Government Printing Office.

National Center for Educational Statistics. (1997). *The condition of education: Indicator 1.* Washington, DC: U.S. Government Printing Office.

National Center for Education Statistics. (2000). *Digest of education statistics.* Washington, DC: U.S. Government Printing Office.

Newell, B. B., & Putman, A. (1924). Pioneers of the Kindergarten in America. New York: Century.

Parker, S. C., & Temple, A. (1925). *Unified kindergarten and first grade teaching.* Boston: Ginn, Newell & Putnam Publishers

Piaget, J. (1952). *Play, dreams and imitation in childhood.* New York: Norton.

Piaget, J. (1969). *Science of education and the psychology of the child.* New York: Viking Press.

Piaget, J., & Inhelder, B. (1969). *Psychology of the child.* New York: Basic Books.

Pilgrim's Scrip. (1911). The first kindergarten in America. *The American Magazine,* November, 123.

Poulsson, E. (1893). *Finger plays for nursery and kindergarten.* Boston: Lothrop, Lee and Shepard.

Ripple, C. H., Gilliam, W. S., Chanana, N., & Zigler, E. (1999). Will fifty cooks spoil the broth? *American Psychologist, 54,* 327–343.

Seefeldt, C. (1993). Social studies: Learning for freedom. *Young Children, 48*(3), 4–10.

Sussman, C. (1998). Out of the basement: Discovering the value of child care facilities. *Young Children, 53*(1), 10–19.

U.S. Government Printing Office. (1999). *Digest of education statistics.* Washington, DC: Author.

Vandewalker, N. C. (1908). *The kindergarten in American education.* New York: Macmillan.

Vygotsky, L. (1986). *Thought and language* (Rev. ed.). Cambridge: MIT Press.

Weber, E. (1969). *The kindergarten: Its encounter with educational thought in America.* New York: Teachers College Press.

West, J., Denton, K., & Germino-Hausken, E. (2000). *America's kindergarten.* Washington, DC: National Council of Education Statistics.

Wiebe, E. (1869). *The paradise of childhood: A practical guide to the kindergarten.* Springfield, MA: Milton Bradley.

Willer, B., & Bredekamp, S. (1992). Of ladders and lattices, cores and cones: Conceptualizing an early childhood professional development system. *Young Children, 17*(3), 17–50.

Wilson, L. J. (1998). Technology in the classroom: Children as software reviewers. *Childhood Education, 74,* 250–253.

Yelland, N. J. (Ed.). (2000). *Promoting meaningful learning.* Washington, DC: National Association for the Education of Young Children.

CHAPTER 2

Understanding Readiness in the Context of Theory and Research

"Ready or not, here I come," children call, playing hide and seek. And ready or not, children come to kindergarten. Are they ready? Will being in kindergarten enable them to be ready for first grade?

Historically, no other issue has troubled the kindergarten as much as that of readiness. Kindergarten teachers, who believe that learning is an ongoing process that begins at birth and continues throughout life, are uncomfortable with the idea of readiness. They know that there is normal variability of skills and abilities in any group of children and believe that each child will have strengths in some areas and not in others. As a group, kindergarten teachers continue to embrace Froebel's belief in the goodness of children. They trust children to grow and learn naturally within the enriched environment of the kindergarten. Rather than being worried about whether children are ready for kindergarten or whether kindergarten will prepare them for the primary grades, they worry that children will be labeled as not ready on the basis of capricious and inappropriate criteria (Kagan, 1999; National Association for the Education of Young Children [NAEYC], 1992).

To be an effective kindergarten teacher today, the concept of readiness and the issues surrounding it must be understood. Readiness is, however, "a murky idea integrally tied to our ideas about how children develop and what we can do to support that process" (Graue, 1998, p. 13). The theories of maturationalism, behaviorism, and constructivism can be used to explain concepts of readiness as well as suggest implications for practice.

The purpose of this chapter is to increase students' understanding of the concept of readiness. In this chapter maturational, behavioral, and constructivist's theories of readiness are presented. The strengths and weaknesses of each theory of readiness are described.

READINESS THEORIES

Readiness is a fact. There is no doubt that some kinds of learning take place more easily and readily at a specific age than another or that the amount of previous learning determines the amount of new learning that can take place.

Nearly everyone has seen the difference a few months or even weeks of growth can mean to a preschool child's abilities and capabilities. It seems as if one day a child cannot copy a square or a diamond, remember three directions given at the same time, or tie a shoe, only to, within a few weeks and without instruction, be able to do so. On the other hand, lack of readiness is equally as observable. One can try to teach a baby to sit or stand or a preschooler to tie a shoe, and because the child is not mature enough to achieve these tasks, he or she will not succeed.

Readiness is defined as being prepared and equipped—arranged for performance, immediate action, or use. Three very different theories explaining readiness have influenced our conceptions of readiness. Each of the theories has strengths and weaknesses, and each has been used as a rationale for implementing kindergarten readiness practices.

Three major theories used to explain readiness are the maturationalist, behaviorist, and constructivist theories. *Maturationists* posit that growth, development, and learning are the result of internal laws of maturation (Gesell, 1940). Thus, all children will learn if given proper time to develop. Directly opposite to maturational theories are those of the behaviorists. *Behaviorists* advocate that growth and learning are external to the child and controlled by the environment. Through direct conditioning, a series of stimuli and responses, or associating the result of one event with another, children learn. To the behaviorist, all children can learn if their learning environment is properly structured. *Constructivists* maintain that both biological and environmental factors affect human development in a reciprocal manner. The role of natural unfolding through maturation is a part of these theories, but children grow and learn through interaction with their social and physical environments.

Maturational Theories of Readiness

G. Stanley Hall (1844–1929) and Arnold Gesell (1880–1961) introduced formal theories of maturation. These theories were at least partially responsible for the replacement of Froebel's ideas and dominated kindergarten philosophy, practice, and methods well into the first half of the 20th century.

Basically, maturational theories hold that growth progresses through a series of invariant stages, with each stage characterized by qualitatively different structures of the organism and qualitatively different patterns of interaction between organism and environment. Growth and learning, according to maturational theories, are due to internal physiological mechanisms and their orderly, sequential growth rather than to the environment.

Gessel conducted careful and systematic observations of children of different ages. On the basis of these observations, he delineated ages and stages of childhood.

Maturationists believe children develop in an orderly sequence.

To support his theories, Gesell observed and studied 11-month-old identical twins. Gesell would carefully instruct and train one identical twin in some skill, such as stair climbing. He would train the twin for six weeks, and finally she could climb the stairs. But within a few weeks the twin without the training could climb stairs efficiently and more effectively than the twin with the training. Within a few days, both were equally as proficient (Gesell & Thompson, 1929).

These findings led kindergarten teachers to questioning whether it was efficient or effective to try to teach children skills that would develop naturally in time and to the conclusions that

♦ readiness is determined by maturation;
♦ development occurs in an orderly sequence, with later abilities, skills, and knowledge building on those already acquired; and
♦ development proceeds in predictable directions toward greater complexity, organization, and internalization.

By the 1960s, Gesell's premise was being challenged for a variety of reasons. First, the children Gesell studied and observed were primarily those of White, middle-class parents of the 1930s. Because children of other cultures, classes, and race or ethnic groups were not included, his work could not be considered applicable to all children, especially those of poor or minority children not from middle-class homes. In answer to this criticism, Gesell's work was replicated in 1974 on a diverse sample representing the diversity of ethnic groups in our nation. In this new edition of *Infant and Child in the Culture of Today* (Gesell, Ilg, Ames, & Rodell, 1974), the same delineation of stages and ages were found as in the 1930s: "We found . . . the unfolding patterns of behavior remain the same as in generations past" (p. i).

Next, Gesell's work ignored the full variability of normal growth and learning. The special needs of children, their culture, and their linguistic skills were not fully addressed by maturational theories. By relying on ages and stages of normal development, children who deviate from the norms could be considered abnormal or thought of as objects to be conditioned, driven, modeled, matured, or staged.

Finally, maturational theories only explain what is. Today's kindergarten teachers are more interested in understanding why children grow and mature, and identifying internal and external conditions that affect and influence children's growth, development, and learning.

In summary, maturational theories place responsibility on the child and the predetermined, internal process of growth and maturation. The emphasis on internal processes that cannot be influenced by the environment has implications for teaching. If growth and development stem from inside the child, then the role of the teacher is to respond to this internal process. Rather than attempting to speed up the growth process, teachers can respond only to the natural unfolding process of sequential development and growth of children.

At their worst, maturational theories could lead to kindergarten readiness practices that do the following:

♦ Apply rigid benchmarks of normal growth and development to determine whether children are ready. This practice has been known to discriminate against children, especially children of color (Baker, 1999). Children who do not exhibit certain, often arbitrarily determined behaviors at a specific age have been kept out of kindergarten. Others, believing in the age-stage theory of maturational theories, deny children access to kindergarten on the basis of their age. Children whose fifth birthdays are in the fall are "red-shirted" and asked to repeat preschool until they are older (Shepard & Smith, 1986).

◆ Confuse what children can do and educational outcomes. Benchmarks of human development could become the curriculum. Because most four-year-olds can learn to jump rope, the curriculum would include rope jumping, or because most five-year-olds can walk on a two-inch balance beam, the curriculum included walking on a balance beam.

◆ Mandate a passive role for teachers. Misunderstanding maturational theories, teachers may simply wait for children to gain skills or learn instead of providing experiences enabling them to learn.

◆ Ignore the role of environment and culture on human growth, development, and learning.

At their best, maturational theories are highly useful in understanding readiness because of the following:

◆ They led to the acceptance that learning is a normal biological function. Children do not have to be cajoled, persuaded, coerced, manipulated, or tricked into learning. Given the opportunity and the appropriate conditions, including readiness, children simply learn (Jensen, 1969).

◆ Children do grow in predictable ways. Even though there is wide variation in children's growth and development, universals of human development cannot be denied. Children all over the world walk at about a year and talk in three-word sentences at about two years.

◆ Knowledge of normal growth and development informs practice. Curriculum practices that are not based on knowledge of maturation can lead to failure. Considering patterns of normal growth and development enables teachers to plan experiences and activities that do not bore children but challenge them to successful learning (Bredekamp & Copple, 1997; Charlesworth, Hart, Burts, & DeWolf, 1993; Marcon, 1992).

Behavioral Theories of Readiness

Behavioral theories of readiness and learning are diametrically opposed to maturational theories. While maturational theories presume that readiness and learning are preestablished within the individual, behavioral theories postulate that readiness and learning are imposed on the individual externally.

In contrast to the maturational theories of readiness, behaviorists believe that all knowledge is derived from sense impressions, either as direct copies of sensory impressions (simple ideas) or as combinations of several simple or complex ideas. Humans, like all mammals, possess the neural structures for the formation of associations between the sensory inputs and outputs. This means that humans have the capacity for acquiring stimulus-response connections or habits, and mental development and learning are viewed as proceeding in an ordered, hierarchical, or progressive fashion.

Edward L. Thorndike (1874–1949), working on animal learning, related the theories of stimulus-response theory to the kindergarten program. He postulated that humans are like a bundle of habits. He said that knowledge is nothing more or less than the habit of sequence among ideas and that the capacity for learning is the possibility of forming a set of habits (Thorndike, 1913). Learning was the result of strengthening and weakening the stimulus-response connections. In experiments with animals, he found that responses to a situation followed by a satisfying experience will be strengthened; responses followed by discomfort will be weakened. This means that any behavior followed by a pleasant, satisfying experience is likely to be repeated; behavior that is not pleasant or that is followed by an unpleasant experience will disappear.

Thorndike told the first kindergarten teachers that if they worked directly for habit formation and measured success by attainment of habits, learning would occur. He saw readiness as taking several forms. If a strong desire for an action sequence is aroused, then the smooth carrying out of that sequence is satisfying; if that action sequence is thwarted or blocked from completion, then such blocking is annoying; and if an action is tiring, then forcing another one would be annoying. He was not referring to reading readiness but rather to how chains of behavior, such as a child going to the cabinet to get a cookie, enhance the learner's readiness for the next steps.

Patty Smith Hill (1868–1946), once a student of Susan Blow, found Thorndike's ideas of interest. Together they wrote *Conduct Curriculum for the Kindergarten and First-Grade* (1923), which consisted of a habit inventory, a list of kindergarten activities, and the behavioral outcomes that they were to produce.

B. F. Skinner (1904–1990), probably the best-known behaviorist, proposed the theory of operant conditioning. Skinner, like Thorndike, hypothesized that behaviors are learned when they are followed by certain consequences. Unlike Thorndike, however, Skinner spoke only about the strengthening of responses, not the strengthening of stimulus-response habits. Skinner proposed a model of operant conditioning. Operant conditioning means that when a response, regardless of the conditions that might or might not have led to its emission, is followed by a reinforcer, the response will occur again. Further, the reinforcer, together with the circumstances surrounding its administration, is a stimulus that can come to have control over that response through repeated presentation. The reinforcer need not be pleasant. Attention, yelling, screaming, or even some form of punishment like a slap or spank could serve to reinforce the behavior, and thus it would be likely to reoccur.

According to Skinner, it simply does not matter whether a child is ready. What matters is how the teacher outlines and specifies the hierarchies of a task and then, with specificity and clarity, breaks the task into its component forms and teaches each in turn. Each new step in learning is dependent on the prior acquisition of certain subskills, and that learning takes place most efficiently when we ensure that all relevant subskills have been mastered prior to the next-to-be-learned skill in the hierarchy.

As Froebel, kindergarten teachers trust children and respect their childish behaviors.

Skinner's theories have had a powerful force on educational methods in elementary and secondary education. The separate subject matter approach, behavioral objectives, stated competencies, lesson plans with specific outcomes specified, scope and sequence charts, and worksheets all have their roots in Skinner's theory. Programs designed to train teachers of parents to reward appropriate behaviors and ignore inappropriate ones stem from Skinner's theories. Direct instruction programs also have their foundation in these theories. Direct instruction breaks learning into specific steps and subskills that must be learned prior to mastering the next skill. Students' responses are carefully observed and the correct ones reinforced. DISTAR, a step-lock programmed curriculum, is an example of one program of direct instruction.

Throughout the years kindergarten teachers have rejected the mechanistic and animalistic nature of behaviorism. They, as Froebel did, continue to trust children, value and respect their childish behaviors, and reject the need to modify or control their behavior or learning.

As with maturational theories, one cannot deny behavioral theories. Each of us can recall some stimulus-response association that continues to influence our lives. One student recalled having been hospitalized as a child. She said that every time someone dressed in a white coat came to her hospital room, some painful treatment took place. Experiencing the pain made her shudder. Now, when she sees a person dressed in a white coat, be it in a delicatessen, a doctor's office, or an ice cream parlor, she shudders.

Operant conditioning is seen every time you observe children running away from their parents in a store or mall. Parents who run after the child serve to reinforce the behavior, and the child continues to run away. Parents who ignore the behavior, even though carefully watching their children, find that their children stop running away and return to the safety of holding their parents' hands.

In summary, behavioral theories give an active role to the environment or external forces in children's growth, development, and learning. This calls for a very active teacher, one who is clearly in control and who can direct children's learning. It is up to the teacher, through some form of direct instruction, to teach children the skills believed necessary for children to be ready.

At their worst, behavioral theories of development could lead to kindergarten readiness practices that do the following:

◆ Reduce readiness to a series of isolated skills taught through drill and practice with appropriate reinforcement. This focus on isolated skills ignores higher-order processes, such as forming concepts, understanding relationships, making generalizations, and problem solving. Although focusing on teaching isolated academic skills improves children's scores on tests of basic skills, this improvement has not been matched with improvement in reading comprehension, writing fluency, or math problem solving (Bredekamp & Rosegrant, 1992).
◆ View readiness as occurring in a sequential, linear, hierarchical process, ignoring the cultural context within which children learn. By ignoring children's linguistic and sociocultural context, the theories fail to accept the variety of ways learning occurs and is expressed.
◆ Manipulate or control children through schedules of external reinforcement, teaching them to rely on someone else to make decisions for them. External reinforcement, which may have short-term benefits, has been shown to lessen children's intrinsic motivation to learn and achieve in the long term (Cesarone, 1998; Dweck, 1986; Kohn, 1993).

At their best, behavioral theories of development could lead to kindergarten readiness practices that do the following:

◆ Are effective. Because the theories demand that teachers specify what children are to learn and how, the theories often lead to successful learning (Gersten & George, 1990). With the outcomes clearly specified, assessment follows readily. One has only to check to see if children can perform the predetermined outcome behaviors to determine their readiness for a given task.
◆ Lead to teachers being able to articulate what their goals are for children and how they will achieve them. Weber (1969) wrote of how difficult it was for the early kindergarteners, once free of Froebelian doctrine, to articulate exactly what they were teaching and what children were learning, a problem that remains today when teachers do not have clear goals and objectives in mind.
◆ Recognize the critical role of the environment and external reinforcement in children's learning and readiness. Too many teachers, misunderstanding classical and operant conditioning, reinforce children's problem behaviors and fail to reinforce desirable learning behaviors.

Constructivist Theories of Readiness

Currently, both the maturational and the behavioral theories are deemed insufficient to explain learning and readiness. Neither fully explain the complexities of human learning or readiness. Cognitive theories of constructivism, which propose that development of the mind is not the result of either maturation or external reinforcement from the environment but rather takes place through a lengthy series of interchanges between individual and environment, are believed more fruitful in explaining readiness.

Constructivist theories imply that individuals develop through a series of stages that must be taken into account, but learners can be helped to construct new understandings through their own social, physical, and mental activity and interactions with the environment. This gives kindergarten teachers an optimistic view of readiness. Once they understand the way the individual child knows the world, they can plan experiences to deepen and strengthen this knowledge. These experiences and interactions will, in turn, lead to new learning and knowledge.

Some claim that Jean Piaget (1896–1980) initiated the study of cognitive development, but many of Piaget's ideas were evident in the philosophy of Jean Jacques Rousseau, who saw the child as active, and the work of the Gestalists and other philosophers and psychologists. Still, it was Piaget who had the greatest influence on the study of constructivism in the United States.

Piaget extended the idea of natural unfolding by maintaining that knowledge is created as children interact with their social and physical environments. Through his observations of children's behavior, he identified the ages and stages of mental thought. He determined that intellectual development is a series of changes in the cognitive structures that progress from the egocentric (inability to adopt another's point of view) to the objective (Piaget, 1965).

Development is the result of the processes of assimilation, accommodation, and equilibration, the processes by which children construct new and better ways of thinking. As children interact with their environment, they form schemata, or organizational patterns. These are the bases for more complex structures as mental activity develops. Children use assimilation and accommodation to organize their thoughts into increasingly complex structures.

Piaget maintained that the infant, child, and the adult all adapt but that adaptation is different and occurs at different times. Thus, the schemata or structures that one uses during a life span vary. These variations represent developmental stages, and each stage is distinct from the others. The stages reflect the interaction of maturation and experiences on the already existing mental structures. Children develop these stages of thinking in the same sequence and at approximately the same time, although the exact age differs from individual to individual and among cultures.

The theories of Lev Vygotsky (1896–1934) are considered relevant today. Whereas both Piaget and Vygotsky believed that development could not be explained by a single factor, such as maturational influences or environmental or social factors, but was dependent on the interaction between these two factors, Vygotsky's emphasis was on the effect that the sociocultural processes had in stimulating development (Vygotsky, 1978). At certain points in the child's life, varying social factors become dominant influences for development and thus better explanations of changes.

To Vygotsky, even though learning and development were interrelated, they were not the same things. At different developmental stages, children learn different things as they independently act on and interpret their environment, but other people interact with children as well, affecting the course of their development. The interaction between adult and child determines both children's learning and their development.

Vygotsky suggested two developmental levels at which children operate. One is the stage at which children can do problem-solving tasks independently. He termed this the *actual* developmental level. The second level of operation is when children can do the same task under the guidance of an adult or a more skilled peer, which he called the *potential* developmental level. As children mature, the potential level becomes the actual level when the child is able to perform the task independently. The distance between the two levels is called the *zone of proximal development* (Vygotsky, 1978).

Vygotsky maintained that "an essential feature of learning is that it creates the zone of proximal development, that is, learning awakens a variety of internal developmental processes that are able to operate only when the child is interacting with people in his environment and in cooperation with his peers. Once these processes are internalized, they become part of the child's independent developmental achievement" (Vygotsky, 1978, p. 90).

Dewey did not call his theories constructivist; he preferred to classify them as experimentalism (Ryan, 1995). He thought that the term "experimentalism" best conveyed his belief that all learning takes place through experience. Bredekamp and Copple (1997) described Dewey's philosophy in their book *Developmentally Appropriate Practice in Early Childhood Programs* when they wrote that children are "active learners who draw on direct physical and social experiences as well as culturally transmitted knowledge in order to construct their own understanding of the world around them" (p. 13).

Dewey also believed that learning is an integrated activity and cannot be separated from children's social, emotional, or physical growth and development. The idea of a whole child learning through integrated experiences with their here-and-now world had a great influence on the kindergarten curriculum. Today these ideas are expressed in the thematic, unit, and project approach to the curriculum— as the whole-language, emergent literacy, and language experience approach to learning to read.

In summary, constructivist theories of learning and readiness place responsibility on both environment (external forces) and maturation and the interaction between the two. This gives kindergarten teachers an optimistic view of readiness and learning. There is a role for teachers. They respond both to children's natural unfolding and maturational level, engaging them in dialogue in order to better understand the children's maturational level, and interact with them, structuring additional experiences, offering information, or instructing children as they guide them to the next level of readiness and learning.

At their worst, constructivist theories of development could lead to kindergarten readiness practices that do the following:

◆ Lead people to focus only on the growth of the mind, ignoring physical and emotional growth and development.

◆ Leave readiness to chance. Because the theories do not specifically articulate how teachers are to interact with children within the zone of proximal development, teachers may leave learning to chance.

◆ Assume that all children are equally interested and motivated to construct new mental structures or to learn how to learn. The theories suggest that learning is a do-it-yourself project, but not all children are motivated or believe themselves efficacious enough to risk new learning.

At their best, constructivist theories of development could lead to kindergarten readiness practices that do the following:

◆ Are grounded in an understanding of how children's thinking is likely to be structured at a given point in time. Teachers can influence children's readiness if they consider their present way of thinking and how the new way of thinking can be acquired.

◆ Lead teachers to base readiness not on what a child can do but on what the child can do with guidance.

◆ Respect the learner. Piaget and Vygotsky considered the learner autonomous, seeking to assimilate environmental situations to his or her present cognitive structures while accommodating those structures to novel elements in the situations being assimilated.

READINESS ISSUES

Current social forces have intensified issues surrounding kindergarten readiness. These have led to serious discussions, questioning, cooperative problem solving, and consensus building. Throughout the process of consensus building, the theories of maturationalism, behaviorism, and constructivism were applied. Ultimately, the issues of kindergarten readiness led to a deeper, more thoughtful conceptualization and understanding of the purpose and nature of the kindergarten.

Social Forces

Despite the 1960s War on Poverty, an expanding Head Start program, Title I, and other early educational projects designed to compensate for the devastating effects of living in poverty, the academic gap between rich and poor has only widened. Schools, under pressure, were asked to make reforms and improve educational outcomes for all children regardless of their socioeconomic backgrounds.

At the same time, increasing anxiety about the future of America's ability to compete in world markets was being expressed (Ravitch, 1995). Research indicating that students in the United States trail their counterparts in many other nations in mathematics and science suggested that we, as a nation, would be ill prepared to compete in future world markets.

The pressure was on. Elementary and secondary school reforms were called for. It was not long before the pressures for reform would trickle down into the peaceful garden for children. The common theme of these reforms was the call for national goals. President George Bush and a cadre of governors, led by then Governor Bill Clinton of Arkansas, responded to the idea of national goals that would have the potential to unify education in America by directly affecting teaching and learning in the schools and appointed a National Education Goals Panel in 1991. Eight goals were written into legislation as Goals 2000 under the Clinton administration.

The first of these goals directly relates to kindergarten. Goal 1 states, "By the year 2000, all children will start school ready to learn" (National Education Goals Panel, 1991). The goal defines readiness in terms of the whole child, using five dimensions of early childhood development and learning: physical well-being and motor development, social and emotional development, approaches to learning, language development, and cognition and general knowledge.

This is a clear statement of high expectations for all children across the curriculum, addressing the child's total development and what he or she should learn as well as supporting positive approaches to education.

The first goal prompted a great deal of concern and discussion about what constitutes readiness to start school. The NAEYC (1990) responded with a position paper on school readiness. The position was that the first goal cannot be understood without considering three critical factors:

◆ the diversity and inequity of children's early life experiences,
◆ the wide range of variation in young children's development and learning, and
◆ the degree to which school expectations of children entering kindergarten are reasonable, appropriate, and supportive of individual differences.

APPLYING THE THEORIES

State legislators, departments of education, and local school systems interpreted the first goal—that all children should enter school ready to learn—in a number of ways. Some mandated that children who were not ready should be denied entrance into kindergarten; other systems instituted developmental or transitional kindergartens for children deemed not ready for first grade or failed children, making them repeat their kindergarten year; and still other states called for reform in the kindergarten curriculum.

Denying Entrance—Kindergarten Entry Age

Those endorsing maturational theories thought that they could ensure children's academic success by making certain that all children were ready for school. Applying developmental benchmarks like those found on the Gesell Developmental Schedules (1954), school systems assessed children's performance in terms of norms, that is, in comparison to the performances of other children of the same age. Those who did not perform according to the norms for their age were denied entrance into kindergarten. Others, again using maturational theories to explain their decisions, moved entry dates back, enrolling only older children who, because they were older, would be "more ready" for school.

All children, regardless of ability, should have access to kindergarten.

Parents reacted as well. Parents, whose views of readiness are somewhat disparate from those of kindergarten teachers, thought that children should enter kindergarten being able to count to 20 or more, know the alphabet, and be able to use pencils and paint brushes (National Center for Education Statistics [NCES], 1995). Parents were so concerned that their children did not have these prerequisite skills and would fail kindergarten that they delayed their children's entrance into kindergarten. About 9% of parents whose children were eligible for kindergarten held them back for a year. More boys than girls were reported being held out of kindergarten, as were more white children than minorities (NCES, 1997).

Surveys found that children who had been held out of kindergarten were indeed "more ready" than those who had not been held back for a year (NCES, 1997). This is no surprise. Older children know more and have greater capabilities than younger children. The process of denying children access to kindergarten on the basis of age or some test is obvious. First, it is unconstitutional to deny children access to public education. Then, by excluding children from early enriching educational experiences, these "unready" children would become progressively "behinder and behinder" (Golant & Golant, 1997).

In truth, all four- and five-year-olds enter school ready to learn. It is up to the school to respond to each individual child's level of readiness rather than making children responsible for meeting school requirements. The NAEYC states: "It is inappropriate to determine school entry on the basis of the acquisition of certain skills and abilities. Schools may reasonably expect that children entering kindergarten will be active, curious, and eager to learn" (NAEYC, 1990, p. 22).

Instead of holding children out of kindergarten because they are too young or not ready, school systems can do the following:

♦ Set a reasonable birth date for entrance into kindergarten where most of the children in kindergarten are five years old and most of the children in first grade are six.
♦ Create kindergartens that are responsive to the needs of individual children by requiring that teachers and administrators understand child development and how children learn.
♦ Offer continuous progress for children from kindergarten to the primary grades.
♦ Include parents in decisions about the best placement for their children.
♦ Implement curricula that are developmentally appropriate and meet the needs and interests of individual children as well as the total group of children (NAEYC, 1990; Peck, McCaig, & Sapp, 1988).
♦ Offer comprehensive services of health, nutrition, and social support for families.

Kindergarten Retention

Other states decided that all children should have access to kindergarten, but if children did not succeed in kindergarten, they would be asked to repeat kindergarten, or be placed in a "transitional or developmental" program prior to entrance into first grade, in order to prevent subsequent failure. "Kindergarten retention" is a generic term used to refer to several different extra-year programs that include a "transition" program before entry into first grade, "developmental" kindergarten before or after kindergarten, or simply repeating kindergarten (Shepard, 1992).

Those advocating for developmental kindergartens claim that they do not consider children to be failures. They want to provide them with a unique curriculum tailored to their needs in order to prepare them for the rigors of first grade. Research, however, suggests that children who are retained in kindergarten or asked to attend a developmental program before kindergarten or first grade have lower self-esteem and poorer attitudes toward school when compared to children in a control group. Parents as well expressed distress about the retention decisions (Shepard, 1992).

Kindergarten Curriculum Reform

Other school systems responded to pressures for reform by changing the kindergarten curriculum. Instead of offering children opportunities for academic, intellectual, social, emotional, and physical growth through a well-rounded program of activities and experiences (Willer & Bredekamp, 1990), legislators and school administrators changed the traditional kindergarten curriculum to one of basic academic skills, including those previously reserved for older children (NCES, 1995).

These school systems, opting to endorse behavioral theories and thinking of learning as occurring in a sequential, hierarchical way, determined the academic content that children were to achieve and master. Teachers were given scope and sequence charts delineating the subskills and skills prerequisite to learning these basic academic skills along with prescribed lesson plans for achieving these. Children who did not master the prescribed skills or learn the content would repeat the sequence until they were successful. Those who could not master the skills by the end of kindergarten repeated kindergarten or were placed in a transitional classroom for a year prior to entry into first grade.

No doubt those who would narrow the kindergarten curriculum to one of isolated academic, basic skills are motivated by the worthy goal of enabling all our nation's children to experience success. However, they ignore the research on school retention and the effects of transitional classrooms. Children who were not considered at risk and who were retained in kindergarten were found to have more school performance problems than children who had not been retained in kindergarten (NCES, 1997; Shepard & Smith, 1989). Placement in transitional classrooms also leads to lowered performance as well as later school failure. Children who may be at increased risk for school failure did not appear to benefit from either delayed entrance into kindergarten, transitional classrooms, or being retained in kindergarten (Mantizicopoulos, 1997; NCES, 1995).

Consensus Building.   Out of the issues of kindergarten entry age and curriculum reform came consensus. Under pressure, the field of early childhood, rather than dividing, unified and reached consensus about the purpose and nature of the kindergarten.

Kindergartens in the United States must be expected to respond to the diversity of children and their educational needs, furnish all children with appropriate activities and instruction, and get each child off to a good start in schooling (NCES, 1997). Thus, the purpose of the kindergarten continues to be to provide a well-rounded program and curriculum in order to meet the needs of all children in the least restrictive environment to enable each child to reach his or her fullest potential (NAEYC, 1990).

Today's kindergarten curriculum is grounded solidly in constructivist theories. On the basis of theory and research supporting the constructivist theory and research, the National Association for the Education of Young Children and the National Association of Early Childhood Specialists in State Departments of Education (1992) articulated support for the rights of four- and five-year-olds to experience a kindergarten program and curriculum appropriate to their development.

This does not mean that every kindergarten in our country is based on a constructivist approach. About a quarter of kindergarten teachers surveyed report using worksheets to teach literary, math, and science skills (NCES, 1997), a practice more congruent with behavioral theories than constructivist ones. Regardless, the majority of kindergarten teachers report that children play in and outdoors every day, listen to stories and songs, use objects to learn math and science concepts, and engage in dramatic play, arts and crafts, and music on a daily basis (NCES, 1997).

TODAY'S KINDERGARTEN CURRICULUM

Today's kindergarten curriculum does the following:

◆ Includes goals for achievement in all domains—social, emotional, cognitive, and physical—in order to prepare children for the role of citizen in a democracy.
◆ Addresses the development of knowledge and understanding and processes and skills, not just isolated facts.
◆ Is grounded on realistic goals that challenge yet are achievable.
◆ Reflects the needs and interests of individual children and the group.
◆ Respects and supports individual, cultural, and linguistic diversity.
◆ Builds on what children already know and are able to do to consolidate their learning and to foster their acquisition of new concepts and skills.
◆ Allows for integration across traditional subject matter disciplines.
◆ Meets the recognized standards of the relevant subject matter disciplines.
◆ Engages children actively, socially, physically, and mentally.
◆ Is flexible so that teachers can adapt to individual children or groups.

IN SUMMARY

Readiness has been a continuing issue in the kindergarten. Theories of maturationalism, behaviorism, and constructivism have been used to explain readiness. These theories, each of which has strengths and weaknesses, have been applied in today's kindergartens.

Growth, learning, and readiness, according to maturational theories, are due to internal physiological mechanisms and their orderly, sequential growth rather than to the environment. Behavioral theories postulate that learning is imposed on the individual externally through reinforcement from the social, physical, and psychological environment. According to Skinner, there is no concern about readiness, only about how to reinforce responses appropriately. Constructivists believe that humans develop through a series of stages that must be taken into account but that learners can be helped to construct new understandings through their own social, physical, and mental activity and interactions with the environment. This gives kindergarten teachers an optimistic view of readiness because once they understand the way the child knows the world, they can plan to extend this knowledge and promote new learning.

Social forces led to increased attention to school readiness. Each of the theories has influenced school readiness practices. Both maturational and behavioral theories led to delaying children's entrance into kindergarten, kindergarten retention, or placement in a transitional class prior to entrance into first grade.

Nevertheless, today's kindergartens are grounded solidly in the constructivists' view of learning and readiness. Kindergarten programs continue to provide children with a well-rounded kindergarten program and curriculum in order to meet the needs of all children.

EXTEND YOUR IDEAS

1. Interview parents of four- and five-year-old children. Ask them what they think their children need to know and be able to do before they enter kindergarten. Discuss your findings in class. What do parents think their children should be able to know and do before entering kindergarten? How do parents' views match those of the theorists and philosophers?

2. Reflect on your own "readiness" experiences. Interview parents or guardians and ask them about their view of readiness. Did they think you were "ready" for kindergarten? Why or why not? What questions did they have about your readiness? Did they take any steps to ensure that you would be ready for kindergarten?

3. Observe a class of four- and five-year-old kindergarters. Record the social and gross and fine motor skills that five-year-olds, but not four-year-olds, exhibit. Next to each, name the theory of development you think best explains these differences.

4. Make a list of your characteristics. Include physical as well as social, emotional, and cognitive ones. Which of these do you think are the result of maturation and which the result of environment influences?

5. Interview two kindergarten teachers and ask them to describe their philosophy of kindergarten readiness and how they apply this philosophy. 🖐

RESOURCES

Publications

Cesarone, B. (1998). ERIC/EECE Report: School entrance age. *Childhood Education, 74,* 184–185.

Golant, S. K., & Golant, M. (1997). *Kindergarten—It isn't what it used to be.* Los Angeles: Lowell House.

National Association for the Education of Young Children. (1992). *Ready or not . . . . What parents should know about school readiness.* Washington, DC: National Association for the Education of Young Children.

Peck, J. T., McCaig, G., & Sapp, M. E. (1988). *Kindergarten policies: What is best for children.* Washington, DC: National Association for the Education of Young Children.

Shepard, L. A., & Smith, M. L. (1989). *Flunking grades: Research and policies on retention.* London: The Falmer Press.

REFERENCES

Baker, B. (1999). The dangerous and the good? Developmentalism, progress, public schooling. *Review of Education Research, 36,* 797–834.

Bredekamp, S., & Copple, C. (1997). *Developmentally appropriate practice in early childhood programs* (Rev. ed.). Washington, DC: National Association for the Education of Young Children.

Bredekamp, S., & Rosegrant, C. (1992). *Reaching potentials: Appropriate curriculum and assessment for young children (Vol. 1).* Washington, DC: National Association for the Education of Young Children.

Charlesworth, R., Hart, C. H., Burts, D. C., & DeWolf, D. (1993). The LSU studies: Building a research base for developmentally appropriate practice. In W. Reifel (Ed.), *Perspectives on developmentally appropriate practice, vol 5 of Advances in early education and day care* (pp. 3–23). Greenwich, CT: JAI Press.

Dweck, C. (1986). Motivational processes affecting learning. *American Psychologist, 41*, 1030–1048.

Gersten, R., & George, N. (1990). Teaching reading and mathematics to at-risk students in kindergarten: What we have learned from field research. In C. Seefeldt (Ed.), *Continuing issues in early childhood education* (pp. 245–261). Columbus, OH: Merrill Publishing.

Gesell, A. (1940). *The first five-years of life* (9th ed.). New York: Harper & Row.

Gesell, A., & Thompson, H. (1929). Learning and growth in identical twins: An experimental study of the method of co-twin control. *Genetic Psychology Monographs, 6*(1), 1–124.

Gesell, A., Ilg, F. L., Ames, L. B., & Rodell, J. L. (1974). *Infant and child in the culture of today.* New York: Harper & Row.

Gesell Developmental Schedules. (1954). The ontogenesis of infant behavior. In L. Carmichael (Ed.), *Manual of child psychology* (pp. 335–373). New York: John Wiley & Sons.

Golant, S. K., & Golant, M. (1997). *Kindergarten—It Isn't What It Used to Be.* Los Angeles: Lowell House.

Graue, M. E. (1998). What's wrong with *Edward the Unready? Young Children, 53*(3), 12–17.

Jensen, A. (1969). *Understanding readiness.* Urbana, IL: ERIC Clearinghouse on Early Childhood Education.

Kagan, S. L. (1999). Cracking the readiness mystique. *Young Children, 54*(4), 2–3.

Kohn, A. (1993). *Punished by rewards.* Boston: Houghton Mifflin.

Mantizicopoulos, P. Y. (1997). Do certain groups of children profit from early retention? A follow-up study of kindergarteners with attention problems. *Psychology in the Schools, 34*(2), 115–127.

Marcon, R. A. (1992). Differential effects of three preschool models on inner-city 4-year-olds. *Early Childhood Research Quarterly, 7*, 517–530.

National Association for the Education of Young Children. (1990). NAEYC position statement on school readiness. *Young Children, 46*(1), 21–23.

National Association for the Education of Young Children. (1992). *Ready or not: What parents should know about school readiness.* Washington, DC: Author.

National Association for the Education of Young Children and the National Association of Early Childhood Specialists in State Departments of Education. (1992). Guidelines for appropriate curriculum content and assessment in programs serving children ages 3 through 8. In S. Bredekamp & T. Rosegrant (Eds.), *Reaching potentials: Appropriate curriculum and assessment for young children: Vol. 1* (pp. 9–27). Washington, DC: Author.

National Center for Education Statistics. (1995). *Readiness for kindergarten: Parent and teacher beliefs.* Washington, DC: Author.

National Center for Education Statistics. (1997). *Digest of education statistics (1997).* Washington, DC: Author.

National Education Goals Panel (1991). *The national education goals report: Building a nation of learners.* Washington, DC: Author.

Peck, J. T., McCaig, G., & Sapp, M. E. (1988). *Kindergarten policies: What is best for children?* Washington, DC: National Association for the Education of Young Children.

Piaget, J. (1965). *The language and thought of the child.* New York: World Publishing Company.

Ravitch, D. (1995). *National standards in American education: A citizen's guide.* Washington, DC: Brookings Institute.

Ryan, S. (1995). *John Dewey and the high tide of American liberalism.* New York: Norton.

Shepard, L. (1992). Retention and redshirting. In L. Williams & D. Fromberg (Eds.), *Encyclopedia of early childhood education* (pp. 278–280). New York: Garland Publishing.

Shepard, L., & Smith, M. (1986). Synthesis of research on school readiness and kindergarten retention. *Educational Leadership, 44*(3), 78–86.

Shepard, L. A., & Smith, M. E. (1989). *Flunking grades: Research and policies on retention.* Lewes, England: Falmer Press.

Thorndike, E. L. (1913). *Educational psychology: The psychology of learning.* New York: Teachers College Press.

Vygotsky, L. (1978). *Mind in society.* Cambridge, MA: Harvard University Press.

Weber, E. (1969). *The Kindergarten.* New York: Teachers College Press.

Willer, B., & Bredekamp, S. (1990). Public policy report. Redefining readiness: An essential requisite for educational reform. *Young Children, 45*(5), 22–24.

PART

II

Ready or Not

CHAPTER 3

Four- and Five-Year-Olds Grow and Develop

"Look what I made," four-year-old Frances points to the row of blocks that she has stacked in random order. With a quick tap, she knocks them all down. "That's great!" says five-year-old Leah as she continues to carefully place blocks in a pattern as she constructs her elaborate city. Leah has carefully arranged the blocks to make walls, doors, and roads. "Hey, what are you making?" Leah asks. "I'm making a house," said Francis. "Do you want to help me build this street?" Leah asks Francis. "No," says Francis, "I'm busy over here."

Although four- and five-year-olds can play side by side in classrooms, they can be at different places in their development. Activities that four- and five-year-olds engage in can be similar, yet the process that occurs within the activity and the outcomes of the activity can vary. Four-year-olds, like Francis, are less planful and goal-directed in their activities. The house that Francis is building can easily transform into a tower if the blocks are arranged in a different way. Five-year-olds, like Leah, are more planful and organized, carefully designing the neighborhood and placing each block accordingly. Four-year-olds still engage in parallel play, whereas five-year-olds are increasingly interested in social interaction with others. Leah welcomed Francis's company, but Francis was satisfied playing next to Leah without playing with her. The challenge for the kindergarten teacher is to design classroom content and activities that meet the developmental needs of both four- and five-year-olds.

This chapter describes (1) the variability in four- and five-year-olds' development; (2) the physical, emotional, cognitive, language, and social development of four- and five-year-olds; (3) the development of the self; (4) behavioral expectations; and (5) diversity in development.

WHAT DO FOUR- AND FIVE-YEAR-OLDS LOOK LIKE?

F our- and five-year-olds come in different shapes and sizes. They grow and develop in many ways. They are physically changing, growing taller and often losing many "baby-like" features. Their language and vocabulary is rapidly expanding. Four- and five-year-olds are extremely curious about the world, and their conversations are filled with questions such as "Why do leaves change color?" and "Why is ice cold?" Typically, four- and five-year-olds enjoy being with other children. At the same time, they are still developing important social skills, such as sharing and cooperation. Four- and five-year-olds love to laugh, giggle, run, and play.

Development for four- and five-year-olds is variable. The tallest child in the class can be the youngest. The oldest child can often be the one that is labeled the most "immature." Girls at this age are often taller than most of the boys. Also, there is great variability in development within an individual child. The tallest child may have the least physical coordination, or the child who is on an average growth trajectory can be advanced in his language and cognitive development. The risk in presenting typical child development and learning is that individual and cultural variations are the norm, not the exception. Growth and development at four and five years of age are variable and change rapidly (Bredekamp & Copple, 1997).

In the next section, physical, emotional, linguistic, cognitive, and social development are described for typical four- and five-year-olds. The goal is to provide early childhood educators with a broad understanding of children's growth and development. Development for four- and five-year-olds should be viewed on a continuum in which there is greater variability at the far ends and more similarities in between. However, there are differences in the development of four- and five-year-olds, and it is important to understand these differences so that expectations about development and curriculum practices are tailored to the appropriate developmental needs of children. In the following section, the similarities between four- and five-year-olds are presented, but the differences in this age are emphasized so that educators understand the uniqueness of children at each of these ages. Understanding the developmental differences for four- and five-year-olds will help with decisions concerning the nature and time spent on activities, the curriculum practices, and the organization of the classes.

PHYSICAL DEVELOPMENT

Four-year-old Sam runs onto the playground and climbs steadily up the jungle gym. Once at the top, he jumps down and dashes toward the slide. Holding on, he climbs the ladder using alternating feet on each step. Sliding down, he yells with delight. Immediately, he is on to the swing, where he jumps on, belly first, and yells for someone to push him. Next to Sam is five-year-old Jason, coordinating his leg movement so that he can pump the swing to go back and forth. Both boys jump off and chase each other around the playground.

Four- and five-year-olds are filled with energy and are constantly moving. As they grow, they are developing and refining their gross and fine motor skills. They can run smoothly and stop easily and love to hop and try to skip. They are beginning to throw a ball with some ease and use two hands to catch, missing frequently. Four- and five-year-olds are developing their balance and sense of equilibrium. They enjoy riding tricycles, pushing and pulling wagons, and scurrying around in little push cars.

Four-year-olds' fine motor skills are advancing. They can stack blocks 10 high and string beads. Completing a simple 10-piece puzzle is no longer a frustration but a victory. Coloring, painting, and tearing and folding paper intrigues children at this age as they develop increasing control over their fine muscles. Development at this time can vary greatly both because of the maturational level and the cultural expectations of the child (Pica, 1997). As one teacher notes, Tony easily slips his arm through the sleeves of his coat, puts the button through the large holes, and pulls on his snow boots. Kent, however, needs help putting on his jacket and adjusting his hat. At this age, cutting is a skill to be mastered. Sally holds the scissors correctly but has some difficulty in cutting completely through the paper, whereas Tommy is struggling to keep the scissors in his hands.

Energy levels are high for four-year-olds, yet impulse control is low. During story time, Nathan is moving around on his mat twiddling a tread on his pant leg, and Kate and Becky are talking about Kate's new Barbie shoes. The teacher asks for the children to pay attention while she is reading and reminds them that it is only a bit longer. Four-year-olds are beginning to develop internal controls, yet their instinct is to keep moving.

Practicing holding a pencil to write is fun yet challenging. Because fine motor coordination is developing, writing skills can vary. Some close approximation of letters scattered on paper is typical for four-year-olds. Attempts at writing one's name can vary from being able to write one letter in their name to writing a few letters to writing their whole name.

Although hand dominance is established by this age, children can still use both hands with ease. Sally mostly uses her left hand to string beads but used her right hand one time. Subsequently, she removed the bead and replaced it using her left hand.

Jason carefully places his softball on a tee. He swings at the ball, misses, swings again, misses, swings two more times, misses, and finally hits the ball across the playing field. He runs with delight, squealing as he reaches first base. His friend in the field catches the ball and immediately drops it.

Five-year-olds have as much energy as four-year-olds, but both their fine and gross motor skills are beginning to be more directed and focused in their actions (Berk, 1997). They find inactivity very difficult. Fine motor skills are becoming more refined. Their control over writing implements is improving, and letters look closer to actual print. Using scissors is less of a frustration, and cutting can be fun. Drawings and paintings are now things that they can talk about and are increasing in their complexity. Human figures are no longer just heads or heads and bodies but include some approximation of arms, hands, legs, and feet. At this age, children become interested in building structures with small blocks and little Lego figures instead of oversized blocks and are graduating to puzzles with 15 to 20 pieces. Dressing is taking on a newfound ease. Most buttons can be placed through their hole; zippers, once started, can be pulled up; and children are developing the dexterity to tie their shoes.

Fine motor skills become more focused.

Gross motor skills are becoming more agile and coordinated. They can combine running with skipping, hopping, and jumping. Depending on the social and cultural context, some five-year-olds begin to ride a two-wheeler and begin to master the eye-hand coordination needed to swing a bat to hit a ball. Five-year-olds do everything with a lot of motion. "Walk, don't run!" is repeated in every kindergarten class numerous times each day. Overconfidence in their physical abilities also presents challenges. A five-year-old teeters on a narrow curb in the park as if he were walking on a balance beam. They want to swing as high as they can and dive down a slide as fast as possible.

Although keeping still is difficult, five-year-olds can be expected to listen quietly while a story is being read, walk carefully down steps at school while using the railing for assistance, and pay attention while someone is speaking to them (Ignico & Wayda, 1999).

EMOTIONAL DEVELOPMENT

Four- and five-year-olds express a wide range of emotions and are able to use appropriate labels such as mad, sad, happy, and just okay to differentiate their feelings. Both four- and five-year-olds' emotional states are very situation-specific and can change as rapidly as they switch from one activity to another. As four-year-olds develop into five-year-olds, there is an increasing internalization and regulation over their emotions.

Four-year-olds' emotions are largely on the surface. At one moment in the classroom, Matthew is laughing uncontrollably about the funny faces that his friend Nathan is making. Within a split second, Matthew is sobbing because Nathan stuck his tongue out at him. "I was just making a funny face," said Nathan. Four-year-olds are beginning to understand the different emotions that they experience, yet they have difficulty regulating these emotions. Their emotions are very connected to the events and feelings that are occurring at that moment (Hyson, 1994).

Four-year-olds also have difficulty separating feelings from actions. If they feel something, they express it. If they want something, they try to take it. Delaying gratification and controlling impulsive feelings are often a challenge. Their natural curiosity can often lead them into trouble. Matthew began building a bridge with blocks. His intense focus and his desire for the blocks did not allow him to see that Nathan was already using the blocks as part of his construction site. A tug-of-war over the blocks evolved into a hitting match. Four-year-olds can often use physical means to solve conflicts instead of verbally negotiating their needs (Hyson, 1994). Teaching children appropriate ways to express their emotions is an important milestone in their development. Conflicts that arise over two children's need for the same object are common; children are learning how to solve conflicts in socially acceptable ways (Hazen & Brownell, 1999).

Four-year-olds are beginning to develop a sense of humor. It is as if the Tickle Me Elmo doll were modeled after four-year-olds. The slightest event can bring uncontrollable laughter. Once they begin, it is difficult to stop them from laughing. They will be amused at the things that adults do. They may laugh simply to make others laugh. This silliness is accompanied by a fascination with "potty" humor where words such as "poop" and "pee" can result in hysterical laughter from a group of four-year-olds.

At this age, children also begin to have fears that they can identify. They want to sleep with a night-light on and will not go down a dark basement alone. Monster books, such as *There's a Nightmare in My Closet* by Mercer Mayer (1969) and *Where the Wild Things Are* by Maurice Sendak (1963), appeal to them. The books affirm what children already believe, "that monsters are really there," but through the books the children are able to keep their fears in place.

At this age, children are also beginning to understand that others have feelings, too (Denham, 1998). One little boy came into Matthew's class with a big bandage on his knee. The teacher asked him what happened, and he said he fell when he was chasing his sister. Matthew said, "It must have really hurt." Matthew touched his own knee where a scrape was healing. He said, "I fell off my bike the other day and cut my knee really bad. It was bleeding. I bet you cried; I did when I fell." Being able to understand how another person feels is emerging.

Separation from parents or primary caregivers can sometimes be difficult, especially at school (Denham, 1998). On the first day of school, Nathan cried and held on to his mother's leg as she tried to leave. When his mother peeked back into his classroom 10 minutes later, Nathan was happily playing at the sand table. Fears concerning separation at this age are typically short-lived and are harder on parents than on the four-year-old.

Five-year-olds are beginning to regulate their emotions and express their feelings in more socially acceptable ways. Sally tells her mom about what happened in school. "I was really mad at Lisa today. She always wants to be the mom when we play house, but I want to be the mom sometimes." Sally's mother asks, "Well, what did you do about it?" "I used my words like you told me to," said Sally. "I told her I wanted to be the mom today and she had to be the baby, but she said, 'no!' I stopped playing with her, but I'll play with her tomorrow because she's my best friend."

Five-year-olds are beginning to separate their feelings and actions (Denham, 1998). For example, Sally is beginning to use her words to express her feelings. This allows her to express her anger or her disappointment in a socially acceptable way. Five-year-olds are beginning to delay their wants and desires. They are learning to wait their turn for a toy and listen when someone is speaking.

Five-year-olds are beginning to internalize socially acceptable behaviors. If they see something that they want, they ask for it (Greenspan

Five-year-olds are beginning to regulate emotions.

& Greenspan, 1994). If they are told that they cannot have something, they are learning to deal with their feelings of either disappointment or anger. Although natural curiosity is strong in five-year-olds, they are beginning to learn the limits of this curiosity. Instead of grabbing a train off a classmate's chair, they may ask if they can see it.

Physical aggression and temper outbursts are beginning to wane. As children are able to express their feelings in words, the behavioral expression of emotions begins to decrease. Unfortunately, verbal insults toward peers can surface at this time. Children often use "potty talk" to express their dislike for a child or situation, calling a classmate a "pee pee face." At this age, children also are learning to distinguish among a wider range of emotions. They can label facial expressions that show when someone is happy, mad, sad, tired, or disappointed.

Five-year-olds are very fun loving and affectionate. They love to laugh and make others laugh. They are discovering jokes, but they do not yet understand the logic or semantics needed to make their own jokes funny. Many kindergarten teachers have heard the one about why the chicken crossed the road. "Because he was a chicken," says five-year-old Matthew, who then laughs uncontrollably. Crying becomes more situation-specific. Five-year-olds are learning to control their tears. Tears are usually the result of feelings being hurt by a peer, physical pain, or frustration. At this age, these incidents are occurring less frequently.

During the first days of kindergarten, there may be tears for some children. Some children are sad to leave their mothers; others are afraid of the unknown situation. These tears, however, do not last long. It is rare to have five-year-olds crying beyond the first month of school.

LANGUAGE DEVELOPMENT

For four- and five-year-olds, it is a time of immense growth in language. Vocabulary is expanding, and the semantic and syntactic structure of their language is becoming more complex. This change in language represents the development of cognitive abilities. Children are becoming more complex thinkers, and as they grow, these changes are reflected in their language. Four- and five-year-olds are curious about language and increasingly rely on language to make their wants and needs known.

At four years of age, children's language development is exploding. Their vocabulary consists of about 4,000 to 6,000 words, and they are typically speaking in five- to six-word sentences. They use language to communicate their thoughts, needs, and demands. However, sometimes they try to communicate more than their vocabulary allows them and extend words to create new meaning (Snow, Burns, & Griffin, 1998). In telling his teacher about their trip to the grocery store, Matthew explains, "We goed to the store and got some food for dinner. We piled all of our food into a baby carriage, oh, I mean cart. I always get them confused." Matthew's use of "goed" instead of "went" is a typical error of overextension of language rules used by four-year-olds. Four-year-olds are learning rules for verb tense, plurals, and pronouns. However, they have not yet incorporated the exceptions to these rules into their language, so "went" is "goed," "kept" is "keeped," and "children" is "childs."

Matthew's confusion with words, using "baby carriage" instead of "shopping cart," is a common error for four-year-olds. They are learning so many new words at this time that there is a frequent misuse of words and mislabeling of objects. Often words that sound the same can be mistaken for each other. Alice said that her father just bought a new blue kayak to go to work. Alice confused the word "kayak" with "Cadillac" and therefore made it appear that her father bought a boat instead of a car.

Talking is a favorite activity of four-year-olds. They talk while they are playing, frequently describing what they are doing while playing (Howard, Shaughnessy, Sanger, & Hux, 1998). They want to share with you their experiences, from how they got up from bed in the morning to how they brush their teeth to what their dog ate for breakfast. Taking turns in conversation is difficult. They want to talk and be heard but have difficulty listening to others talk. At this age, some children talk incessantly, and teachers need to help these children learn to regulate their talking to allow others opportunities to speak.

As mentioned in the section on emotional development, "bathroom" talk is a common part of four-year-olds' language. Four-year-olds are pushing the boundaries of their language and are learning what words are socially acceptable and what words are not. Four-year-old Liz yells to her friend, "Nanny, nanny, poo, poo. You can't get me!" Liz is discovering new ways to express herself. Teachers need to help children understand that there are more appropriate ways to express themselves than through "bathroom" talk.

Five-year-olds' language continues to grow, and their vocabularies are expanding to 5,000 to 8,000 words. The number of words in sentences is increasing, and sentence structure is becoming more complex. As a result of adult feedback, five-year-olds begin decreasing their use of overextensions of rules for verbs and plurals, frequently correcting their own errors. Remarking about his trip to the beach, Seth said, "I put my foots, I mean feet, in the water, and it was cold." Five-year-olds are also using pronouns correctly. Seth used "I" to identify himself instead of using his name or the pronoun "you," which is used by others to identify him.

Five-year-olds become increasingly more sophisticated in their ability to communicate their ideas and feelings with words (Ninio & Snow, 1996). Asking what happened in school can be answered with elaborate stories ranging from what they had for a snack to who spilled the paint all over the floor. As five-year-olds' language becomes more complex, they often misuse words in a humorous way. Bryan told his mother that he was afraid to go to the doctor because he heard that he would get a shot with an arrow. He thought it would really hurt.

Five-year-olds also enjoy talking. They are also learning the conventions of conversation and are interrupting less frequently, learning to take turns, and listening to others while they speak. At this age, children enjoy using language to act out plays and stories. Through this, they show their skills of using conventional modes of communication, complete with pitch and inflection. A group of five-year-olds can perform the "Three Little Pigs" complete with songs and voice changes to imitate the various characters. Opportunities such as "show and tell" allow the children to talk in front of a group for a limited amount of time and use language to express themselves.

"Bathroom talk" is still a big part of five-year-olds' playfulness with language. However, they are learning to control its use so that they are not caught using it by an adult. They are also fascinated with big words not typically found in their everyday vocabulary, such as "Stegosaurus" and "tarantula." It is not uncommon for five-year-olds to learn the difficult vocabulary words that are associated with things that they are interested in, such as dinosaurs or Star Wars.

COGNITIVE DEVELOPMENT

Four- and five-year-olds experience important changes in cognitive growth. In general, four- and five-year-olds are beginning to problem solve, think about cause-and-effect relationships, and express these ideas to others. As four- and five-year-olds' cognition matures, they begin to make the distinction between private thoughts and public expressions.

Four-year-olds are actively manipulating their environment and constructing meaning from their world. One of the most important cognitive shifts from three- to four-year-olds is the development of symbolic thought. Symbolic thought is the ability to mentally or symbolically represent concrete objects, actions, and events (Piaget, 1952). The most obvious sign of the development of symbolic thought in four-year-olds is the significant increase in their use of make-believe play, which becomes more elaborate as they grow. "Do you like my horse?" Sam says as he rides around his classroom on a makeshift broom. "He's really fast and loves it when I brush his hair."

Children begin to problem solve and think about cause and effect.

At this age, children are very egocentric in their thinking. Egocentrism is the tendency to be more aware of their own point of view than that of others (Piaget, 1952). This explains why four-year-olds have difficulty understanding how the world looks to other people. It is difficult for them to understand why others are not happy when they are happy, sad when they are sad, and hungry when they are hungry. A four-year-old gave her teacher her favorite teddy bear because the teacher said that she was not feeling good. The teddy bear made the four-year-old feel better when she was sick, so the same must be true for her teacher. Because four-year-olds think egocentrically, it is best to present information that is hands-on and is relevant to their own experiences.

Four-year-olds' thinking and reasoning are concrete, and they typically reason from the particular to the particular (Siegler, 1997). Four-year-old Seth reasons that his dog is friendly, so the dog he passes on his way to school must be friendly, too. Seth likes chocolate, so everyone in his family must like chocolate. At this age, children presume a causal relationship if two events are closely associated in time or in some other way. Bryan sees his teacher at school when he arrives in the morning and leaves her there when he returns home in the afternoon. He reasons that his teacher must live at school.

Concept development is another important aspect of the cognitive development of four-year-olds. They are organizing information into concepts (e.g., chair or animal) based on attributes that define an object or an idea. However, at four years of age, the categories that the concepts are based on are derived from the appearance or the action of the object. Seth calls a small goat that he is allowed to pet at the zoo a "dog." In his mind, the goat fits all the criteria needed to be a dog: small, furry, and having four legs (Gelman, 1999).

Similarly, when four-year-olds classify objects into categories, they tend to focus on one aspect of the object and ignore the other features. Mary is trying to tell her mother that she does not want fruit for a snack; she wants an apple. She is having difficulty understanding that an apple is a part of the larger category of fruit. Because four-year-olds are beginning to understand part/whole and hierarchical relationships, they have difficulty grasping that objects can be in more than one class. Also at this age, when children are asked to sort objects into specific categories, they are beginning to sort objects on the basis of one attribute (Gelman, 1999). When asked to sort the blocks into groups, Nathan started to put all the blue blocks in one pile and the red blocks in another. At one point, he had put a circular red block in the blue pile because the last block he picked up was circular, and that one was placed in the blue pile. For a moment, Nathan needed to think about what feature of the block he was focusing on for sorting. He confused the shape with the color and soon corrected himself. This ability to focus on one attribute of an object to classify is developing in four-year-olds.

Time is a concept that four-year-olds have difficulty comprehending (Piaget, 1969). Four-year-olds view time as events occurring immediately or taking a very long time. Anyone who has ever told a four-year-old that they will be taking a field trip in a week knows that the child will ask every day if they are going on the trip that day.

Four-year-olds are developing their memory skills. They can, with some prompting, remember what they did last weekend. Salient events such as birthday parties, class trips, and a child breaking his or her arm on the playground can easily be remembered. The child can recall main events in a story and can retell a story with some accuracy of the sequence. Four-year-olds have difficulty remembering lists or isolated information. Learning and remembering things at this age are easier if information is presented in a context that is meaningful to the child. Learning and remembering about spiders is easier if the child can study a spider that was crawling on the playground.

At four, children are also beginning to develop a sense about what is real and what is not. This is called the appearance/reality distinction (Flavell, 1992). Four-year-old Kate was very frightened of the clown that was at her friend's birthday party, and she clung to her mother's leg. As the clown did a magic trick and made her laugh, she said to her mother, "The clown is like a real person. I love her." Children are beginning to understand what is real and what is not real, what is a dream and what is not a dream.

Five-year-olds think about things. Lee watches the leaves fall off the trees and says that the leaves look like they are dancing. Then he asks, "Why do the leaves fall off the trees?" Five-year-olds are filled with questions about how things work, how things are made, and where things come from. This reflects their interest in understanding the world around them. Their imagination continues to develop, and their play centers around pretending. However, they begin to make distinctions between when they are pretending and when they are not. Classrooms are filled with children saying, "Look at me, I'm pretending to be a kite, or a dog, or a snake."

Although five-year-olds are egocentric in their thinking, they are beginning to be aware of others' feelings and points of view (Siegler, 1997). At this age, children can begin to understand that they can be happy when others are not and begin to accept that others do not have to play the exact game that they are playing. They are beginning to understand other children's likes and dislikes. Gary said at snack time, "You can give me Sam's graham crackers because I like them and he doesn't."

Five-year-olds' reasoning is still concrete, yet they reason less from the particular to the particular (Gelman, 1999). They may reason that because their dog is friendly, all dogs are friendly. However, they are quick to understand when an adult explains that that may not be the case with all dogs. They are beginning to understand that there are general rules, yet also exceptions to the rules. Also, five-year-olds' reasoning about concrete information, such as dogs that they see, is easier to accomplish than it is for more abstract information. Understanding that both whales and humans are mammals is a difficult concept for five-year-olds to grasp because it is difficult to demonstrate the similarities of the two in a concrete way.

Five-year-olds continue to become more sophisticated in their development and organization of concepts. With things that children are very familiar with, they can begin to see how different objects fit into different categories. Matthew has both a bunny and a turtle in his classroom. He understands that the bunny is soft and cuddly and eats carrots. The turtle lives in water, and his shell is hard. But when his teacher says that it is his turn to take the animals home for spring vacation, he understands that this means both the turtle and the bunny. He says, "Even though the bunny cannot swim, it still is an animal." Matthew is developing criteria for his concepts and refining his concepts on the basis of each new experience. His concept of "animal" is becoming more refined as he interacts with other animals and objects and begins to construct his notion of similarities and differences among things.

Five-year-olds are interested in sorting and grouping (Flavell, Miller, & Miller, 1992). They can successfully sort objects on the basis of a single feature, such as color, shape, and size. Sorting things on the basis of more abstract concepts, such as an object's use, is more challenging. Kim proudly showed her teacher how she sorted all the beads into different color groups. When asked to sort all the toys in the dramatic play area that could be used in the kitchen, the group included spoons, artificial foods, as well as a doll and teddy bear. Kim explained that she frequently played with her doll and teddy in her kitchen at home.

Understanding the concept of time is still a challenge for five-year-olds (Flavell, Green, & Flavell, 1995). They talk about things that happened in the past, yet yesterday means the same thing as last month or last week. However, they are able to understand time in terms of things that they are familiar with. To explain how long it will take to get to the zoo, the teachers say that it will take as long as it takes you to get home from school. Time is relative to things in the children's immediate experiences. Calendars posted in classrooms and in homes begin to help children conceptualize how long it will be until the field trip or their birthday.

At this age, children have not developed strategies for remembering information. However, with help, they can employ some strategies for remembering (Siegler, 1997). In remembering where they left their sneakers, the teacher can ask specific questions about what and where they were last playing, trying to help them reconstruct events to help them remember. Learning in context and in meaningful ways will increase their chances of recalling information. Five-year-olds can learn the alphabet if it is connected to experiences that they are familiar with. Also, they can recall parts of a story after two readings of a story (Morrow & Smith, 1990).

Five-year-olds are becoming more certain about what is real and what is pretend. At the classroom Halloween party, Jake stood and stared at the frightening witch who entered the room. Then he said, "Hey, Tina, is that you under there. You didn't fool me." At this age, children love to play pretend games, and their imaginations are boundless. They are fascinated with magic and think that things really can appear and disappear. Five-year-olds typically believe in the tooth fairy and the magic of Santa Claus. However, they are beginning to ask important questions about how the tooth fairy gets into their house and how she knows where the tooth is. These questions represent the evolution of their thinking and attempting to make concepts fit into what they know about the world.

SOCIAL DEVELOPMENT

Four- and five-year-olds are becoming social beings and often prefer the company of other children to that of adults. Children will begin to express their preference for playing with some children over others. Playing and getting along is an important aspect of social development for four- and five-year-olds.

Developing social relations is an important milestone for four-year-olds. For many four-year-olds, the school experience will be the first time that they will have to negotiate getting along with a group of children their own age. Although four-year-olds still engage in parallel play, they are becoming increasingly interested in playing with other children. Along with playing with others comes the need to play cooperatively and fairly. These are skills that four-year-olds need help in developing. They have difficulty sharing and often believe that things need to be their way and no other. When conflicts do arise, they want to solve them but lack the verbal skills to do so. Helping children understand turn taking, sharing, and being respectful of their peers is a major challenge when working with four-year-olds. Activities can be structured to facilitate cooperative social skills.

Four-year-olds are beginning to make distinctions between children who they prefer to play with and those who they have no interest in. Although most friendships at this age are controlled by parental choice and proximity, children are beginning to make requests and clearly play better with some children than they do with others (Rubin, Coplan, Nelson, & Cheah, 1999).

Five-year-olds are very social and frequently prefer other children's company to that of adults. They have developed some effective cooperative skills and have learned, for the most part, how to get along and play with others. They are beginning to internalize social rules. Jake understands that if he hits his friend because he wants to pitch the ball, his friend will become angry and will not want to play at all. Play activities typically occur in one-to-one situations or in small groups. At this age, children are also expressing preferences over children who they want to play with and those who they do not. Friendships are becoming more clearly defined. Five-year-olds also are beginning to understand the power of social rejection. In the middle of arguing about the rules of a game they were playing, Lee says to Evan, "If you don't play the right way, you can't be my friend anymore, and you can't come over to my house." Children at this age can be loving, affectionate friends and also have the ability to say things to one another that can be very hurtful. Teachers need to be aware of the social structure of the relationships among children in their classroom. It is important to help children become aware of other children's feeling and develop a sense of respect for others.

Social relations can affect children's cognitive and emotional development. A socially rejected child will be a child that is not happy at school. Helping children get along with one another will promote a positive classroom attitude and instill a love of learning in all children.

BEHAVIORAL EXPECTATIONS

In the previous sections, the physical, emotional, linguistic, cognitive, and social development of four- and five-year-olds was described. As teachers of four- and five-year-olds, it is also important to understand how development translates into behavioral expectation in the classrooms. What behaviors should be expected of four- and-five-year-olds in school? Can they be expected to sit and listen for a sustained amount of time? Should they work only in small groups? Teachers' expectations of four- and five-year-olds influence the way classroom activities are planned and organized.

Anyone who has spent time with four- and five-year-olds understands that they have limited attention spans. Typically, children at this age can sit and listen to a story or watch a science demonstration that precedes a hands-on activity for about 10 to 15 minutes. Anything longer, and they are fidgeting, looking around the room, or talking to a friend. In order to keep on task and focused, four- and five-year-olds need to be actively engaged in their learning.

Children at this age are filled with energy and need to be active. They are filled with energy and need productive avenues to direct this energy. Keeping a steady and even pace to the activities in the classroom will help channel children's energy in the appropriate direction. Too many activities that require sustained attention will result in the children losing interest.

At this age, children can follow simple directions. Mrs. Hope asks the children in her four-year-old class to clean up the activity areas and line up to go outside. The children scurry because they are anxious to play on the playground. Simple two-step commands can be met with success. However, when children are given too many directions to follow, they will not be able to process all the information. Situations that request more than what a child can do result in frustration and give the appearance that children are not following directions. This is especially true when children are transitioning from one activity to another, as following directions can be difficult with the added activity in the room.

Learning to get along with other children is one of the most important milestones for four- and five-year-olds. Children need to learn how to work and cooperate with one another. Aggressive behavior can be seen in the way in which some four- and-five-year-olds express their anger or frustration over a situation. However, it is not acceptable classroom behavior. At this age, children need to understand that using words instead of actions is the more effective way of communicating their feelings. Behavioral interventions such as removing the child from the situation coupled with a verbal explanation are the most effective ways to deal with aggressive behavior.

At this age, children find comfort and security in the repetition of routines. Having a routine that the children follow helps them feel that they have control over their environment and helps them anticipate events. Mrs. Hope begins to sing the "Clean-up" song, and everyone begins to put his or her things away. "It's my turn to help with the napkins today," said Melissa. Melissa knows that after they clean up the toys, it is snack time. Routines help children understand how their day is organized.

Four- and five-year-olds can benefit from working in various groups, be it small groups, whole groups, or one-to-one. The activity typically dictates the grouping that is most appropriate. For some circle-time activities—for example, when the teacher is demonstrating how to weigh sand—a whole group can work. When the children are weighing the amount of sand in their shoes from playing in the sandbox, a small group works better. With five children, the teacher can help them pour the sand from their shoes onto the weighing plate and watch as the child adjusts the scale to the weight of the sand. One-to-one works best when the teacher is listening to what the child wrote in his or her journal about weighing sand. The one-to-one attention helps the child focus on what he or she has written. Varying the different group configurations helps learning work in different settings and allows the appropriate amount of teacher attention to be given according to the specific task.

DEVELOPMENT OF THE CONCEPT OF SELF

Annie poses in front of the mirror in the dramatic play area. "Look at me; I look like a princess, and my daddy calls me princess, too." Four- and five-year-olds are developing a sense of self. They are beginning to understand things about them that are unique to them. They can recognize themselves in mirrors and in pictures. They are learning things about themselves and beginning to compare themselves to others. "Sally has the same hair color as I do, but Nancy has more of a yellow color," says Andrea. "Majia's skin is darker than mine," says Dora. At this age, children want to explore the characteristics that make them special. Four- and five-year-olds understand that boys and girls are different. When describing a classmate, they can always identify if the child is a boy or a girl. They also understand that gender is constant. If you are a boy today, you will be a boy tomorrow.

At four and five years of age, children still have difficulty understanding what their "whole self" includes (Siegler, 1997). Playing hide-and-seek, Steven crouches behind a tree. His head is covered, and he cannot see David, who is counting to 20 before he searches for his friends. However, Steven's entire body is sticking out from behind the tree. His other friend, Leo, is hiding his eyes behind a narrow pole from the swing set. Because Leo cannot see David, he assumes that David cannot see him. At this age, children's concept of their physical self can be limited to what they can and cannot directly see.

Classroom environments can support the healthy and positive development of a child's concept of self (McClellan & Katz, 1997). Activities that encourage body self-awareness help young children understand how their bodies move and work. Art activities that allow children to draw pictures of partners and themselves help children conceptualize their own image as well as those of others. Photos of children next to their artwork or displayed on a bulletin board help reinforce children's images of themselves. Providing a full-length mirror in the classroom where children can watch themselves play or see how they look in their dress-up clothes facilitates the development of the concept of self. Games such as "Simon Says" and "Head, Shoulders, Knees, and Toes" help develop children's perceptions of their bodies. Have the children document their growth in a diary over the course of the year. Weigh and measure them, have them trace their shoe and their hand, and have them draw a picture of themselves. Repeat this activity again at the end of the year to see the changes in each child.

DEVELOPMENT OF SELF-EFFICACY

As young children are learning and interacting with others, they are developing a sense of self-efficacy. Self-efficacy is one's perception of his or her ability and competence to do things. Four- and five-year-olds have a genuine sense that they can do anything. They are eager and motivated and typically think that they are good at any task set before them. When Katie's teacher asked if she needed help tying her shoes, Katie quickly replied, with an air of confidence, that she could do it herself. The teacher watched as Katie tangled the shoelaces to look something like a balled knot. Within 10 minutes, the shoe was untied again. Katie's teacher asked again, "Do you want me to help you with that shoe?" "No, thanks," replied Katie,

"I'm really good at tying my shoes." Even in the face of failure, children at this age are optimistic about their abilities and skills. Like Katie, they will persist at things, even if they need to try the same task over and over again before they achieve success. Persistence and feeling that they are competent contributes to the development of self-efficacy.

Providing children with opportunities to be independent helps foster the development of positive self-efficacy. As four- and five-year-olds begin to try more things on their own, they develop a greater understanding of what they can accomplish. In many cases, children at this age are beginning to assert their independence. Like Katie, they want to try to do things on their own, and they feel a great sense of satisfaction when they are successful. Having children put materials in the appropriate place after an activity, put on their boots, or cut paper are ways in which they are asserting their independence.

Adults working with young children need to understand that patience is the most important attribute in developing independence in young children. Doing the activity for a child will certainly be accomplished in a shorter period of time. However, the value in having the child learn from the process of completing an activity will never be achieved if the child is not provided with the opportunity to try things on his or her own.

INDIVIDUAL DIFFERENCES IN DEVELOPMENT

In a kindergarten class, children are graphing their heights and shoe sizes. Nancy says to her friend Sally, "You have bigger feet than I do, but I am taller than you." Four- and five-year-olds come in various shapes and sizes and grow in all areas at different rates. Some children are cutting out paper dolls with no assistance at four years old. Others are struggling with this as they turn six. Some children are reading in kindergarten; others are beginning to identify letters.

Teachers need to be sensitive to the great variability in development in four- and five-year-olds. There are considerable individual differences in children's learning abilities and physical development in these early years. Although children share the common experience of the classroom, each child comes to school with his or her unique experiences. They bring with them the experiences of their own families, their previous school or caretaking experiences, their ancestry, and other variables that make them who they are.

Although teachers teach a group of children, it is important to be aware of children's individuality. Although children share many similarities, they are not all alike. Children have different learning styles (Saracho & Spodek, 1984). Some children learn better visually, some learn better tactilely, and still others learn best with a combination of these two modes of learning. Awareness of ways that children learn will help tailor the classroom instruction to meet the needs of all children.

Cultural Diversity

Today's classrooms are melting pots of children from many diverse backgrounds. Children come from a variety of ethnic and racial backgrounds. It is becoming increasingly more common for children to enter school not speaking English and not being familiar with the ways of the majority culture. How can schools meet the needs of such diverse groups of children?

One of the important steps in helping schools meet the needs of all children is to help teachers understand how culture affects development. In some African cultures it is disrespectful for children to make eye contact with adults. In the majority culture in the United States, not making eye contact can be interpreted as a sign of disrespect. Similarly, in many Spanish cultures, independence in young children is not considered an important part of early development. Because of this, four- and five-year-olds are not typically asked to do things for themselves. This is very different from typical American kindergartens that foster independence in young children. Not understanding the expectations and values of other cultures can result in misinterpretation of behaviors. Teachers need to try and understand the cultural differences of students to help children negotiate the school culture.

Children with Special Needs

Since Public Law 99-457, the Federal Preschool Program and Early Intervention Program Act of 1986, which extended rights and services to infants, toddlers, and preschoolers with disabilities and their families, the opportunities for four- and five-year-olds to come to school have significantly increased. Teachers working with special needs children need to provide the least restrictive environment that supports children's learning. In order to do this, teachers need to consider the following factors related to development in order to effectively integrate children with special needs into the classroom.

One important factor to consider is that although children with special needs are often delayed in development or follow an atypical developmental path, they grow and change like all children. Teachers need to understand the skills and abilities that children with special needs bring to the classroom. Given the child's current skills, the teacher needs to work with the child toward improving those skills and work on progressing in areas that need improvement. A goal for a four-year-old with language delay may be to learn 30 vocabulary words and construct three-word sentences. A five-year-old with cerebral palsy who uses a walker may be working on ways that he can play with his peers in the playground during recess. Like all children, children with special needs have strengths and weaknesses in all aspects of development. Through careful planning and working with other special education personnel in the schools, teachers can provide special needs children with opportunities for growth and development.

A second essential factor is that teachers need to make accommodations in lesson planning and physical arrangement in the classroom. If you are taking a nature walk with your class, accommodations need to be made for the student in a wheelchair. An autistic child who can't transition well from one activity to another will need your help in guiding him or her through transitions. Arranging furniture and setting up centers so that children with walkers, wheelchairs, or other equipment can negotiate through the room will be important.

Helping children understand and relate to children with special needs is an important responsibility of teachers. Children are very curious about anyone who looks or acts differently from them. Having a child with special needs in your class-room provides a wonderful opportunity to teach children to be accepting of people's differences. Children who play and work side by side with children with special needs are more tolerant and understanding of children with disabilities (Kochanek & Buka, 1999). Encouraging children to play and work together will foster a sense of a respectful, caring classroom.

IN SUMMARY

There is great variability in the growth and development of four- and five-year-olds. A child's age does not necessarily predict the competencies of the child. However, in this chapter, typical similarities and differences of the physical, emotional, cognitive, and social development of four- and five-year-olds are outlined.

Four- and five-year-olds are filled with energy and are constantly moving. As they grow, children's gross and fine motor skills are becoming more precise and their ability to perform tasks that require coordination, such as bike riding and throwing a ball, improve. Five-year-olds developing increasing control over their physical abilities are able to sit quietly for longer periods of time.

Four- and five-year-olds express a wide range of emotions. Their emotional states are situation-specific and can change rapidly as they switch from one situation to another. As four-year-olds develop into five-year-olds, there is an increasing internalization and regulation over their emotions. Five-year-olds are learning more internal control over their emotions and have developed language skills that allow them to articulate their emotional states verbally.

There are important changes in the cognitive growth of four- and five-year-olds. Four-year-olds begin the development of symbolic thought, which results in make-believe play. Egocentric thought is a hallmark of four- and five-year-olds' thinking and they have difficulty taking other people's perspectives. Four- and five-year-olds are thinking and reasoning concretely and have difficulty thinking hypothetically. As four- and five-year-olds grow, they begin to become more certain about what is real and unreal and begin to refine their organization and development of concepts.

Social development plays a part in the development of four- and five-year-olds. Children are beginning to learn how to get along with other children and are beginning to develop friendships. Also, children are beginning to develop negotiation strategies to get along with others. As children interact with others, they begin to develop a sense of self-concept and self-efficacy. Teachers need to develop a realistic sense of behavioral expectations for four- and five-year-olds' structure curriculum that is in line with the developmental level of the children.

Individual differences in children's development need to be respected, and classroom adaptations need to be made to accommodate these differences. This is especially important for children from various cultures and with various disabilities who need to be assimilated into the classroom. All children have unique learning styles and make their own contributions to the class. Teachers need to be aware of differences in children and adapt classroom experiences to meet diverse needs.

EXTEND YOUR IDEAS

1. How are four- and five-year-olds in your class the same , and how are they different? Observe four- and five-year-olds in a similar play activity and document their similarities and differences.

2. Observe a group of four- and five-year-old boys and girls in two situations: on the playground and in the art center. Record the different activities that boys and girls engage in and how they interact with one another.

3. Interview three kindergarten teachers regarding their views on four- and five-year-olds in their classes. Explore their perceptions and beliefs about age and development and how it relates to children's performance. Are teachers' expectations and beliefs the same for all children, or do they differ for children with disabilities and children with English as a second language?

4. Observing a group of kindergartners, try to identify the youngest and the oldest child. What are you basing your decision on: physical size, verbal skills, or physical coordination? Confirm you decision with the teacher. What attributes were indicators of children's maturity?

5. Review your district's policy on the age criterion for admission into kindergarten. Find out the rationale for the specific age criterion that is used in your district. Can parents request that a child who does not meet the age criterion be admitted to kindergarten on the basis of other information? 🖐

RESOURCES

www.childdevelopmentinfo.com
This Web site provides information on expectations for children's development from birth through 12 years. The site is comprehensive and outlines the expectations for four- and five-year-olds.

www.journals.uchicago.edu/SRCD/
This is the Web site for the Society for Research in Child Development, a professional organization that disseminates research on issues in child development.

REFERENCES

Berk, L. (1997). *Child development* (4th ed.). Boston: Allyn & Bacon.

Bowman, B. T., Donovan, M. S., & Burns, M. S. (Eds.). *Eager to learn.* Washington, DC: National Academy Press.

Bredekamp, S., & Copple, C. (1997). *Developmentally appropriate practice in early childhood programs (Rev. ed.).* Washington, DC: National Association for the Education of Young Children.

Denham, S. (1998). *Emotional development and young children.* New York: Guildford Press.

Flavell, J. H. (1992). The development of children's understanding of the appearance-reality distinction between how people look and what they are really like. *Merrill-Palmer Quarterly, 38,* 513–524.

Flavell, J. H., Green, F. L., & Flavell, E. R. (Eds.). (1995). *Young children's knowledge about thinking.* Chicago: University of Chicago Press.

Flavell, J. H., Miller, P. H., & Miller, S. (1992). *Cognitive development.* New York: Prentice Hall.

Gelman, S. A. (1999). Categories in young children's thinking: Research in review. *Young Children, 53,* 20–26.

Greenspan, S. I., & Greenspan, N. (1994). *First feelings: Milestones in the emotional development of your baby and child.* New York: Penguin.

Hazen, N., & Brownell, C. (1999). Peer relationships in early childhood development: Current trends and future directions. *Early Education and Development, 10,* 233–240.

Howard, S., Shaughnessy, A., Sanger, D., & Hux, K. (1998). Let's talk! Facilitating language in early elementary classrooms. *Young Children, 53,* 34–37.

Hyson, M. (1994). *The emotional development of young children: Building an emotion-centered curriculum* (Early Childhood Education Series). New York: Teachers College Press.

Ignico, A. A., & Wayda, V. K. (1999). The effects of physical activity programs on children's activity level, health-related fitness, and self-esteem. *Early Child Development and Care, 154,* 31–39.

Kochanek, T. T., & Buka, S. L. (1999). Influential factors in inclusive versus non-inclusive placement for preschool children with disabilities. *Early Education and Development, 10,* 191–208.

McClellan, D. E., & Katz, L. (1997). *Fostering children's social competence: The role of the teacher.* Washington, DC: National Association for the Education of Young Children.

Morrow, L. M., & Smith, J. K. (1990). The effect of group size on interactive storybook reading. *Reading Research Quarterly, 25,* 213–231.

Ninio, A., & Snow, C. E. (1996). *Pragmatic development.* Boulder, CO: Westview Press.

Piaget, J. (1952). *The origins of intelligence in children.* New York: Norton.

Piaget, J. (1969). The child's concept of time. (A. J. Pomerans, Trans.). New York: Basic Book.

Pica, R. (1997). Beyond physical development: Why young children need to move. *Young Children, 52,* 4–11.

Rubin, K. H., Coplan, R. J., Nelson, L. J., Cheah, C. S. L., & Lagace-Sequin, D. G. (1999). *Developmental psychology: An advanced textbook* (4th ed.). Mahwah, NJ: Erlbaum.

Saracho, O., & Spodek, B. (1984). Cognitive and children's learning: Individual variation in cognitive processes. In L. G. Katz (Ed.), *Current topics in early childhood education.* Vol. VI. Norwood, NJ: Ablex.

Siegler, R. S. (1997). *Children's thinking.* Upper Saddle River, NJ: Prentice Hall.

Snow, C. E., Burns, S. M., & Griffin, P. (1998). *Preventing reading difficulty in young children.* Washington, DC: National Academy Press.

CHAPTER 4
Are Schools Ready for Four- and Five-Year-Olds?

As four-year-old Claire and her mother were leaving kindergarten one afternoon, Claire said,"Oh mother, I wish there weren't any doors in my kindergarten."When her mother asked why, Claire replied, "Well, you see, if there weren't any doors, then I could stay here all day long."

There's no doubt about it. Like Claire, four- and five-year-olds are ready to separate from their family and eager to go to school. The question is, are schools ready for young children?

Yes! Schools are ready. Guided by state and local policies grounded in knowledge of child growth, development, and learning, Claire and many other four- and five-year-olds find kindergartens happy places in which to learn, grow, and blossom.

The purpose of this chapter is to describe the structural policies that guide and direct overall kindergarten goals, group size, teacher/child ratio, and the basic philosophical underpinnings of the curriculum and assessment. Local and district policies directing the use of space, schedules and routines, working with resource and auxiliary staff, and family involvement are also discussed.

STRUCTURAL POLICIES

tate legislatures, government agencies, or state boards of education establish structural policies for kindergarten programs. Among the structural policies developed at the state level are (1) the overall goals of kindergartens, (2) teacher/child ratio, (3) the philosophical underpinnings of the curriculum and the benchmarks of what children should learn, (4) assessment methods, and (5) family involvement. These policies mirror society's concern that all children experience academic success when in school, outlined in Goals 2000.

Overall Goals

Historically, goals have guided the nature of kindergarten programs. Designed to fulfill the goals of helping immigrant children and their families become assimilated into the culture of the United States, the first kindergartens involved mothers and provided health, nutritional, and social services for both children and families. Likewise, following the advent of Head Start, more school systems added both four- and five-year-old kindergarten programs to achieve the goal of offering children living in poverty the type of early, enriching educational experiences that would ready them for academic success in later years. Other systems revised and redesigned existing programs in order to do so.

Goals continue to influence today's kindergarten programs (Bredekamp & Copple, 1997). Established at the state level, the overall goals for kindergarten throughout our nation are multidisciplinary and multidimensional. Typically, these goals revolve around fostering children's knowledge, skills, and attitudes and dispositions (Graue, 1993).

Knowledge.   Kindergarten programs are designed to clarify, expand, and extend children's knowledge and understanding of the world in which they live. Content from every discipline area is a part of the curriculum (Fromberg, 1995). This knowledge provides the substance for learning to read, write, think, and create.

At the end of the kindergarten year, children should

◆ have a store of concepts and understandings of the world around them;
◆ understand concepts of mathematics, the biological and physical sciences, social sciences, and the arts;
◆ know the characteristics of the symbol system necessary for learning to read, write, and compute;
◆ have mastered knowledge of basic vocabulary and grammar; and
◆ have an understanding of how their bodies work and of sound health and safety practices.

Skills.   Kindergarten programs are designed to give children the opportunity to develop and practice their thinking, language, problem-solving, emotional, social, and other skills.

At the end of the kindergarten year, children should have developed the following:

◆ Sensory skills necessary to explore their world through observing, listening, touching, tasting, and smelling.
◆ Skills using and experimenting with tools, materials, and equipment, including drawing, painting, constructing, and writing skills.
◆ Thinking, reasoning, and creative and problem-solving skills.
◆ The skills of enunciation and pronunciation, auditory discrimination, and others involved in communicating. They should be able to express themselves verbally and in drawing and writing and take meaning from the oral and written language of others.
◆ Emotional skills, including being able to express emotions constructively.
◆ The social skills required to cooperate, share, and build positive relations with others; recognize his or her own rights and responsibilities; and respect the rights of others.
◆ Skills involved in self-care, such as dressing, hand washing, eating, and toileting.

Attitudes and Dispositions.   Academic success depends on more than just knowledge and skills. Children must have positive attitudes and dispositions about learning and school. The beliefs that they can exercise control over their own learning and hold positive expectations for academic success are necessary as well.

At the end of the kindergarten year, children should have developed the following:

◆ A positive attitude toward learning.
◆ Curiosity in the world around them.
◆ A positive self-concept—valuing themselves as unique and worthy individuals.
◆ Confidence in others, including those with special needs, as well as feeling safe in their physical environment.
◆ The ability to accept and adjust to opposition or lack of success.
◆ Dispositions necessary to be able to take the initiative and persist in learning.
◆ Feelings of self-efficacy—believing that they are in control of their own learning.
◆ Positive expectations for their academic success.

Group Size and Teacher/Child Ratio

There is overwhelming agreement among educators, administrators, researchers, and policymakers that the overall goals of the kindergarten can be achieved only with small groups of children and sufficient numbers of adults (Williams & Fromberg, 1992). Kindergarten children, unlike older ones who can care for themselves, depend on adults to help them dress and care for their other physical needs. Four- and five-year-olds are ill able to learn while sitting still in a large group listening to a teacher talk. They seem to learn best when they can act on objects and things in their world while interacting with others, both adults and peers. This type of learning calls for teachers to be continually available to interact with children on a one-to-one basis or in a small group.

Therefore, most states and school systems recommend that no more than 20 four-year-olds and 24 five-year-olds be in a group. The adult/child ratio, which often includes the teacher and an assistant or regular volunteer, is 1 to 10 for four-year-olds and 1 to 12 for five-year-olds. In the case of mixed-age grouping, group size and adult/child ratios should not exceed the youngest age classification.

Curriculum

The basic philosophical underpinnings of the curriculum are often articulated at the state level. In general, this philosophy stems from constructivist or interactional theories, such as those of Dewey, Piaget, Vygotsky, and other cognitive psychologists, as well as current views of child growth and development. Thus, the

The curriculum engages children's hands and minds.

kindergarten curriculum is filled with ideas and ways of knowing that engage children's hands and minds (Bredekamp & Rosegrant, 1995).

Based on the overall goals for kindergarten, the curriculum addresses the social, emotional, physical, and intellectual well-being of children. As the goals are multidimensional and interdisciplinary, an integrated curriculum, organized through thematic units or projects, is usually recommended. This allows for a curriculum that is not only meaningful but also ongoing and continual with one learning experience building on the other. To help teachers plan a continual, meaningful, and child-relevant curriculum, some states have identified concepts from a wide range of content areas that children are to gain while in kindergarten (Bredekamp & Rosegrant, 1995).

Assessment

Assessment strategies are also recommended at the state level. The recommended strategies are integral to the curriculum and are continual, strategically planned, and meaningful (Kagan, 1999). Assessment must be meaningful, and it must have a purpose. The results should benefit children in some way. A curriculum may be adapted to meet the developmental learning needs of children, the results communicated to families, or overall program improvement planned (Bredekamp & Copple, 1997).

LOCAL AND DISTRICT POLICIES

States offer broad, overriding policies that local districts and schools can use to create exemplary kindergarten programs. Local districts and schools establish additional policies. These include policies about (1) entrance age and retention, (2) the use of physical space within a school, (3) length of the school day, (4) schedules and routines, (5) working with resource and auxiliary staff, and (6) how to involve families.

Entrance Age and Kindergarten Retention

School districts set the kindergarten entrance age and make policies negating kindergarten retention. The National Association for the Education of Young Children believes that systems should set a uniform kindergarten entrance age whereby most children attending kindergarten are five years old and most first graders are six years old (Bredekamp & Shepard, 1990).

Based on the research, it is recommended that school systems do not retain children in kindergarten. Kindergarten retention does nothing to boost subsequent academic achievement. Further, retention results in a social stigma for children who attend an extra year, regardless of whether the class is called a *transition* class, *pre–first grade*, or *readiness group* and fosters inappropriate academic demands in first grade (Shepard & Smith, 1989).

Physical Spaces

When the kindergarten became a part of the public schools in 1973 in St. Louis, schools were built to accommodate Froebelian programs. Kindergarten rooms were huge. They were so large that each contained a sandbox, a swing set, and a slide. Because the purpose of the kindergarten was to provide for the physical and intellectual needs of children living in poverty, bathrooms, complete with showers, were located next to kindergarten classrooms.

Even though today's schools are designed for flexibility, kindergarten rooms are rarely as large as those in the first public school kindergartens. Nor are they always equipped with bathrooms or spaces for children to store personal belongings, for child-sized equipment, or for teachers' equipment and supplies.

Teachers, however, have found that they can do much to maximize spaces they are given. Some arrange for children to work in hallways or out of doors under the supervision of aides or volunteers. If sinks and bathrooms are not in the room, teachers work with school administrators, parents, and community representatives to provide these.

Because kindergarten rooms are sometimes placed in a separate wing of the school, on a different floor, or even in a separate building, such as an Early Learning Center, teachers and children may feel isolated. Teachers have solved the problem of isolation by making certain that they are considered a part of the school. They take children on walking trips throughout the school to observe older children or office workers, media staff, building engineers, and others at work. Documenting children's learning, growth, and progress by displaying their work throughout the school helps familiarize others with the kindergarten.

Outdoor spaces must be considered as well. Four- and five-year-olds need outdoor spaces to run through; things to climb in, out, and under; and spaces in which they can build large, complex structures. They also need a variety of surfaces for their work and play. A grassy area for sitting, thinking, and reading; a hardtop so that they can ride wheeled toys; and someplace to dig or work with sand, dirt, and mud are essential.

School systems initiating kindergarten programs after the advent of Head Start found that they had to redesign outdoor spaces to accommodate the needs of four- and five-year-olds. One school designed play spaces connected to the kindergarten classrooms. Doors leading to an outdoor fenced area were added to existing rooms. Within the fenced area, teachers designed hardtop pathways for bike riding. They planted grass around the fence, keeping some open spaces for children to dig in and plant gardens. They filled the middle space with sand and one small table made from a large spool that once held telephone cables. With creative planning and the cooperation of school administrators, these teachers demonstrated how physical spaces could be designed to meet the special needs of kindergarten children.

Length of School Day

More than half the school districts in the United States have elected to hold full-day kindergarten programs. Full-day kindergartens are not new to our nation. The early kindergarten programs in St. Louis were full-day programs, partially in response to society's needs. In order to offer the type of total physical, emotional, and social care they thought children needed, the early initiators of the kindergarten arranged full-day kindergarten programs complete with lunch, naps, and showers.

Today, as in the past, full-day kindergartens are popular because they meet societal needs for the full-day care of young children as well as for economic and academic reasons. Districts, during the past years of a flush economy, were able to afford the extra costs involved in full-day kindergarten programs and were willing to do so because they believed children would have the potential to achieve more in a full-day kindergarten.

Schedules and Routines

Schedules and routines provide a sense of order, safety, and security for both children and adults. This does not mean, however, that all are suitable for kindergarten children.

"Good morning boys and girls," a voice from the box on the wall shouts. "Today is Wednesday, May 10." The voice continues by reciting the Pledge of Allegiance and giving some announcements and warnings about proper behavior. None of the children attend to the voice. Some look around as if they are trying to figure out where the voice is coming from. More giggle and squirm in their seats, and a few try to engage one another in some sort of pinching game.

Kindergarten teachers make decisions about which school routines and schedules are appropriate for the children they teach. Some, like the morning announcements, have no use or meaning to four- and five-year-olds. Just as teachers work to adjust the physical environment, they adjust the routines and school schedules so that they match the needs of young children.

Other school-wide routines can also be negotiated. Arrival and departure times, which may be set by bus companies, have been negotiated by some kindergarten teachers so that children do not have to leave home in the dark (Fromberg, 1995).

Because few school cafeterias have been designed for four- and five-year-olds, teachers can arrange for snacks (and in the case of full-day kindergarten, lunch) to

Children's attention spans are considered when assessing their learning.

be served in the classroom at an appropriate time. Served in the room, snacks and meals have a greater potential to be incorporated into the total curriculum and do not disrupt the children's day.

Children's short attention span and inability to think abstractly is taken into account when deciding which school assemblies are suitable or appropriate for young children.

Once the daily routines of the school have been taken into account, kindergarten teachers can design their daily schedule. The daily schedule is based on children's

SAMPLE HALF-DAY SCHEDULE

Arrival

Materials—perhaps puzzles, peg boards, books, or sociodramatic play materials to work with as children arrive. When all the children have arrived, the group is called together for morning opening. Announcements and news are shared, and the plans for the day are discussed. Songs, poetry, stories, and review of fieldwork motivate children for center work.

Center Time

Children select the centers they wish to work in. This is when children will engage in art, math, block construction, sociodramatic play, and other activities revolving around content from every discipline area. Teachers work with individual and small groups of children on literacy, math, and other skills. Serving open snacks, with children choosing when and where they will take a nutrition break, can be a part of center time.

Center time ends with cleanup and another short group meeting to review the work of the morning. If snacks are not available during center time, they could be served after group discussion.

Outdoor Play

Vigorous outdoor play, fieldwork on the play yard, follows center time.

Group Work

Together, the class engages in fieldwork, discussions of fieldwork, music, literacy, mathematics, or other special topics.

Closing Activities

The morning or afternoon is reviewed, songs are sung, and stories and poetry are read. Children are readied for leaving.

SAMPLE FULL-DAY SCHEDULE CONTINUES

Preparation for Lunch

The morning is reviewed, songs are sung, and stories and poetry are read. Children are readied for lunch, washing hands.

Lunch

As children finish eating, stories are read, songs are sung. Playing quiet games, reading books, or listening to tapes, CDs, or videos take place as children brush their teeth, wash, and prepare for rest.

Quiet Time

Children do not have to actually sleep; they can read books or engage in quiet play on their cots, but there

needs to be a time in which everyone is quiet and resting.

Outdoor/Indoor Center and Project Work

Time for vigorous outdoor play, field trips, and project work either in or out of doors.

Group Work

Music, learning activities, and project work.

Closing Activities

The day is reviewed, songs are sung, and stories and poetry are read. Children are readied for leaving.

developmental level, culture, school, family, and community resources and is designed to meet the short- and long-term goals of the total program.

Daily schedules differ, depending on the school's schedule and routines and whether the program is full or half day or for four- or five-year-olds. When schedules are planned, balance and pacing are considered. Times of high physical activity are balanced with quiet activities. Teacher-directed activities are balanced with child-initiated activities. Children's attention spans are also considered, and group times are paced accordingly.

WORKING WITH OTHERS

Today's kindergarten teachers are members of a team of professionals working together to provide the best educational experiences possible for all children. Being a part of a team means establishing communication with everyone who has contact with children. You will want to talk with bus drivers about how children are adjusting to the trip, and even ride the bus in order to suggest ideas for talking with and gaining the cooperation of children. Likewise, you will want to talk with cooks, custodians, secretaries, school counselors, social workers, and others about children's needs and progress (Seefeldt & Barbour, 1998).

Close teamwork between the principal and other teachers is necessary. You will want to ask the principal how to handle parents' requests or complaints, what kind of reporting should take place, and how much autonomy you will have in your classroom. In turn, principals, who are responsible for the total school, need to be kept informed about your goals, how you plan to achieve these, and children's learning and growth (Barbour & Barbour, 1997).

Even though the principal is the official leader of the school, others may have assumed a measure of authority. A teacher who has seniority may be another leader in the school. The parents go to him or her with their problems, as do other teachers. Sometimes one of the teachers will act as a representative for a group of teachers. One kindergarten teacher may assume authority for the others, ordering materials or telling you "how things have always been done" or when certain themes, projects, or units are best taught.

Take some time to observe the culture of the school. Your observations may uncover a complicated informal structure of authority within. Observing a while gives you an understanding of what is and is not expected of you by other teachers. It is not that you need to comply, but you will want to know what is expected and condoned. This information gives you the opportunity to express your uniqueness and establish your autonomy without confrontation.

Working with specialists will be necessary. These include teachers of English as a second language (ESL), those who work with special needs children, and curriculum area specialists.

ESL Teachers

Working closely with the ESL teachers helps you provide the most appropriate educational experiences for any non-English-speaking children in your class. Some ESL teachers may want to work with the child outside the classroom. This may not

Close teamwork and creative planning enables teachers to assess children appropriately.

always be the most productive practice. Pulling children from the group may make them feel different from the others or isolate them from the others. Then, too, when children are pulled from the group, they miss taking part in the language-rich activities of the classroom. Involving ESL teachers in your planning and finding ways they can work with individual children in the classroom may be more productive (Seefeldt & Barbour, 1998).

For example, creative planning between one team of kindergarten teachers and ESL teachers in Virginia led to the development of a family literacy night. While volunteers worked with children, the ESL teachers worked with parents. The goal was not to teach parents English but to familiarize them with the vocabulary they needed to know in order to feel comfortable in school. Words such as "backpack," "PTA," "portfolios," "delayed two hours," "parent conference," and "snow days" were explained. Parents found the meetings so helpful that many followed up by enrolling in ESL classes themselves.

Special Needs

When you have children with special needs in your class, you will become a member of a team of professionals whose goal is to design and implement an individual educational plan (IEP) for each child. The team may be comprised of medical, speech, hearing, or other specialists and the child's family. The team will look to you to inform them about how the child functions within the context of the classroom as well as to inform them about the normal growth, development, and learning of all children.

Curriculum Area Specialists

Specialists in curriculum areas, such as music, physical education, art, or some other curriculum area, are invaluable. Because most state and local policies recommend a unified, integrated approach to the curriculum, you will want to coordinate your planning with these specialists. You can inform specialists about the themes and projects taking place in your classroom and ask for their suggestions for resources and ideas on how to extend and expand on these themes. Ask the specialists whether they can arrange to work with the children in the classroom. This way, children do not have to waste valuable time getting ready to go to another area of the building, going there, and returning to the classroom.

Often chosen from the community, the assistant brings knowledge of the culture and traditions of the families to the kindergarten. As such, the assistant can interpret the values and goals of the community to teachers who may be unfamiliar with these. An assistant with knowledge of the language spoken in the community is especially helpful.

Each assistant and teacher will have to develop his or her own method of working together. Assistants will probably have participated in some form of training or orientation program and may even be supervised by a special administrator. Still you will have the major responsibility for directing and supervising the assistant. One way to increase effectiveness is for you and the assistant to clarify your roles and responsibilities. Each day you and your assistant will need to be clear about what is to be done and by whom.

Sometimes new, young teachers are assigned an experienced assistant, one who misses working with the teacher you replaced. If you take time to listen to the assistant, respond to his or her concerns, and observe how he or she works with children, you will have a better idea of how to best utilize your assistant's strengths while establishing your own autonomy.

INVOLVING PARENTS

Historically, parents' involvement in kindergarten has always been considered necessary. True, in the past, involving parents often meant instructing them in habits of cleanliness, child training, and how to keep their children "safe against the temptations of the lower senses" (Vandewalker, 1908, p. 104). Nevertheless, there has always been an emphasis on involving parents as partners in their children's education.

Parents' involvement and cooperation is believed even more critical today. On the basis of research relating parents' in-home and at-school involvement and children's academic success (Seefeldt, Denton, & Galper, 1999), nearly every state and most local school districts have policies mandating parent involvement in programs and activities; not just in the kindergarten but also throughout children's experiences in elementary, junior high, and high school (Epstein & Sanders, 2000).

Some school systems have a director of parent involvement who helps schools plan and implement parent involvement activities. Schools may also have a counselor or social worker who is in charge of parent involvement in the school. These people can assist kindergarten teachers in establishing a variety of parent involvement activities.

Many different levels, forms, and types of involvement have the potential to benefit children, parents, and schools. All involvement, however, is built on a foundation of effective communication and confidence and trust that in turn leads to full cooperation and collaboration between school and home.

Communication

Parents want to know how their children are doing in kindergarten. Parents want their children to be successful in kindergarten and socially and academically ready for their next grade placement. Perhaps this is why parents are anxious to be involved in their children's education both at home and in school.

Even so, there is limited time for families to be involved in their children's kindergarten education. Parents are busy. So are teachers. Parents may have a moment or two to chat with you when they drop off or pick up their children, but when children ride the bus, even this brief encounter is not possible.

Across the country kindergarten teachers have found ways to establish effective communication with families even though time is limited. Communication begins as soon as teachers receive their class list in late summer by sending a letter, along with a self-addressed postcard. The letter welcomes children to kindergarten and asks children to list the things they want to learn on the postcard and send it back to their teachers. As with any other written communication, teachers make certain that this letter is not only clear and understandable for all families but also translated into the family's primary language. The ESL teacher in the school or other ESL teachers in the system will be pleased to take on this responsibility.

Next, teachers visit the home of each child. Home visits benefit everyone. Children feel honored and respected when teachers visit their homes. Parents have concrete evidence that teachers are concerned about them and their children. Teachers benefit because they gain knowledge of children's strengths and an initial understanding of the culture and traditions of children's families.

During the visit teachers share information about arrival and departure times and other kindergarten procedures, such as snack and rest times. The overall goals of the kindergarten can be shared, as can some of the methods you will use to achieve these.

Teachers continue making home visits throughout the year. Calling ahead, one teacher would visit children in their homes on a special occasion. When children were ill, she would take them a blank book titled "My Flu Book" or "My Broken Arm Book" along with a sample box of markers or crayons. Children were to

HINTS FOR SUCCESSFUL HOME VISITS

- ◆ Feel free to meet outside, on the porch, or under a tree.
- ◆ Take along an ice breaker—maybe a small book, a finger puppet, or a small box of crayons that the child and other siblings can play with and you can leave with the child.
- ◆ Take a photo of you and the child so that the child can be reminded of the teacher as school approaches.
- ◆ Have materials about the school, its policies, and its procedures to leave with the parents.
- ◆ Ask parents about their dreams and goals for their children, taking notes so that they know you are really interested in what they have to say.
- ◆ Ask the child what he or she wants to learn during the coming year.
- ◆ Find out about any special needs of parents and children and discuss how the family wants you to meet these needs.
- ◆ Make sure that you know the child's name and how to pronounce it and whether the child has a nickname he or she likes to be called.

record their experiences in the book. Or she would visit the new baby, taking along a small, inexpensive book for the kindergarten child to "read" to the baby.

E-mails and telephone calls keep communication between teachers and parents alive. Parents feel honored and respected when teachers e-mail them about the progress their children are making or how their child helped another, solved a problem, or coped with a frustrating challenge. Parents in turn are encouraged to e-mail you with their comments, concerns, and ideas. Phone calls work even better because communication is instant and hearing one another's voices is even more meaningful.

A kindergarten Web site is another good way to keep lines of communication open. A Web site from a kindergarten in Alaska includes a copy of an ABC book made by the children, a parents' page, Ms. F.'s page (about the teacher), Ms. R.'s page (about the principal), and pages for Our Season's Projects, Things You Need to Know, and Linkages to Resources. Even when all families have computers available, follow up by writing the same information in written form.

Families are interested in receiving news about the kindergarten. Newsletters informing families of schedule changes, bus schedules, and weekly plans and a monthly calendar of events or themes you are working on is helpful, as is other information and news from the kindergarten.

The curriculum itself communicates to parents. Writing notes explaining children's invented spelling, what they were saying as they were painting, or a note telling how children counted or classified a group of objects informs families about children's progress. The whole-language approach to literacy learning is a form of communication as well. The books that children make, their journals, and poems, either dictated or written, when accompanied by notes pointing out the specific skills the children were practicing or have mastered, informs parents about children's language learning.

One kindergarten teacher spends her duplicating budget copying class books. These books revolve around a theme and contain a page about the theme drawn or written by each child. One book was action words. Each child picked a letter of the alphabet, identified a verb that began with the letter, and illustrated it. The book began with "A" for "Arriving" and ended with "Z" for "Zipping." A copy was made for each child.

Look for other examples of language activities and other curriculum experiences that communicate to parents throughout this book. These are marked with "CF" to indicate that they communicate and inform families about their children's school day.

Confidence and Trust

Good communication is the foundation for building confidence and trust between families and schools. Research shows that parents' confidence in themselves to teach their children and be a part of the school is related to children's academic success (Hoover-Dempsey & Sandler, 1997). Further, parents who feel confident that they can exercise control over their children's education seem to be more involved in their children's education, both at home and school, than those who do not have this confidence (Seefeldt, Denton, & Galper, 1999).

Teachers continually demonstrate their confidence, trust, and respect for parents throughout the day, saying things like, "Let's save this for your mother, she'll want to see it." Or they might say, "Won't your family be proud of you when I tell them how you helped Sarah today?" Comments like this serve to reinforce children's sense of self-worth, dignity, and esteem. This demonstrates that they and their families are important to you.

Attitudes of trust and confidence can also be shared through daily activities. Children know that you are proud of their parents when you talk about what their parents are doing during the day. Stories describing mothers and fathers at work and depicting the cultural background of the families are read to children. Props the parents use in their work, such as cell phones, computers, pencils, paper, receipt books, boots, tool chests, and lunch boxes, can be added to the dramatic play areas so that children can act out being a parent at work.

Communicate trust to parents by establishing an open-door policy. When parents are free to drop in and observe, volunteer, or work in the classroom whenever they have the time, they know that you respect and trust them.

Let parents know that they are doing a good job in raising their children. Through notes, calls, and any other means of communication, inform parents of how well their children are doing, of their strengths, and of progress and attribute their successes to the family. "Mark has a sure sense of himself—you must have a strong family." "I can tell you're reading to Natasha—she's so interested in books."

Cooperation and Collaboration

Parents and teachers are partners in the education of their children. This partnership involves full cooperation and collaboration through parent-teacher conferences, parent meetings, and service on advisory boards (Grolnick & Slowiaczek, 1994).

Parent-Teacher Conferences

Parent-teacher conferences, held several times, offer the mechanism for informing parents about children's progress, the school's way of doing things, and seeking parents' support and involvement. Teachers report that conferences are productive for giving insights into the children. Parents as well believe that conferences are beneficial because they have the opportunity to ask questions, have their questions answered, and exchange ideas related to children's needs (Barbour & Barbour, 1997).

Before the Conference.   Successful parent-teacher conferences are planned. Before the conference, send parents an agenda listing the time and place and the things you want to cover. Leave room for parents to respond. Ask them what things they will want to discuss during the conference and whether they have any concerns or questions.

Go over each child's portfolio and make notes about his or her progress in the kindergarten. Pick a few products from the portfolio to use as examples. Invite parents to do the same. They may list the things the child does at home and bring with them photos of them caring for pets or completing other tasks or things they have written or painted (Barbour & Barbour, 1997).

Arrange the furniture in a way that establishes equality and promotes open communication. For example, sitting at a round table helps each participant feel equal.

During the Conference. Set a positive tone to the conference, beginning with a warm greeting followed by telling something of the child's accomplishments. Perhaps parents will want to tell you something about the child's progress at home. Using samples of work from children's portfolios or digital photos on a computer, you can discuss the child's progress. Make sure parents know they are free to tell you their concerns so that a discussion takes place. If parents seem reluctant to ask questions during the discussion, encourage them to tell you of their dreams for their children or their concerns or disappointments. And listen as they do so. Reflect on what parents say. You might say something like, "Tell me if I heard you correctly—you are concerned that Sabrina is not learning her ABC's" or "You want Alberto to wear a hat when he goes outside to protect him from the sun."

If you do not understand what the parents' real concerns are, ask. "I still do not understand what is bothering you, can you tell me in another way?" "What do you mean when you say you're not happy with Shawn's progress? Can you give me an example?"

Know, too, that your tone of voice, the way you say things, and your non-verbal behaviors communicate your confidence and trust as well. A soft voice is useful in calming yourself and parents. Silence speaks. Sometimes silence is a form of disapproval: "I don't like what you're saying so I won't respond." Other times silence is used to reflect on what the parents have said, to think about it, and then respond with an idea that builds on the ideas they have expressed.

Professionals need to watch the use of educational jargon when speaking with parents, especially those new to the United States. Rather than telling a parent his child needs more "peer association," simply say how good it is for children to play with one another outside of school. It is disrespectful to talk down to parents, but it is important that the words you use do communicate.

Think of the messages we send through our body language and behaviors. The gestures we make and our physical and facial expressions all communicate a message. For example, eye contact is important in many cultures. In general, in most cultures eye contact is believed to foster good communication. If eye contact is too intense, however, people begin to feel uncomfortable. Then, too, in a number of cultures, looking another directly in the eye is considered aggressive or disrespectful.

There are times when you will want to discuss problems children are having. If you need to do so, be direct. Instead of labeling the child—calling the child "disruptive" or "inattentive"—give specific examples of the child's behaviors that are troublesome. "Shawn has a habit of shouting at other children. Yesterday he yelled at Kim, calling her a stupid dodo." Then describe how you are handling the situation and together brainstorm strategies to teach Shawn other ways to communicate his needs, wants, and ideas to others.

Some kindergarten teachers involve children in conferences. Before the conference they meet with the children and go through their portfolio with them, asking children to pick out work that they want to show their parents. Then the first part of the conference takes part with parents, teacher, and child. The child will tell parents about the selected work. The child then leaves to play with others, and the teacher and parent talk together.

End the conference by reviewing or summarizing the major points you made and those made by the parent and child. Restate what you plan to do and what the parents said they would do to resolve any problems or issues that arose during the conference. Thank the parents for coming, letting them know how valuable the meeting was to you as their child's teacher.

Follow-Up.   Follow-up with a written thank-you note. In the note include the things you said you would be responsible for and those the child's parents said they would take care of. Restating some of the things shared during the conference confirms the importance you place on meeting with parents.

Advisory Boards

Head Start and any program receiving federal funds or those receiving foundation grants are mandated to involve parents in decision making. Even when this is not federally mandated, many kindergarten teachers meet with the total group of parents to help them and the school set kindergarten policies. Parents might discuss and offer solutions to bus schedules, the routines of the school, activity or field trip fees, or other issues.

Home Involvement

Full collaboration and cooperation also means parents continue the work of the school in their home. When families and teachers are partners in children's education, children seem to have a better chance to achieve academic success (Epstein & Sanders, 2000). Kindergarten teachers involve parents in learning activities across the curriculum.

Teachers may assign "homework." These form a direct link to school learning and serve to create continuity of learning between home and school. Parents might be asked to look at the night sky and chart the changes they observe in the moon with their children, collect samples of soil in their neighborhood to return to school, read books together, or count the number of chairs, tables, or other things in their homes.

One kindergarten teacher sent home a stuffed brown bear along with Bill Martin's *Brown Bear, Brown Bear, What Do You See?* (1969) and a blank notebook in a backpack. The directions were for the children and parents to read the book together and then write their own story in the notebook about how Brown Bear spent the night in their home. Other kindergartens send home literacy bags that include a variety of materials, games, and books to use at home (Barbour, 1999).

Parent workshops might be held to remind parents of their role in children's education. Parents need to understand the importance of the traditional rhymes, chants, and incantations that are a part of their cultural heritage and family. Informing parents of the link between reading and rapping with children, singing traditional nursery rhymes, or reciting traditional poetry lets parents know how important they are to children's school success (Barbour & Barbour, 1997).

Other workshops could revolve around the learning that occurs when parents and children play games together, talk, or interact. Teaching parents how to respond to children's questioning and expanding on children's curiosity is also fruitful.

If the school does not provide a toy, game, or book-lending library, you might start one in your kindergarten. Donations can be obtained from the PTA, Reading Is Fundamental program, or a local business to provide materials that can be sent home.

IN SUMMARY

Just as four- and five-year-olds are ready for kindergarten, so are schools ready for them. Guided by state and local policies, today's kindergartens are specifically designed to meet the needs of young learners.

Structural policies set at the state level reflect the intent of Goals 2000: that all children will succeed when in school, and to determine the overall goals of kindergartens, teacher/child ratios, the philosophical underpinnings of the curriculum, assessment methods, and family involvement.

Overall, the goals of the kindergarten are multidimensional and revolve around fostering children's knowledge, skills, and attitudes. These are believed best achieved through a curriculum grounded in the philosophy of constructivism or the interactional theories of Dewey, Piaget, and Vygotsky in classrooms with small teacher/child ratios. Evaluation and assessment follow the theories of constructivism with policies recommending authentic assessment techniques.

Local districts and schools set other goals. These determine how the physical space within a school is used, the schedules and routines of the school and kindergarten, working with resource and auxiliary staff, and how parents are to be involved.

Working with local and state policies, kindergarten teachers have found that they are able to create appropriate classroom and outdoor spaces for children's learning. They have adjusted the schedules and routines of their schools and learned to fully utilize the resource people within their school in order to meet the needs of four- and five-year-olds.

Understanding that parents must be involved in their children's education, kindergarten teachers find a plethora of ways to effectively involve today's busy parents as partners in their children's education.

EXTEND YOUR IDEAS

1. Obtain copies of your state's and school system's kindergarten policies. Review these. How would they affect your planning and teaching? Obtain a copy of Goals 2000 and match the state and local policies with those of Goals 2000.
2. How do kindergarten teachers adjust school schedules to meet the needs of four- and five-year-old children? Interview a kindergarten teacher, asking him or her which scheduled school routines he or she finds appropriate and which he or she does not. How did he or she adjust these? Discuss your findings in class.

3. Visit your local school to find out what kinds of resources are available for kindergarten teachers. Interview an ESL teacher, a music teacher, and an art teacher to find out how they work with kindergarten teachers and children. Now interview a kindergarten teacher, asking how he or she best utilizes resource people within the school to maintain an integrated, meaningful curriculum. In class determine how you would use resource personnel.

4. Most kindergartens will have aides. Observe a kindergarten classroom. Note how the teacher and aide communicate, cooperate, and collaborate.

5. Review the parent involvement policies of a local school or school district. Talk with parents to find out how and whether these policies are being implemented. In class discuss which of the policies parents find most productive. 🖐

RESOURCES

U.S. Department of Education
www.ed.gov/pubs/index.html
Contact the U.S. Department of Education for information about Goals 2000. While you are at the site, look under Early Childhood Education for free information for parents and teachers on working with and teaching young children.

National PTA Children First
www.pta.org/programs/index.htm
A wealth of information for parents and working with parents is on this Web site.

REFERENCES

Barbour, A. C. (1999). Home literacy bags promote family involvement. *Childhood Education, 75,* 71–75.

Barbour, C., & Barbour, N. (1997). *Families, schools, and communities.* Upper Saddle River, NJ: Prentice Hall/Merrill.

Bredekamp, S., & Copple, C. (1997). *Developmentally appropriate practice in early childhood programs* (Rev. ed.). Washington, DC: National Association for the Education of Young Children.

Bredekamp, S., & Rosegrant, T. (1995). *Reaching potentials: Transforming early childhood curriculum and assessment* (Vol. 2). Washington, DC: National Association for the Education of Young Children.

Epstein, J., & Sanders, M. G. (2000). Connecting home, school and community: New directions for social research. In M. Halliman (Ed.), *Connecting home, school, and community* (pp. 128–145). New York: Plenum Press.

Fromberg, D. P. (1995). *The full-day kindergarten: Planning and practicing a dynamic themes curriculum* (2nd ed.). New York: Teachers College Press.

Graue, M. E. (1993). *Ready for what? Constructing meanings of readiness for kindergarten.* Albany: State University of New York Press.

Griffin, J. (1996). Relation of parental involvement, empowerment, and school traits to student academic performance. *Journal of Educational Research, 90,* 33–41.

Grolnick, W. S., & Slowiaczek, M. L. (1994). Parents' involvement in children's schooling: A multi-dimensional conceptualization and motivational model. *Child Development, 65,* 237–252.

Hoover-Dempsey, K. V., & Sandler, H. M. (1997). Why do parents become involved in their children's education? *Review of Educational Research, 67,* 3–42.

Kagan, S. L. (1999). Cracking the readiness mystique. *Young Children, 54*(4), 2–3.

Seefeldt, C., & Barbour, N. (1998). *The early childhood curriculum: An introduction.* Upper Saddle River, NJ: Prentice Hall/Merrill.

Seefeldt, C., Denton, K., & Galper, A. (1999). Fostering Head Start parents' efficacy and the relationship between efficacy and children's achievement. *Early Childhood Research Quarterly, 14,* 99–109.

Vandewalker, N. C. (1908). *The kindergarten in American education.* New York: Macmillan.

Williams, L., & Fromberg, D. (Eds.). (1992). *Encyclopedia of early childhood education.* New York: Garland.

CHAPTER 5 Classrooms Are Ready

"So you're going to kindergarten next week," an aunt said to her niece. "What do you think you'll do in kindergarten?" "Well," replied Casey, "I don't know what kindergarten will be like. But I know there'll be housekeeping because I saw the housekeeping area when my Head Start went to see kindergarten. And there'll be books and puzzles, and there's a block center too."

Casey was astute to recognize that the classroom environment communicates what takes place in kindergarten. The physical environment alone does not make up the kindergarten curriculum or program, but it does determine, at least in part, the behaviors of teachers and children alike. How a teacher uses the physical environment of the classroom, how he or she arranges things within the set environment, will affect the curriculum, program, and how children will learn and behave.

Just as Casey seemed to organize her thinking about kindergarten around centers of interest, teachers find that arranging the classroom with centers serves to organize their curriculum and program. Centers of interest are clearly delineated, organized thematic work areas. In the centers, materials are displayed openly, inviting children to try activities for themselves.

This chapter describes why and how to arrange indoor and outdoor spaces with centers of interest. The teacher's role in establishing the centers—observing and evaluating children's interactions with the materials in the center and with others—is illustrated.

THE WHAT AND WHY OF CENTERS OF INTEREST

In every kindergarten there will be areas set aside for centers of interest. These permit children to make choices during free play and initiate much of their own learning. Centers of interest devoted to art, a library, writing, music, socio-dramatic play, mathematics, science, blocks, media, and technology are typically present in today's kindergartens. Materials within the centers are juxtaposed in ways that challenge children to ask "Why?", "How?", "What if?," and "Let's find out."

These centers are not static but rather are flexible. Centers change. Not all centers may be in place at the same time because of space constraints or because children have lost interest in one or another center. The materials within the centers are also changed to meet children's changing interests, skills, and abilities. Changing themes dictate other changes in centers. After a trip to a plant nursery, a special center, a garden shop, is arranged. Other trips lead to other centers so that children are able to reflect on and make sense of their experiences.

Some centers lose their appeal to children and are narrowed or changed. Others are set up to meet the needs of a small group of children. For instance, two boys who found airplanes fascinating were provided with a table, some chairs, model airplanes, books on making paper airplanes, and other building materials.

Involving the children in planning optimum room arrangements is one way for children to make decisions that directly affect them. Mallory (1998) suggests that asking children to give their suggestions about how to arrange the room to accommodate the needs of children with disabilities is also a way of teaching children to advocate for others. "Suggestions regarding the placement of furniture and materials, the assignment of classroom responsibilities . . . to make them accessible to all children are examples of ways in which young children can advocate for their peers with disabilities" (p. 229).

Centers of interest are designed to foster the broad goals of the kindergarten. Centers do the following:

◆ Meet children's needs to learn through play and their physical, social, and mental activity and make plans and decisions.
◆ Provide for full inclusion for all children, regardless of their special physical, emotional, or learning needs. Wide pathways are designed to accommodate wheelchairs, work spaces are sheltered from intrusion and interference, textures permit visually impaired children to participate fully, and the needs of hearing-impaired children are met through increased visual stimulation, such as felt pads on tabletops, carpeted shelves, and other work surfaces.
◆ Promote cognitive development by permitting children to take the initiative, make choices and decisions, and experience the consequences of these. Children decide which center they will begin working in, what they will do in the center and with whom, and when they have finished.
◆ Recognize individual needs, interests, differences, and the ways children learn. Children choose centers to develop or learn to master a skill. Because children do the choosing, their individual needs are at least partially met.
◆ Promote children's language usage and hence development through varied print and nonprint materials and the opportunity to communicate with others (Loughlin & Sunia, 1987).
◆ Set boundaries on children's behaviors. The physical boundaries of the centers subtly direct children's actions, as do the pathways between centers.

CENTERS OF INTEREST

Socio-Dramatic Play Area

The socio-dramatic play area is a place loved by children. Here they have the opportunity to reenact their experiences in their homes, neighborhoods, and communities. Here they can play house, taking on the role of mother, father, baby, or big sister. Or they can reenact any of their daily experiences, replaying their experiences in fast-food restaurants, grocery stores, churches, department stores, or any other place. They might turn the area into a magical, make-believe place as well, acting as if they were characters in favorite books or even movies, taking on the roles of a wicked witch, giants, Little Red Riding Hood and the wolf, or any other character.

Even though the socio-dramatic play area is a place where children can take on many roles, four- and five-year-olds seem to like playing house the best. A study designed to reveal Head Start children's ideas about kindergarten confirmed the children's love of playing house. About 98% of the over 300 children interviewed said that they hoped they would be able to "play house" when in kindergarten. "I think there's housekeeping," said one. "I'll be real sad if there isn't." So frequently was the housekeeping area mentioned that it almost seemed as if the Head Start children had read about the relation between reenacting their home experiences through socio-dramatic play and their growth, learning, and development (Seefeldt, Galper, & Denton, 1997).

Centers of interest enable individual children to meet their needs.

During the 1940s and 1950s, psychologists believed that housekeeping and other socio-dramatic play was necessary if children were to understand and clarify the events of their lives. Playing "as if" they were the mom who was in control or as if they were the baby in need of loving care was thought essential for sound psychological health.

Today, psychologists agree that socio-dramatic play, whether playing house or fast-food restaurant, is a way that children can work their way through feelings and come to understand and release strong emotions, but they believe that social dramatic play is important for other reasons.

One important reason is that language is demanded. Not just to keep the play going—"Now I'm putting out the fire, hose, hose"—but also to convince others of their role—"Get in the truck now, and put on the siren." Research suggests that both second-language speakers and English-only speakers gain vocabulary when they participate in socio-dramatic play (Fassler, 1998; Tabors, 1998) and that all children gain vocabulary and learn necessary skills of syntax and grammar (Dyson, 1988).

Socio-dramatic play is a highly cognitive activity. Playing "as if" the block were a scissors means that children hold images and ideas in their minds. When playing with others, they must not only hold these images in their minds but also convince the others that the block is a scissors. The abstraction of the play has been related to children's cognitive development and academic success in their later schooling (Howell & Corby-Scullen, 1997; Trawick-Smith, 1998). Piaget and Inhelder (1969) also believed that play was the way children come to develop the ability to use symbols and understand their world. As children play with objects and things in their environment, they are gaining knowledge of the physical properties of the world in which they live.

Social skills are also gained when children engage in socio-dramatic play. In contrast to solitary play, socio-dramatic play requires playing with others. Together children create the scenario, communicate and cooperate in carrying it out, solve problems, and coordinate their roles.

Equipping the Socio-Dramatic Play Area.   Discarded boxes that children have painted with suggestions of knobs to turn or doors to open can represent stoves, dishwashers, refrigerators, or other items. Some teachers give children large hollow blocks to build housekeeping furniture. Because the use of blocks is not dictated by any realism, the only limit to their use is children's imaginations. With blocks and boxes, children are the ones who must do the thinking. They are the ones who must decide on goals for the blocks and how they will achieve these goals and monitor their progress toward reading them. In the end, they are the ones who gain the joy and satisfaction of achieving their goal and the joy of creating any kind of building.

Children have arranged hollow blocks to create a post office, store, fast-food restaurant, doctor's or dentist's office, plant nursery, airport, or any other place they have experienced. One Native American group of children used the hollow blocks to create benches and a village plaza so they could watch traditional dances (Fayden, 1997). These areas may last a day or two or a couple of weeks.

Because children reenact experiences in their home and community, equipping the dramatic play area differs from region to region—for example, snow books in cold regions, certain regional foods, or things representing life in rural or urban areas.

Some things, however, seem universal. In addition to furniture or suggestions of furniture, dress-up clothing is found in most dramatic play areas. Suggestions of clothing, such as a piece of lace or discarded curtain, are enough to stimulate children's thinking and direct them to take on any variety of roles.

Things that are real have appeal to children. Stock the shelves with real cans of food or real pots and pans. Fill empty cereal boxes with styrofoam peanuts or pegs. Parents can donate discarded coffee pots, microwaves, and other cooking equipment. Safety proof everything, however, before adding to the play area.

Add things common to children's homes, such as the following:

◆ Tools—wrenches, pipes, oil cans, pieces of hoses, and gardening equipment
◆ Health aides—band-aids, cotton, bandages, and a stethoscope
◆ Purses and wallets with "credit cards" and play money, or children can make money
◆ Road maps and suitcases
◆ Cooking equipment that reflects their backgrounds

Think about the literacy environment of a home and include the following:

◆ Clipboards, with paper and markers attached
◆ Parts of the Sunday newspaper meant for children

- ◆ Magazines for children or other picture newsmagazines
- ◆ Books—reference as well as children's books
- ◆ Address books for children to consult and write in
- ◆ Pads of paper and pencils
- ◆ Receipt books and discarded checkbooks
- ◆ Stamps, trading stamps, stickers, envelopes and stationary, greeting cards and address labels
- ◆ Rubber stamps
- ◆ Cookbooks
- ◆ Junk mail that looks official, with things to fill out
- ◆ Paper and pencil

Math up the dramatic play area. You could add the following:

- ◆ Handheld calculators
- ◆ Cell phones
- ◆ Cash register receipt tapes
- ◆ Plastic numbers
- ◆ Calendars
- ◆ Measuring cups, spoons, tape measures, and rulers
- ◆ Scales—bathroom and kitchen
- ◆ Store coupons

Blocks

Blocks, one of the original gifts of Froebel, are traditional in kindergartens. Block play has been related to fostering children's spatial learning, mapping skills, language usage, mathematical knowledge, social skills, and concepts of height, weight, size, balance, and others (National Council of Teachers of Mathematics [NCTM], 1999; Newcomb, 1997).

Every kindergarten needs to have a complete set of unit blocks with arches, semicircles, triangles, and double arches as well as a set of large and small hollow blocks. These are stored on open shelves, usually by size and type of block. A hard surface building area, separated from other areas, enables children to construct large, tall buildings and to keep building them for several days.

Increase the complexity of block play by adding additional materials. If you have visited a farm, add wooden farm animals. If you have visited an airport, add planes and so on. Rocks, sticks, and pieces of wood are used by children to add reality to block building. Brown strips of paper lend themselves to children creating roads and blue paper to ponds, lakes, and rivers. Clipboards with paper and markers, available anywhere, let children sketch their buildings, make signs, or record how many blocks they can stack before the building falls.

Library Area

The library area is a place where books are arranged along with tables, chairs, or cushions enticing children to stay and read. This area is more than a shelf of books and a table. It is a place located away from other distractions where children will find every type of book—poetry, stories, folktales, picture books, reference books, and materials—even sections from the newspaper specifically designed for children as well as children's newspapers and magazines.

All children should find themselves reflected in these books. Books depicting the lives of children with special needs, as well as children of diverse cultural, racial, and ethnic backgrounds, will be selected.

Catalogs are fun to include. Children can use these as "wish books," or if you place two or more of the same catalog in the area, children will play games with them. "I'm looking at a toy, it's red and black, and children ride on it. Can you find it?"

Mounted pictures cut from magazines and chosen because they depict a topic the children are studying are fun for younger children to sort through and carry around with them. Books dictated or written by the children or photo albums and stories written by the teacher are other favorites. Some library areas also include a flannel board with cutout stories for children to sequence or retell a story by themselves or with a group of children.

Some books may be organized as a take-home library for the children so that children's learning experiences can continue when they are at home. A simple checkout sheet can be mounted above the books with two markers attached. The children can place a check by their name with the red marker when they take a book out and a check in black when they return it.

Books will also be displayed and arranged throughout the room. In one Head Start center, children observed a construction site and were fascinated with the trucks, cranes, and earth-moving equipment they saw. When they returned to the room, the teacher placed several books on trucks and construction vehicles in an open box next to the blocks. Children were seen consulting these as they created their own building.

In another classroom, teachers added Mother Goose and other nursery rhyme books in the housekeeping area. Children used these to read their babies to sleep (Seefeldt & Galper, 2000).

Writing Area

A shelf and table and chairs can become a writing center. Here children will be able to write, spelling words just the way they sound (Adams, 1998). On the shelf are all kinds of paper, journals, blank books created by stapling a couple of sheets of plain paper between construction paper covers, stationary, envelopes and stamps from junk mail, file folders, all kinds of pencils, pens, crayons, and markers. A box of alphabet rubber printing blocks along with ink pads, a box of plastic letters, small chalkboards and chalk, carbon paper, and other writing materials are also available on the shelf.

Even though children are encouraged to invent their own spelling, it is productive to provide children with models of the ABCs and of numerals in the writing center instead of tacked to the top of a wall. Providing a booklet of the ABCs or individual letter cards that children can use as models is useful. Children have also been intrigued with a set of name cards of the children in the class. They use these as models for writing or just for picking out the names of their friends.

Teachers may create a hanger upon which to attach words that reflect children's experiences. For example, on Halloween, the word hanger contained the words "bat," "cat," "witch's hat," and "pumpkin," and after a trip to the airport "flight attendant," "pilot," "plane," and "runway."

Box dictionaries can be started as well.

Art Area

Rather than there being just one center for art, there are many. Art activities take place throughout the room. Children need to find clay, boards to work on, and other clay tools stored on one shelf, always waiting for them. Fresh paints can be at easels or in cans in a six-pack carrier to take anywhere. All kinds of paper, markers, scissors, glue, and collage materials are located together on an open shelf so that children can see their choices and select the tools and materials they need for any project they have in mind.

Drawing tools and paper are also a part of the writing center. These allow children to draw pictures to illustrate their stories and other writing.

Board games develop children's mathematical understanding.

Math Area

Good kindergarten classrooms have a host of materials for children to manipulate. In the math or manipulative area, there are small blocks; things to sort and classify, such as bottle caps, buttons, seeds, and paint or wallpaper squares; as well as puzzles, peg boards, parquet, and Lego blocks.

A few sets of regular decks of cards and other materials for sorting, counting, and categorizing, such as large beads and buttons, nuts and bolts, washers, seashells, and objects, are good additions. Things for children to string on shoestrings or pipe cleaners, such as beads, macaroni, bottle caps with holes in them, and pattern cards, give children practice in making and following patterns as well as developing fine muscle skills. All are stored on open shelves in clear containers near a table and chairs. Children have access to the materials and select the ones they wish to work on.

Board games, such as Hi Ho Cherry Oh and Chutes and Ladders, and all types of bingo games are important in gaining mathematical understanding. When playing these games, children must count, take turns, and follow rules.

In British infant schools, the math table includes scales and things to weigh, tools for measuring things, clear plastic boxes of things to classify and categorize along with sorting trays to do so, plastic numerals, and sets of number cards. Task cards are hung in an apron on the edge of the table. These, color coded by difficulty, suggest tasks that children can try.

Materials in the manipulative or math area are chosen to meet the specific goals and objectives of the mathematics program. There are materials to foster children's concepts of numbers and operations, patterns, geometry, measurement, data analysis, problem solving, reasoning, connections, and representations. The complexity of the materials provided will increase as children's thinking and understanding of mathematical concepts increase.

Science Area

There are materials throughout the room to permit children to engage in scientific inquiry; nevertheless, there are specific places within the room where children can examine, explore, and solve problems in both the life and the physical sciences.

Use the science area or areas to fulfill the goals and objectives of the kindergarten curriculum and the life and physical sciences performance standards.

Life Sciences. To fulfill the life science goal of introducing children to the variety of plant and animal life on earth, you could set aside a couple of areas in the room to grow things. Provide children with packets of seeds. Have them find the smallest and the largest seeds. Try growing the seeds. Sprinkle Timothy grass seeds on dampened sponges or paper towels and watch a sea of grass grow. Other seeds can be planted in cups.

Seeds are not always necessary to grow things. In another area you could grow plants from cuttings of a part of a plant. Pussy willow, forsythia, and other bushes and plants will root in water or soil and can then be planted in the school yard. Cuttings of root vegetables will also grow. Carrots, turnips, and radishes, cut about an inch from their top with the greens removed and anchored in a dish of water and gravel, will produce lacy, new green plants. Cut the top off a pineapple and, letting it dry a day or two, plant it in the same manner.

Keep clipboards handy so that children can sketch the growth of the seeds, vegetables, and fruits. Children can record which seeds or vegetables sprouted first, which grew the tallest, and which died.

Physical Sciences. Water and sand are considered key components of learning about the physical nature of earth. Both are considered science centers. It is not necessary to have large, freestanding water tables. A plastic dishpan set on a table covered with plastic, a chair, or even the floor covered with plastic is all that is necessary, along with things to use with the water. Plastic hoses, funnels, strainers, spoons, cups, or anything that will not break can be used. Ask children to find out which container holds the most water, how much it weighs, and which containers hold the least or no water at all. Help them graph their findings.

Things to wash—dolls, dolls' clothes, windows, tables, or other furniture in the room—give children another use for water. With a few focused questions from a teacher, children can find out where things dry the fastest (in the shade or in the sun), how long it takes things to dry, and what happens to the water. Clipboards with paper and markers permit children to record their findings. They could draw, paint, or write about their ideas of where the water goes when clothes dry.

Sand play offers much the same type of sciencing as water. Sand is pourable, it fills things, and it can be a building material. After children are familiar with sand, they can be asked to find out how much sand fills one container and compare this amount to the sand in another. Ask them to weigh different containers of sand. Give children water in squirt bottles so that they can build with sand. Add pebbles, sticks, play people, vehicles, animals, marbles, and other props and watch children build castles in the sand.

One science center could contain things to look through. Ask parents to give you old lenses from their glasses or ask the science department in your school for lenses from discarded telescopes and old magnifying glasses or sheets. Show children how to look through these. Five-year-olds may notice that some of the lenses have a bump in the middle. These are convex lenses. Another day add a prism to the center. Now children can catch rainbows of light. Have paper and markers ready so that they can record what they see and describe how the world looks through the lenses.

Music Area

Some area of the room can be set aside as a music center. A small table, perhaps holding a listening station with a selection of CDs and perhaps a video player or tape recorder, could be located in the center. Here children can listen to and watch tapes or videos of themselves singing, dancing, and moving to music as well as listen to their favorite songs.

Provide a few musical instruments to experiment with, or a selection of sound makers, to give children the opportunity to listen to as well as make music. Not all musical instruments should be made available at all times. Select one or two. You might select an autoharp, drum, guitar, shakers, or tone blocks. Introduce these to the group one at a time, demonstrating how children can make music with them and how to care for them.

Picture songbooks can be another choice in the music center. Music paper with lines and staff and a container of markers can allow children to write music as well.

Technology Center

At least several computers with programs appropriate for kindergarten children should be available in every kindergarten. Make certain that the programs you select do the following:

◆ Relate to the program goals and objectives, but are also more effective in extending or expanding children's knowledge or in providing children with practice in a skill than using less expensive traditional methods and materials.
◆ Involve higher thought processes and are not simply rote drill and practice but require judgment, evaluating, analyzing, or synthesizing information (Wright & Shade, 1994).

Computers are available in today's kindergartens.

◆ Include materials which are age and developmentally appropriate based on your judgment, not simply on what is printed on the box.
◆ Include materials which are accurate—do not emphasize war, violence, or stereotype or discriminate by gender, race, or age (Wright & Shade, 1994).
◆ Involve children in cooperative learning.

A Place to Be Alone

Kindergarten children, like all humans, need space to be alone. It may just be a few pillows or a comfortable chair in one of the corners of the room, a small nook in the library area, or a small table and chair away from the other centers. Wherever or whatever it is, this space is set aside where children can go to be away from the group to think, relax, or calm themselves (Hubbard, 1997).

Reality

In reality, no kindergarten or pre-kindergarten classroom is large enough to hold every center all the time. Nor would you expect young children to make choices from the full array of centers. Nevertheless, everyday children should be able to use the following:

◆ Drawing, painting, writing, modeling, or constructing materials to express themselves
◆ A variety of books to look at, consult, read, or listen to

◆ Dress up materials and other props that enable them to take part in socio-dramatic play
◆ Opportunities to work with manipulatives
◆ A shelf or table of math and science materials to work with and explore
◆ A computer station
◆ A place to make or listen to music

OUTDOOR LEARNING SPACES

Recess is another opportunity to fulfill the goals of the kindergarten program. True, this is a time for children to release pent-up energy, run, yell, roll down hills, and climb to the top of the jungle gym. However, it is much more than just physical activity and emotional release (Rivkin, 1995).

Research suggests that recess facilitates school learning (Bjorklund & Brown, 1998). The National Institute of Child Health and Human Development (2000) suggests that physical play alters brain development in positive ways and that physical play, combined with social pretend play, seems to serve a number of functions in addition to giving children a break from intellectual work (Bjorklund & Brown, 1998).

Recess provides children the opportunity to do the following:

◆ Act out concepts and ideas they are learning or have already learned.
◆ Develop large muscles and skills in using these muscles.
◆ Increase their powers of observation. The natural world is filled with things for children to observe. Clouds, rain, sprouting seeds, falling leaves, birds, insects, shadows—all are experienced out of doors.
◆ Fostering children's autonomy and independence.
◆ Expand and develop social skills. Recess gives children additional opportunities to cooperate with others. Complex schemes for rearranging equipment, digging gardens, making cities in the sand, or building structures develop and bloom out of doors (Pellegrini & Smith, 1998).
◆ Promote language use. Outdoors, children can sign, shout, yell, and use language in ways that differ from being inside.

Physical Activity

Space and a variety of equipment foster boisterous running, jumping, and climbing out of doors. Some equipment that promotes social interactions, the use of language, and cooperative play that is rich with potential for children to form concepts of the physical properties of their world include the following:

◆ Large wooden crates and boxes, boards with cleats, and large hollow blocks. The size of these materials demands that two or more children work together to build or construct with these materials (Odoy & Foster, 1997).
◆ Climbing equipment that comes in several movable sections, such as a trestle unit, climbing gate, or Λ-frame unit, that can be arranged and rearranged to meet children's changing interests or needs is a good investment.

◆ Cable tables of assorted sizes, tree trunks, with sharp branches removed, along with sturdy wooden barrels, give children an opportunity to use large muscles as well as work cooperatively with others.
◆ Balance beams. An old log, several logs placed end to end, a board placed on its side, or stepping-stones, patio stores, or old tires placed in a series give children several different ways to balance themselves in space.
◆ A wide assortment of balls of all sizes and weights.
◆ Things to push and pull give children a sense of control over their environment. Large wooden or cardboard boxes, planks, old tires, and even small cable tables can be rolled to new locations, stacked to make a tower, or pushed around the yard.

Other Outdoor Activity

The out of doors is really an extension of the stimulating, well-arranged indoor learning environment. The added richness of the natural surroundings and the open spaces enhance possibilities for learning experiences. Centers of interest found indoors can be arranged in varying forms out of doors.

Socio-Dramatic Play.   Any kind of structure will do to stimulate socio-dramatic play. It can be a playhouse, but more often a wooden platform, a tepee of bamboo stalks, or a couple of boxes arranged with a blanket over them motivate children to housekeeping play. Add a couple of metal muffin tins, wooden spoons, pots and pans, plastic dishes, and a hat or two, and dramatic play flourishes out of doors.

Wheel toys placed near the housekeeping center add to the complexity of dramatic play. Parents can leave for work on bikes or in wagons, deliveries can be made, or firefighters can come to rescue the "house" and the people in it.

Art.   Any art activity can take place outside. From painting with water to hanging large brown paper strips on a playground fence and putting a six-pack of paint next to the paper, children can enjoy painting out of doors.

Children can draw with large chunk chalk dipped in water on the hard surfaces on the play yard. Their creations will wash away with the next rain. Or you can provide crayons or markers with large pieces of paper spread on the yard or tables. Clay and modeling with other materials is fun to do outside, as is constructing with large boxes, found objects, and other materials.

Science.   With nature surrounding them outdoors, children approach science with dynamic curiosity and vivid interest. Experiences with the biological as well as physical sciences are plentiful.

The life cycle of living things can be directly observed and recorded in photographs, pictures, and graphs. Birds, insects, and mammals can be watched, fostering the concept of the variety of life on earth. Seeds and bulbs can be planted and cared for. A few butterfly nets aid in the study of insects (Rivkin, 1995).

Experiences with simple machines are abundant outdoors. The principle of the wheel can be introduced through wheeled toys and the lever through a seesaw. The use of simple machines, such as an inclined plane or a lever, can be demonstrated in moving heavy boxes or other equipment. The physical properties of light can be introduced outdoors. A prism can be used to catch the sunlight, or the refraction of light can be observed in water and bubbles.

Water and sand play can expand out of doors. On a hot and sunny day, children can play with water and hoses or run through a sprinkler. Or they can wash dolls' clothes and hang these in the sun to dry or hold a car wash and wash all the tricycles, wagons, and wheel toys. Add a trickling water hose and plastic squirt bottles filled with water to the sand area, and children can create large structures in the sandbox.

Music.   When the teacher brings an autoharp or ukulele outdoors, children can join her in singing familiar songs. Sitting in the shade of a tree or gathered around a picnic bench adds variety to outdoor time. By observing children running, skipping, and hopping, an astute teacher can pick up the children's natural rhythm by beating a drum or other instrument.

Math.   Counting, classifying, ordering, and other mathematical concepts are made real outdoors. The smooth stones a child gathers, the acorns another child collects, the sticks or cups in the sandbox, and the number of children waiting to ride a new tricycle all give children something meaningful to count. Clipboards and markers on the play yard permit them to record their classifications of the stones, insects, seeds, or acorns they find or the way they sequenced them from smallest to largest and heaviest to lightest.

Organized Games.   Organized games that begin and end spontaneously, such as "Ring around the Rosy," "Frog in the Middle," "Did You Ever See a Lassie?," "Punchinello," and others are a part of outdoor play and experiences. Traditional games, such as marbles and jacks, are included (Casbergue & Kieff, 1998). The values of playing organized games are many. By playing a game together, children gain concepts of the following:

◆ Cooperating—learning to give up some of their individuality for the good of the group
◆ Sequencing—learning and remembering what to do next
◆ Structured language—Introducing children to concepts of grammar through the repetitive language found in organized games

ROLE OF THE TEACHER

Teachers teach during center time. More complex types of teaching interactions take place when teachers can work alone with a child or small group during center time (Kontos & Keyes, 1999). Clearly, they observe and supervise, but their major role is to interact with individuals and small groups of children in ways designed to promote children's learning and development.

Teachers enter into discussions with children about what they are doing. This is not the talk of an interviewer—"What color is the truck?", "How many do you have?"—nor the talk of a lecturer—"This truck is yellow, this one is green. Blue and yellow together make green."

Rather, teachers enter into what Vygotsky (1986) termed an "educational dia-logue." This implies a give-and-take between teacher and children. The teacher does have goals in mind, does tell children information, and does question them to guide them to achieve the goals of the program or their own personal goals (Berk & Winsler, 1995; Bodrova & Leong, 1996). Primarily, however, teachers talk with children in order to lead them to correct their misconceptions, discover meaning, and avoid dead-end lines of thinking.

A few thought-out questions can open communication and lead children to think. Teachers can ask the following:

What do you think of. . . ?

Can you find some ways. . . ?

Can you find another way. . . ?

Why do you think that happened. . . ?

I wonder why. . . ?

What might happen if you. . . ?

What else could you do. . . ?

In addition to questioning, teachers reinforce children's talk by expanding on their ideas. A teacher might respond to a child who says, "Bunny's nose wiggles," by saying, "Look at it wiggle. What do you think she's doing?" Depending on the child's answer, the teacher can respond again or suggest consulting books or experts to find out why rabbits wiggle their noses.

A child who says, "I took a trip on an airplane this weekend," might be rein-forced with a statement like, "You went on an airplane to visit your grandmother and father on their 50th wedding anniversary. What did you do on the plane? Did you see the ground below?"

Teachers encourage children to solve problems. A child trying to join two boxes is engaged in conversation. The teacher first tries to determine the child's goals, then may suggest alternate ways of achieving these. Or she may ask a question helping the child to find a solution to the problem. To a child who is frustrated, the teacher may suggest, "Have you tried . . .?" Finally, teachers encourage children to stay with a task or project until the child's goal is achieved: "Try this piece here."

Teachers listen to children, respecting children's ideas. Listening is more than hearing. Active listening means stopping what you are doing, looking directly at the child who is talking, and reflecting on what he or she has said or is trying to say. Waiting a few seconds to reflect on what the child has said is helpful. This lets the child know you are thinking about his or her statements and ideas. Then re-spond in several ways. You might repeat what the child has said: "Understandably, you were really frightened when it thundered last night," "You like red," or "You are telling me that Tommy is bothering you." This nondirective technique helps children work out their own problems and gain an understanding of their own feelings and will increase communication between you and the child.

Or you could respond by commenting on the theme or the important points the child has made. You might answer, "Yes, the paper is difficult to work with; your fingers are too sticky from the paste."

Teachers give feedback as well as enter into dialogue with children. Giving feedback lets children know how they are progressing. Generally, productive feedback does the following:

◆ Describes what the child has done rather than placing a value judgment on it. "You completed three puzzles" or "You started from the middle and worked out with the puzzle pieces" is more reinforcing than saying, "I like the way you worked with puzzles."
◆ Is specific rather than general. "You wrote all the letters of your name" rather than "Good job."
◆ Directs children toward something they have control over and can do something about. "Put these three dishes here" is more helpful than "Pick up."
◆ Is well-timed. Feedback needs to be juxtaposed with the child's actions and given while children are actually working or achieving.
◆ May be non-verbal. A wink, a nod of the head, or a smile communicates to children that they are on the right track or that you noticed how well they are doing.

Without even knowing so, teachers teach through their every action, nonaction, and reaction. Every bit of verbal and non-verbal behavior of the teacher is noted by the children. And because children adore their kindergarten teachers so much, they want to be like them and will copy, or model, their teachers' behaviors.

Sometimes teachers deliberately model a skill, attitude, or procedure as a means of teaching. During indoor and outdoor work time, teachers will model how to hold a tool, feed the fish, turn on the computer, safely carry a chair, or wash out paintbrushes. At times they may direct children's attention to a specific task— "Watch me, I put the pegs in the board like this. Now you do it" or "Watch me as I thread the needle, first I do . . . now you do it."

EVALUATING INDOOR AND OUTDOOR SPACES

Daily, teachers observe children interacting in their environments. These observations are the basis for evaluating the effectiveness of both the classroom and the outdoor environments. Teachers can ask themselves the following:

◆ Do the centers, both indoors and outdoors, reflect the goals of the program and objectives for children's learning?
◆ Are children making choices and decisions about which centers they will work in and what they will accomplish when in the centers?
◆ Are the provisions made for children with special needs effective? Are children with special needs able to participate fully with others in all or most of the centers?
◆ Can the equipment be used by children with different interests and differing levels of maturity? Are there enough open-ended materials, like blocks, art materials, books, and dramatic play equipment, that can be used in different ways by children of differing abilities and maturity?

◆ Are storage areas clearly defined? Are children using the materials and equipment independently?

◆ Is there a balance between high physical activity both inside and outside and activities that require thinking and cognition?

◆ Are traffic patterns clearly defined so that children are not running and bumping into one another as they move from center to center?

◆ Can children work alone or with others?

◆ Are both indoors and outdoors equipped with materials and things that offer children a challenge that they can successfully meet? How are you increasing the complexity of the materials and spaces on a daily or weekly basis?

◆ How safe are the spaces and materials for all children? Is outdoor equipment checked daily for loose or sharp or dangerous parts? Is indoor equipment sanitized daily?

◆ Do the spaces respect children by being ordered, clean, and filled with beauty? Outdoors, children should find a variety of textures and aesthetically pleasing equipment, growing plants, and animal life. Indoors, the beauty of living plants, prints of genuine art, displays of their own work, and other beautiful objects surround children.

IN SUMMARY

Froebel's belief that children learn through play and activity is as current today as it was in the past. Today's kindergartens are based on research and theory, demonstrating that children learn best through play and social, mental, and physical activity.

To enable children to learn through their own activity, classrooms are arranged with centers of interest. Center time has been called the heart of the kindergarten. Clearly children adore center time, especially housekeeping. But center time is more than just enjoyable for children. This is a prime learning time for them.

Typically, centers include a socio-dramatic play area; blocks; library; writing, art, math and manipulative, music, and technology areas; and a place to be alone. The materials within the centers are chosen to fulfill the goals of the kindergarten. Content from every discipline as well as skills and attitudes are taught as children work and play together or alone in centers.

Outdoor play is just as valuable a learning time as indoor center work. Although outdoor play offers children opportunities to develop large muscles and motor skills and release pent-up energy, content from every discipline area is taught during outdoor play. Materials and equipment for children to participate in art, music, socio-dramatic play, and the sciences are found on the play yard. Teachers find that by rotating centers for outdoor play, they can achieve their goals and keep children's interest and motivation high.

Center and outdoor play time is a busy time for teachers. As Dewey (1938) suggested, the role of the teacher is more complex and more intimate when children are actively engaged in learning. During center time and outdoor play, teachers interact with individuals and small groups of children, teaching them new skills, guiding them to solving problems, and introducing new vocabulary and concepts from every discipline area.

Teachers also observe and evaluate during center and outdoor play time. They observe not only to supervise and understand children's growth, learning, and progress but also to evaluate the centers and learning spaces. They note which centers and outdoor areas are being ignored and could be made more complex and which are troublesome and should be removed or replaced with more appropriate centers or spaces.

EXTEND YOUR IDEAS

1. Observe in kindergarten classrooms and make sketches of the floor plans for both the indoor and the outdoor physical environments. In small groups in class, evaluate the rooms and spaces using the evaluation questions at the end of this chapter. Make suggestions for how you would improve the environments.

   Now make a floor plan of your ideal kindergarten classroom. Share these with the class.
2. As a class, generate a list of the centers of interest you might include in your kindergarten. Discuss how these could be combined and used in ways to integrate the curriculum.
3. Observe in a kindergarten. Analyze how children make choices of activities and materials. How does the physical environment help or hinder children from selecting their own activities?
4. Scour your neighborhood for hidden treasures you might use to equip indoor and outdoor learning spaces. Go to a drugstore, florist, gas station, grocery store, or any other businesses in the area. Ask for materials they throw away and would be willing to give you to use with children. You might find packing cases, corrugated papers of all kinds, signs, posters, or other materials to use to equip a kindergarten.

RESOURCES

Some good books on arranging the physical environment follow:

Play for All Guidelines: Planning, Designing and Management of Outdoor Play Settings for All Children, by Robin C. Moore, Susan M. Goltsman, and Daniel S. Iacofano (New York: MIG Communications, 1992). This is a valuable resource for creating play settings.

The Complete Learning Center Book: An Illustrated Guide for 32 Different Early Childhood Learning Centers, by Rebecca Isbell (Silver Spring, MD: Grypon House, 1995).

This book gives you new and unique ideas for learning centers.

The Great Outdoors: Restoring Children's Right to Play Outside, by Mary Rivkin (Washington, DC: NAEYC, 1995). This book validates the power of outdoor play while suggesting ideas for arranging for play.

The Right Stuff, by Mary Bronson (Washington, DC: National Association for the Education of Young Children, 1995). This book gives teachers all they need to know to equip kindergarten play spaces.

A web site devoted to school planning is the following: *http://www.schoolclearinghouse.org/right.asp* Here you will find every type of assistance in planning school buildings, publications on the school facilities, and other information that might stimulate your thinking and ideas of arranging indoor and outdoor spaces.

REFERENCES

Adams, M. J. (1998). *Beginning to read.* Cambridge MA: Massachusetts Institute of Technology.

Berk, L. E., & Winsler, A. (1995). *Scaffolding children's learning: Vygotsky and early childhood education.* Washington, DC: National Association for the Education of Young Children.

Bjorklund, D. F., & Brown, R. D. (1998). Physical play and cognitive development: Integrating activity, cognition, and education. *Child Development, 69,* 604–607.

Bodrova, E., & Leong, D. J. (1996). *Tools of the mind: The Vygotskian approach to early childhood education.* Upper Saddle River, NJ: Merrill/Prentice Hall.

Casbergue, R. M., & Kieff, J. (1998). Marbles anyone? Traditional games in the classroom. *Childhood Education, 74,* 143–147.

Dewey, J. (1938). *The School and society.* New York: McCure, Phillips & Co.

Dyson, A. H. (1988). The value of time off task: Young children's spontaneous talk and deliberate text. *Harvard Educational Review, 97,* 396–420.

Fassler, R. (1998). Room for talk: Peer support for getting into English. *Early Childhood Research Quarterly, 13,* 379–410.

Fayden, T. (1997). Children's choice: Planting the seeds for creating a thematic sociodramatic play center. *Young Children, 52*(3), 15–21.

Howell, J., & Corby-Scullen, L. (1997). Out of the housekeeping corner and onto the state: Extending dramatic play. *Young Children, 52*(6), 82–85.

Hubbard, R. S. (1997). Creating a classroom where children can think. *Young Children, 53*(5), 26–31.

Kontos, S., & Keyes, L. (1999). An ecobehavioral analysis of early childhood classrooms. *Early Childhood Research Quarterly, 14,* 35–50.

Loughlin, C. E., & Suina, J. (1987). *The learning environment: An instructional strategy.* New York: Teachers College Press.

Mallory, B. (1998). Educating young children with developmental differences: Principles of inclusive

practice. In C. Seefeldt & A. Galper (Eds.), *Continuing issues in early childhood education* (2nd ed., pp. 213–238). Upper Saddle River, NJ: Merrill/Prentice Hall.

National Council of Teachers of Mathematics. (1999). *Mathematics in early childhood.* Reston, VA: Author.

National Institute of Child Health and Human Development. (2000). Child Development Report to the NACHHD Council. Washington, DC: Author.

Odoy, H. A. D., & Foster, S. H. (1997). Creating play crates for the outdoor classroom. *Young Children, 52*(6), 12–16.

Pellegrini, A. D., & Smith, P. K. (1998). Physical activity play: The nature and function of a neglected aspect of play. *Child Development, 69,* 577–599.

Piaget, J., & Inhelder, B. (1969). *The psychology of the child.* New York: Basic Books.

Rivkin, M. (1995). *The great outdoors: Restoring children's right to play outside.* Washington, DC: National Association for the Education of Young Children.

Seefeldt, C., Galper, A., & Denton, K. (1997). Head Start children's conceptions of and expectations for their future schooling. *Early Childhood Research Quarterly, 12,* 387–406.

Tabors, P. O. (1998). What early childhood educators need to know: Developing effective programs for linguistically and culturally diverse children and their families. *Young Children, 53*(6), 20–26.

Trawick-Smith, J. (1998). A qualitative analysis of metaplay in the preschool years. *Early Childhood Research Quarterly, 13,* 433–451.

Vygotsky, L. (1986). *Thought and language* (Rev. ed.). Cambridge: MIT Press.

Wright, J., & Shade, D. (1994). Young children: Active learners in a technological age. Washington, DC: NAEYC.

CHAPTER 6 Teachers Are Ready to Guide Children's Social Behavior

Teaching kindergarten is unlike teaching at any other level. Kindergarten children seem to experience life with more exuberance, enthusiasm, and joy than children of any other age do. With "batteries attached" (Kaiser & Rasminsky, 1999), kindergarten children are filled with boundless energy, spirited animation, and lavish imaginations. And they bring all this with them to the kindergarten.

Living and working with children so full of energy, so exuberant, and so in love with life and learning truly is a joy and pleasure. Regardless, it does require a special kind of person to teach four- and five-year-olds—one who not only respects and values the vibrancy of young children but also has the ability to guide the behavior of these exuberant, vivacious children in ways that promote their full growth, development, and learning.

Understandably, each child is an individual, and each child's behaviors are influenced and directed by the cultural context within which they live. Still, understanding the normalcy of four- and five-year-old behavior enables you to respect and value the childishness of children.

FOUR-YEAR-OLD BEHAVIOR

Four-year-olds have earned the label "out of bounds." It begins with their language. Loving to play with language, they often use what teachers have termed "bathroom language." They do so because the words are fun to say and then, once they find out the power of the words, to shock others. In a way, the language of four-year-olds is typical of their behavior. Four-year-olds are testing themselves, their boundaries, and at the same time anyone who has authority over them. Just as they seem to go overboard with the language they use, they run too fast, climb too high, and boast and boss others way too much.

Emotions are close to the surface in most four-year-olds. They become angry easily, fly off the handle, and have difficulty in sharing and the normal give-and-take of playing and working with others. Their play is often wild and out of control; still, however, they want to play with others, want to please friends, and are developing self-regulating behavior.

FIVE-YEAR-OLD BEHAVIOR

On the other hand, most five-year-olds enter kindergarten with a sense of confidence, certain of their competence to learn and ready to assume more and more responsibility for their own care. Unlike four-year-olds, five-year-olds want most of all to please others. After teaching four-year-olds, working with five-year-olds seems peaceful and relaxing.

Five-year-olds are, as A. A. Milne wrote in his poem *The End* (1961), "just alive." They are just alive with wonder about their world and eager to learn more about ants, worms, astronauts, animals, insects, and themselves. They really do seem to be truly alive.

This does not mean, however, that five-year-olds do not have emotional outbursts. Even though they have more control over their emotions, five-year-olds can have sudden, short temper tantrums or become angry at a moment's notice. Socially, they play well with others, and many five-year-olds have a special friend. They can be bossy and assertive, but they are beginning to play cooperatively.

GUIDING THE BEHAVIOR OF FOUR- AND FIVE-YEAR-OLDS

"Nanny poo-poo to you," a four-year-old told her kindergarten teacher. An astonished student teacher said, "I would never permit that kind of language in my kindergarten. That girl would be disciplined—you can count on that."

Guidance to many means discipline or some form of punishment—a reprimand or a time-out. The actual meaning of "discipline," however, is to guide or instruct to act in accordance with the rules of proper conduct or action. Teachers who believe in guiding children's behavior think beyond conventional classroom discipline, the goal of which is to literally and figuratively "keep children in line" (Gartrell, 1997, p. 34). Their goal is to guide children's behavior in order to enable them to become autonomous beings, in control of their own behaviors regardless of whether an adult is present. Teachers plan ways to guide children's behavior that (1) foster children's sense of self, (2) develop their social skills, and (3) use specific guidance techniques when problems do arise.

GUIDANCE THAT FOSTERS A SENSE OF SELF

Children who feel good about themselves believe that they are competent beings who can and will learn, are able to control their own behaviors, and relate effectively with others. Thus, a first step in guidance is to ensure that children do know themselves and hold positive feelings toward themselves.

Research suggests that kindergarten can do much to foster children's confidence in themselves and build the foundation for future relationships with others (National Institute of Child Health and Human Development [NICHD], 2000). They do not shame, ridicule, or punish but rather support, guide, and teach children in ways that enable them to maintain their dignity and feelings of self-worth while they learn new and more effective ways of behaving (Eaton, 1997).

Teachers Are Supportive

A supportive teacher who communicates genuine and unconditional respect for children does much to foster children's self-confidence, identity, and esteem. Rogers (1951) called this *unconditional self-regard,* meaning that teachers give love and support freely, without wanting love, admiration, or anything else in return. This does not mean that adults are permissive and accept anything a child does (Marion, 1995). Supportive adults are authoritative—they set and maintain clear limits for children's behaviors, teach children how to work with others, and keep them from hurting themselves or others.

Teachers Are Positive

Respecting children, teachers are firm and consistent but do not threaten or force children to good behavior. For example, Sekai's behavior was out of bounds. One morning as she dashed around the room, she knocked into Alberto, making him fall, and stopped her running only long enough to splash paint on Claire's painting. Taking Sekai aside, the teacher said, "You cannot run in this room because you hurt others. You cannot destroy the property of others. What do you think you can do about this?" Sekai, feeling threatened, said, "I don't know and I don't care." The teacher responded, "We care," and asked more specifically, "Is there some way we could arrange the room differently so you would remember not to run and hurt others?" Sekai, gaining some time and security, offered several suggestions, ending with "I won't run and I won't touch the paint." The teacher did not let it go at that but asked, "How can I help to keep you from running in the room or hurting others?" Sekai, with feelings of confidence restored, said, "Well, you could shake your head at me when I think I'm going to run. Then I won't."

Teachers Acknowledge Children's Feelings

Acknowledging children's feelings lets them know they are respected. Shawn yelled, "I hate you! I hate you! You stupid head!" at Todd, who had accidentally run into Shawn's block castle, knocking it down. Neither child was reprimanded; instead, the teacher acknowledged Shawn's anger. "You are angry with Todd. Tell me about it." After Todd explained what had happened, she said, "You have a right to be angry with Shawn because he destroyed your block castle." Because kindergarten children do not understand the difference between intentional and accidental behaviors, the teacher did not ask either child to apologize to the other. She did, however, work with Shawn by teaching him to express his feelings in ways that were assertive yet did not hurt others. Then she talked with Shawn about the effects of running, asking him to control his behavior.

Teachers Model and Guide

Teachers who let children know that they really care for them and respect their needs and ideas are in turn beloved by the children. Because children love and trust their teachers, they want to be like them. Thus, teachers serve as powerful, if subtle, models of behavior. One teacher's way of interacting with a Spanish-speaking child new to the kindergarten was modeled by the children. While observing Juan's adjustment to kindergarten, the teacher noticed a number of children taunting Juan, calling him "funny talk." Instead of reprimanding the children, she chose to serve as a model. In front of the children she would ask Juan to say the Spanish name for different things in the room. She looked to Juan for the correct pronunciation, putting Juan in the role of teacher. The other children then began to ask Juan, "Is this the way you roll r's?" They laughed and giggled together as they practiced rolling r's as Juan taught them Spanish words (Seefeldt & Barbour, 1998).

Teachers Deliberately Confront Stereotypes and Prejudices

The old saying "Sticks and stones may break my bones but names will never hurt me" is not at all true. Names do hurt (California Tomorrow, 1999). Just as teachers do not allow children to bully, tease, or taunt one another, they do not allow children to call one another names, especially those that deride or disparage children's ethnicity, race, or special needs.

California Tomorrow (1999) advocates helping children understand that some words are very hurtful by asking children who call others names to name the words that hurt their feelings and to tell you why. Then mention that the words he or she used were just as hurtful to other children and find words that do not hurt when they are angry.

Teachers can do the following:

◆ Immediately address a child's response to a cultural difference (Derman-Sparks & the A.B.C. Task Force, 1989). "You have beautiful straight blond hair, Tonja has beautiful black curly hair."

◆ Help the child understand why he or she is uncomfortable. Children who have not known others of differing racial or ethnic groups or have never seen children with a special need may find differences frightening. They need to have their fears accepted while learning to be comfortable with others (California Tomorrow, 1999).

STRATEGIES FOR TEACHING SOCIAL SKILLS

One day during the first week of kindergarten, five-year-old Joshua sat alone at a table, sighing from time to time. Andrea, sensing Joshua's distress, darted to him and tried to push a cup and spoon in his hands. In a loud, demanding voice, she said, "Here—eat your breakfast or you'll be late." Joshua's sighs turned into quiet sobs.

In each kindergarten there will be children like Joshua and Andrea. Many, like Andrea, enter the group well socialized and sensitive to the needs of others. Even so, they may still be unclear about how to behave in a given social situation. Others, such as Joshua, may have only limited understanding of what it takes to be a part of the group and are anxious, even frightened, at the prospect of joining one.

Each child brings a different level of social understanding to the kindergarten.

Because each child brings a different level of social understanding and skills to the group, socialization, the process by which children are transformed from individuals into social beings, takes place continually. In the kindergarten setting, socialization involves (a) learning to accept others; (b) being able to form close, affectionate friendships with others; and (c) developing the skills necessary to become a cooperative, participating member of a democratic society.

Socialization is a contradiction. To accept others, children must first find acceptance themselves. To form affectionate friendships with others, they must first know affection. Only then will they be able to give up some of their individuality and develop the social skills necessary for participation in the small democracy of their classroom and the culture in which they live.

Acceptance

Acceptance begins with respect for whatever level of socialization children bring with them to the kindergarten. By four or five years of age, children become increasingly social. When children have experienced responsive, loving care as infants, they are in control of their social behavior and are able to play and work with others cooperatively. They can manage the dynamics of working with small groups of children and take part in discussions, music, and listening to stories as a member of the total group.

Not only do teachers accept the social skills and knowledge children bring with them to the kindergarten, but they ensure that each child finds a measure of acceptance from the group. One kindergarten teacher asked children how they could make their classroom a place where children would feel accepted, welcome, and comfortable and safe in school. The children responded to the prompt "I feel welcome when . . . " by saying, "When someone says play with me . . . is nice to me . . . I play with the teacher . . . someone says 'Happy Birthday' " (Froesch & Sprung, 1999).

Research shows that groups reject some children because they behave aggressively (Kemple, 1991). Research shows that aggressive children benefit from discussing "what if" conflict situations that encourage a wide range of potential solutions (Beatty, 1999). Some teachers use hand or finger puppets to present a problem situation. After they act out the conflict, teachers ask the child to come up with a solution using the puppets.

On-the-spot guidance during conflict situations seems helpful as well. As children fight over toys or over who can and cannot play with them, teachers teach. Using Vygotsky's (1978) idea of scaffolding, teachers support children's existing social skills while guiding them to more sophisticated behaviors. Teachers might help children voice their opinion ("Tell her you do not want to be the baby"), generate solutions ("Shawan will use the trike first, then it will be your turn"), and help children reach a mutually accepted solution to their problem ("If you hold this piece and Ashok holds it here, you can balance the building").

Research from the University of Oregon suggests that some children may benefit from changing groups (Stromshak, 1999). Shy and withdrawn children, who may find it difficult to feel accepted when in a group filled with boisterous, assertive, and even aggressive children, might find more acceptance when in a quieter, gentler group.

Helping each child achieve recognition and prestige within the group can also enhance his or her acceptance. Children feel honored and recognized when the class makes them a "get well" book or a birthday or other celebratory book. These books consist of pictures and stories by the children stapled together between construction paper covers. And prestige is the reward for children who can explain to others how they were able to balance a tall block building, make a dinosaur from clay, or describe the rules for the woodworking area.

Research suggests that some children with special needs can improve social skills with the help of their teachers. Lowenthal (1996) found that special needs children can be taught to observe others and model appropriate social skills and that teachers can help them through problem situations with verbal prompts— "Tell her you want to play"—or a simple gesture. Specific training with puppets or dolls has also been useful. Finally, peers can be taught how to engage the special needs child in their work and activities. Teachers can ask resource people in their school for other suggestions on how to foster the social skills of children with special needs so that they are fully included in the social world of the kindergarten (Crowley, 1999).

Forming Affectionate Friendships

A part of the socialization process is being able to form close, affectionate friendships. Research shows that children who have close friends are popular, well-liked by others, and successful in later school and life (Burk, 1996; Ladd, 1996; Ramsey, 1991). Observing these children, researchers found that they have good communication skills. They call other children by name, look at others (Bost, 1999), and touch those they are talking or listening to (Kemple, 1991). They also reply appropriately when spoken to. Instead of ignoring the speaker or rejecting another child, they suggest alternatives or give a reason for rejecting their ideas. When asked to play robbers, they might say something like "Let's be space monsters instead," or "We played that yesterday."

Making sure that children know one another's names is a first step. In addition to singing name songs and chants, teachers serve as models using children's names as they talk with them. Observing children having trouble making friends is the next step. This helps you pinpoint the specific problems and strengths of a child. A child who ignores others when playing can be taught to look at children who are talking to them (Bost, 1999). One who looks at

Enabling children to form affectionate friendships is a goal of today's kindergartens.

others but does not reply or does so inappropriately can be coached to reply appropriately.

One study paired friendless children with those who were socially competent. By doing so, the friendless child had an opportunity to observe and then model a more competent child's social skills. Isolated children also benefit from playing with socially competent children. This seems to give them the confidence they need to reach out to, and accept the social overtures of, others.

Teachers have also found that giving a friendless child a large cardboard box, space in a loft, or a card table covered with a blanket as their "own" is helpful. All children are attracted to playing in these small, safe places, and it is up to the child given the box to decide who will be his or her friend for the day. Others find that they can help friendless children get started making friends by giving them a special task. "I've asked Mary Kim to pick two friends to help her take these things to Ms. Smith."

Literature has always helped people understand social relationships (Bhavnagri & Samuels, 1996). Books can be chosen to help children infer and respond to emotions (*Making Friends*; Rogers, 1987), initiate friendships (*Will I Have a Friend?*; Cohen, 1967), or learn to cooperate and share (*Tom and Pen*; Iwamura, 1984).

Participating and Cooperating

With a foundation of acceptance and affectionate friendships, children are ready to assume responsibility, not just for themselves but for the group as well. This is not easy. With their thinking centered around themselves, kindergarten children really are developmentally unable to consider the welfare of others. By living in the democracy of the early childhood classroom, children have a multitude of opportunities to develop the social skills of participating and cooperating so necessary for socialization into their culture.

Rooms are arranged so that children can take responsibility for themselves. Kindergarten children are capable of assuming responsibility for their own dressing, toothbrushing, and washing and for the care of toys and other equipment. With assistance, they are able to participate in setting tables, serving food, cleaning up after play and work, and caring for the plants and animals that belong to the group. After they have adjusted to kindergarten, children are asked to assume greater responsibility for one another. They may directly be asked to care for others: "Ask Sabrina to join you" or "Cassy, you hold Bryan's hand when we walk to the park." As a group, children are taught to consider the feelings of others. One group made a tape of songs and sent it to a child who was hospitalized.

Children participate and cooperate in establishing and keeping rules for their group. To begin the habit of voting, teachers engage children in practice voting. At first each child receives his or her choice. For example, children could vote for the snack they prefer—vanilla or strawberry yogurt—with each child receiving his or her choice. They may vote on the books they want to read, board games to play, or songs to sing. In any case, the votes are recorded, and the option the group liked best is discussed; no child is made to feel as if he or she has lost. After a lot of practice, voting groups can vote on what to name the new guinea pigs, where to go on a field trip, what to do for a special celebration, and even what snack they will eat (Seefeldt & Galper, 2000).

Children learn what they live. Whether or not children have social skills when they enter the classroom does not matter. What matters is the acceptance of the skills they do have and the ability of teachers to use these as the foundation on which to build increasingly complex social skills. Children who live with affection are able to form affectionate friendships. And if they live in a democratic classroom, they will learn the skills of cooperating and participating in a democracy.

PREVENTING PROBLEMS

When children have developed a strong sense of self and have developed the social skills required to live in a democratic group, there are few discipline problems. Other problems are prevented before they begin by (a) an arranged environment; (b) a fantastic curriculum; (c) implementing consistent, dependable routines; (d) clear and consistent expectations for behavior; and (e) skilled guidance when children are in a group.

The Environment

Arranged to set clear limits for children's behaviors yet permitting them to move about freely and safely without disrupting others, the environment is like another teacher. Problems can be avoided by separating active, loud centers, such as the block or construction area, from quieter areas, such as the library area or manipulative area. Traffic patterns are considered. Drawing a floor plan of the room, you can ask yourself the following: Are the pathways clear? What things might block children's seeing pathways? What will happen if the easels are placed near the windows? Will children have access to the sink or drying racks? How will children see the path to the library area? What about children with special needs? Will they be able to manage to navigate throughout the room?

Too much space or not enough causes problems. Large open spaces that seem to shout "Let's run" are divided with boundaries or some sort of physical limit. Too little space and too many children leads to frustration, bumping into one another, and other problems. Limiting the number of children who can work in a given area, the availability of materials, and the activity may be necessary (Kaiser & Rasminsky, 1999; Reinsberg, 1999).

Too much equipment or not enough causes other problems. With too many toys or materials to choose from, children have difficulty making choices. If materials and toys are limited, children will have trouble sharing.

An aesthetically pleasing environment seems to calm children. Soft colors, soft lights, prints of works of art, growing plants, and materials that are clean and ordered beautify kindergartens. Too much noise or blaring music disrupts children, especially those who are tired or overstimulated.

Even when teachers plan and think ahead, they still need to adjust and rearrange the physical environment from time to time. It takes experimentation. Trying the room arranged one way, changing it to accommodate differences or growth in children, and moving equipment and furniture may be necessary before the ideal room arrangement is reached.

A Fantastic Curriculum

When the curriculum is filled with meaning, it engages children's minds and hands, negating any need for overt discipline of any form. Because curriculum goals are realistic, achievable, and individualized, every child experiences success and believes in him- or herself as learners.

The curriculum is balanced as well. It provides periods of intense work, followed by relaxing times for play or less intellectually demanding work. The content is balanced. It introduces children to knowledge and ideas from every discipline area, motivating them to want to learn more and more about the world in which they live.

Routines and Schedules

The daily routines and schedules act as guides to discipline. The consistency of the daily schedule helps children know what behaviors will be expected and what behaviors are acceptable in different situations. Further, routines that children can depend on enable them to develop independence and autonomy. With a clear idea of what they will do, children can carry on independently, without adult assistance.

When teachers plan for smooth transitions between routines, they eliminate the need for discipline. Children are not asked to wait until the milk is delivered to the room, wait for the music teacher, or wait at their seats until everyone is ready. Rather, smooth transitions, engaging children in some activity, are planned.

Clear, Consistent Expectations

Being clear and consistent about expected behaviors is necessary. One teacher found this out when she said to a group of four-year-olds, "Now it's cleanup time." When the children failed to start cleaning up, she repeated, "I said to clean up, now! It's story time." A few stopped what they were doing and ran to sit on the story rug. Once more she demanded that children clean up. Now the children waiting on the story rug got up and started running around the room. Others started to randomly toss the housekeeping materials in cupboards. Chaos began. Giving up, the teacher said, "Okay, come and sit on the story rug."

This teacher stated her expectations clearly: "It's time to clean up." On the other hand, she failed to do the following:

◆ Prepare children for the transition. Young children as adults need some time to adjust to a coming change. She might have rotated through the centers, saying to small groups of children, "In a few minutes it will be story time. You might want to think about stopping and begin cleaning up."
◆ Be specific in her expectations. The term "clean up" for this group of four-year-olds was vague and general. The teacher needed to be specific, informing children of the expectations for cleaning up. She might have said things like "Elaine, Sabrina, and Morgan, put the blocks back on the shelf" and "Timmy, will you help Alice put the puzzles back together and on the shelf?"
◆ Enforce her expectations. Instead of giving up and beginning story time before the children cleaned up, she could have called all the children to the rug and asked them how they planned to clean up. This would have given the children

time to think how they would clean up and, by offering suggestions, put them in control of the situation. It would have given the teacher the opportunity to specify exactly what was meant by "cleaning up" and to help individual children with the task.

Effective teachers are aware of the total group. They are alert to the sounds or stillness that signals that something is wrong. They constantly observe and while doing so can enforce limits. Most often a look, shake of the head, hand signal, or raised eyebrow is enough to remind children of a limit and stop them from hitting or pushing or following through with an unacceptable behavior. Sometimes singing a refrain from a song ("Slow down, you move too fast") or quoting lines from a poem ("It was an awful morning") stops negative behaviors. If this does not work, then teachers, without reprimanding, simply state the desired behavior: "Walk here," "Soft voices inside," or "Tell her what you want, she doesn't know what you want her to do when you hit her." If the request is refused, teachers repeat it. If children persist, they physically stop the behavior. They might hold a child's hand, take the scissors away from the child, or step in between children preparing to fight, stopping unacceptable behavior before it begins.

Giving children choices is an effective strategy for working with four- and five-year-olds who are striving to achieve autonomy and want to accept more responsibility for their actions. A child who is taking puzzle pieces from another is told, "You can put this puzzle together, or you can leave the puzzle table and choose another center to work in, but you cannot hide Saundra's puzzle pieces." Or you might say to a four-year-old who tells you "NOT! NOT! I'm NOT coming to story time," that "You may sit quietly on this chair and this table, or you can join us for story."

By involving children in making choices about their behaviors, you are giving them a measure of control. Because you have determined the two choices, each of which are equally as safe, acceptable, and appropriate, you are still very much in control.

Four- and five-year-olds are fully capable of setting and enforcing limits for their own behavior. After a particularly difficult morning in one kindergarten, the teacher called a meeting of the entire class. She began saying, "This morning was very difficult," and continued recalling the instances of name calling, shouting, throwing blocks, hitting, and fighting that were unacceptable, concluding, "This can't go on—we can't learn like this. We need to have rules for work time. Who has a suggestion?" Like all five-year-olds who love to set rules, the group offered dozens of rules. Finally, one child said, "I know what the rule should be. The big rule is 'be nice'." The others agreed, "Okay," they said, "just be nice."

Working with a Group

Different strategies are useful when working with children in groups. Children, like all humans, are social beings and take pleasure in being a part of a group. They enjoy being together as a group for stories, poetry, music, group meetings, being the audience for creative dramatics, and project work.

Call the group together. Do not wait for the children to "get ready." Rather, begin immediately with a song, a finger play, a game, or even a story. Using a quiet

Teachers help children understand social situations.

low voice makes children curious to find out what is happening, and they come and listen. Remember that children's attention spans are short. Even though they can attend for long periods of time when working individually or in small groups, four- and five-year-olds cannot sit still for long in a group. And their egocentric thought gets in the way of their understanding of what others are saying.

Five-year-olds can be helped to develop the skills of interacting with others in a group. They can be encouraged to keep to the topic, to listen and attend to one another, and to ask each other questions. Before a group meeting or discussion, make the topic clear to the children. They may even want to do some research or think about the ideas they want to share with the group. Just like adults, children will divert from the topic or purpose of the group. Gently bring them back with comments such as "We'd love to hear about your new turtle. Can you wait until we finish our discussion of the astronauts?"

Children will interrupt each other as well. "Sabrina, hold your thought until Ashok is finished, then it's your turn" is all that's needed. Encourage questioning. Ask, "What do you think of that?" Or you could even have pairs of children practice asking each other questions and listening to responses in preparation for a group meeting.

Make certain that all children are included. You can say, "Saundra, you look like you have something you need to tell us." Dividing the class into small groups and assigning each a topic to report back to the total group has been productive. One kindergarten studied dogs and cats. Depending on children's interest, the teacher divided the class into four groups. The first group was to review books about dogs and the second group was assigned books about cats. The third group was asked to find resources about dogs and cats on the computer, and the last group was to design a print, using the computer, of dogs or cats. After a great deal of discussion, arguing, and teacher support, the four groups presented their findings to the total group.

WHEN MORE IS NEEDED

Generally, limits stemming from an arranged environment and respectful, sensitive teachers who guide and teach children to behave appropriately are sufficient. Still, children with developmental delays or attention-deficit disorders, aggressive children, or those who are shy and withdrawn will be in kindergarten. These children, like others who have difficult temperaments, may require more direct guidance.

A number of approaches can be used effectively to help all children gain control. These include (a) behavior management, (b) psychoanalytic approaches, and (c) social cognitive methods of guiding children's behavior.

Behavior Management

In America, Thorndike (1913) hypothesized that any behavior followed by a reward or reinforcer would likely be repeated; any behavior not rewarded or reinforced would recede. Following this basic principle, teachers have rewarded children's good behavior by giving stars to children who completed assigned work, tokens that can be collected and traded for a candy bar to those who sit still and listen, or stickers for cooperating.

Behaviorism is an effective and efficient way of changing children's behaviors. But it is far from as simplistic as giving stars or candies to children who behave in desirable ways. Changing a child's behavior through rewards first means uncovering the antecedents of the behavior, fully understanding the behavior, and then identifying the consequences of the behavior.

Antecedents. Uncovering the antecedents of children's behaviors—that is, what takes place just before disruptive behavior—helps teachers answer the question of why a child is behaving negatively.

To find out what precipitates behaviors, teachers observe the child. They begin by making a chart with spaces for the child's name, date, and time and place and for recording the disruptive behavior and the event that took place just prior to the behavior. Throughout the day they observe the child, recording the information on the chart. Others who work with the child may record their observations as well. Or, if there is a psychologist, guidance counselor, or social worker in the school, you might ask them to conduct the observations. These will give a picture not only of what the child is doing but also of how your interactions with the child affect his or her behavior.

After you have completed a number of observations, review them. You should be able to see a pattern of behavior. One teacher found that Bryan, a child who was constantly in trouble, was being taunted by the others. Bryan seemed to lash out when others jeered at him, teased him by hiding pieces of a puzzle he was working on, or ridiculed him, calling him "double trouble."

Specifying the Behavior.   It is necessary to be able to specify the behavior you want to change. Saying that Bryan is always "in trouble" does not describe his behaviors very well. Trouble could mean a number of things. By observing, the teacher found that she was able to describe Bryan's behaviors that troubled her and the other children. Among these were whining, poking other children to get their attention, and hitting and yelling at others when they did not respond.

Consequences.   Next, teachers observe to find out what the consequences of the behavior are. What is the payoff? Observing Bryan, the teacher noted that after Bryan hit or yelled at others, the children yelled or hit back or ran to the teacher, saying, "Bryan's in trouble again." The teacher, in turn, observed that after an incident she would hold Bryan close to her and talk to him about what had happened, giving him a great deal of attention.

This scenario illustrates how reinforcement works (Duncan, Kemple, & Smith, 2000). Bryan, by yelling and hitting, was reinforcing the taunting behaviors of children. Finding that their taunting had a "payoff," the children continued to taunt him. The teacher, in turn, by focusing on Bryan following an incident, was reinforcing his hitting and yelling.

The teacher's sharing of her observations with the school psychologist did a number of things. First, she found that when she was able to stop others from teasing and taunting Bryan, she negated a lot of his troublesome behaviors. The psychologist pointed out that the children teasing Bryan provided him with attention, and were being rewarded in some way. She also pointed out that when Bryan reverted to yelling or hitting others, the teacher spent time reinforcing Bryan by holding him and talking to him. She suggested that the teacher ignore Bryan, removing whatever payoff he was receiving by hitting, and to focus her attention on the children being hit. The psychologist also showed the teacher how she could use puppets to teach Bryan the skills of handling the taunts of others by ignoring them or through an appropriate response.

Even though most kindergarten teachers reject the idea of giving stars or candy to reward or bribe children, they understand their role in reinforcing and rewarding children's behaviors. One teacher who said that she would never use behavioral methods was observed during circle time. She reprimanded a number of children to sit still and listen and sent several to their tables for a time-out. At the same time she ignored the children who were sitting still and listening. Not once did she praise a child for attending, expand or extend a child's appropriate comments, or compliment a child for participating in the group. In effect, she was using principles of behaviorism. But because she did not understand these principles, she was inadvertently increasing negative behaviors through the reinforcement of attention and eliminating desired behaviors by ignoring them.

Teachers need to understand that punishing children in any way—with reprimands, spankings, even time-outs—serves to reinforce the behavior being punished. Research shows that punishment has a payoff for children. Probably it is the attention they receive, even though it may be a very negative, even painful, reinforcer. Whatever the reason, research has demonstrated that punishment not only is ineffective in stopping negative behaviors but also serves to increase them rather than eliminate them.

The techniques of clearly specifying the behaviors that are troublesome and observing the antecedents and consequences of challenging behaviors help teachers enable children to gain control over their own behaviors by modifying their own behaviors. They also help teachers gain control of themselves. Four- and five-year-olds, who for the most part are delightful to be with, have been known to bite, spit, kick, and hit one another. Teachers have probably built strong emotions about these children. These emotions can get in the way and interfere with attempts to help the child gain control.

Psychoanalytic Approaches

Psychoanalytic theorists claim that all humans are driven to seek perfection. How a person strives to gain perfection is the basis for the way that person deals with problems (Dreikurs, Greenwalk & Pepper, 1982). Children, like all humans, are believed to create their own style of striving for perfection rather than being motivated through external rewards, such as praise, stickers, or other tokens.

One morning, four-year-old Alisha stomped into the room, pushing Shawn in the process. Not stopping to take off her coat, she then ran to the easel and started splashing paint, not only on the easel paper but also on anyone who happened to be near her. This was not the first time Alisha acted out. Yesterday she tossed sand at children passing the sandbox, and the day before she clobbered Andrea with a book she had been reading.

Children may do so by doing the following:

◆ Getting attention
◆ Achieving power
◆ Getting revenge
◆ Displaying inadequacy

The role of the adult is to try to identify children's goals. This begins, as with the theories of the behaviorist, by observing the child to determine the goal of the disruptive behavior and then to react in a way so that the child will cease that disturbing behavior. Instead of trying to change the child's behavior, the theory suggests that adults change their way of reacting to the behavior.

To stop Alisha's negative behaviors, teachers would first try to understand Alisha's goals in striving to seek perfection. After attending to the children who had been splashed with paint, the teachers took Alisha's coat off, and the aide sat with her, trying to soothe and calm her. During nap time, the aide and teacher met with the school counselor and together tried to solve the problem of Alisha's behavior.

First, they advanced hypotheses as to why Alisha was behaving so negatively. They knew that Alisha's mother had left her father and that she and her mother were living with her maternal grandparents. Was Alisha's goal that of trying to get attention? Or was she seeking revenge or power? Maybe she was feeling left out, angry, and powerless.

If attention and power were Alisha's goals, it would be important for the adults to understand this and not fight back. If they had tried to punish Alisha by scolding, pushing, or splashing paint on her as she had done to the others, she would have achieved her goals of getting attention and power. Achieving her goals, her negative behaviors would accelerate.

What were Alisha's teachers to do? Surely they could not continue to let Alisha harm others. But because they did not want to give Alisha any attention or power, they decided to change her behavior by letting her experience the logical consequences of her behaviors.

In the case of splashing paint on others, the logical consequences would have been for Alisha to assume the responsibility for washing and cleaning those she had splashed. Or, if Alisha could not play in the sand without throwing it in others' faces, she would be denied the opportunity to play in the sandbox.

When logical consequences are given, teachers do the following:

◆ Express the reality of the social order, the rules of behavior, or procedures that are to be followed in the kindergarten. "You may not hurt others" or "You can only use paint to paint with."
◆ Relate the misbehavior. The idea is to make certain that the child, Alisha in this case, clearly understands the consequences of her behavior. Punishment is not necessary because the consequences of behavior are so clear. A child who dawdles misses out on the next activity. A child who spills milk cleans it up. A child who leaves a mess at the easel cleans it up. A child who hits others plays alone for a period of time.
◆ Be nonjudgmental. Misbehavior is just that. It is not a sin. Rather than preaching, scolding, or threatening, the teacher neutrally removes a child who is hitting from the group while attending to the others. Following the incident, measures are taken to prevent future hitting. The social order—"No one is permitted to hit"—is made clear. The consequences of hitting—"No one will want to play with you because you hit"—are made equally as clear.
◆ Focus on what *will* happen, not on what *did.* Punishment is concerned with the past; logical consequences are concerned with the present and future. "Now what will you do?" or "Now how can we help you from splashing paint on others?" The purpose of logical consequences is to help children become more effective—to learn effective and appropriate ways of getting attention and feeling powerful and in control.
◆ Eliminate anger, either open or concealed. It is hard not to express anger when a child splashes paint on others, but it is necessary not to. Catching her breath, the teacher might have said to Alisha, "You are angry. Let's begin by helping wash the paint off of Alberto and Kim. You get the paper towels, and I'll get a bowl of warm, soapy water." Throughout the day and coming weeks, the teacher would help Alisha find a way of appropriately expressing anger and controlling her behavior.

Social Cognitive Approaches

Those endorsing the social cognitive point of view of guidance claim that the children's ability to relate effectively in a group and behave in accordance with the rules of society are based on their cognitive understanding of the situation.

A four-year-old who scribbles on another's paper is not punished because her behavior reflects her cognitive maturity. Rather, the teacher attempts to teach the child, saying, "Color on your paper, here. Do not color on other children's papers." By evaluating children's social cognition, teachers have a better understanding of what they can and cannot expect children to do at any given age.

Another principle of social cognition is the idea that the individual is in charge of his or her own learning. Although growth stems from the interaction of maturation and experience, the individual must construct social knowledge. Stimulating children to think about social relations and offering them suggestions to enable them to construct knowledge of social skills are viewed as important.

With this framework, teachers guide children to talk about social situations or problems and come up with their own solutions. Instead of offering solutions to a child who grabs a toy from another by saying, "Use your words instead of grabbing so she'll know what you want," or offering alternative solutions by saying, "Give her a turn now," the idea is to develop children's skills of thinking of solutions for themselves. There is no recrimination. Shaming or blaming children for behavior is not acceptable in a democratic classroom.

Spivack and Shure (1978) developed the Cognitive Approach to Interpersonal Problem Solving. Inherent in this approach is the assumption that the ability to think clearly paves the way for emotional relief and healthy social adjustment. When children have problems relating socially, teachers are supposed to ask them what happened, how they felt in the situation, what they did, and what other ways they could act in similar situations. In addition to the scripted learning experiences that constitute their program, Spivack and Shure (1978) continue to maintain that the dialogues teachers have with children informally and in connection with ongoing events are even more important in developing children's social skills.

IN SUMMARY

Children come to kindergarten with "batteries attached." They are eager to learn and full of exuberance and vitality. It takes a special kind of person to guide these vivacious children. Teachers need to understand and accept the children's level of social maturity and their childish behaviors. And they need the skills necessary to guide children's behaviors in ways that permit them to maintain a healthy sense of self, learn social skills, and use specific guidance techniques when the need arises.

Children who feel good about themselves are usually able to control their behaviors and relate effectively with others. They need teachers who are supportive, positive, acknowledge children's feelings, model appropriate behaviors, and challenge stereotyping.

The level of social skills children bring with them to the kindergarten is accepted. These are extended and expanded by helping children make and keep friends and by teaching the skills involved in participating and cooperating in a group.

If you observe in a kindergarten, you will probably have a difficult time noting the teacher's discipline techniques because most discipline problems are prevented before they start. Teachers arrange the environment; establish consistent, clear routines; plan a super curriculum; set and enforce clear limits to children's behavior; and develop strategies for working with children in groups.

Problems do arise. Children who are angry, aggressive, withdrawn, or shy will come to kindergarten. Using the techniques of behaviorism, psychoanalytic approaches to guidance, and social cognitive theories, teachers are able to work with these special cases in ways that enable all children to feel successful in kindergarten.

EXTEND YOUR IDEAS

1. Recall a time when you were disciplined as a child. What had you done, and how did the adults react? Did they act in ways that enabled you to learn? Or did you feel shamed and ridiculed? Relate your feelings to the ways you will guide kindergarten children's behaviors as a teacher. Discuss your feelings with your classmates.

2. Children's books can help children sort through their feelings, relationships with others, and behaviors. Go to the Web or library and identify children's books that could be used as tools for teaching children how to enter a group, solve social problems, or relate effectively with special needs children.

3. Observe in a four- and five-year-old kindergarten class. Note the ways that teachers guide children's behaviors. How do they state limits? How do they arrange the environment to prevent problems? What do they do and say when problems arise?

4. Ask a principal or teacher for the school or district's discipline policies. Review these in a group. Which can be appropriately applied to young children and which cannot? Why?

RESOURCES

Meeting the Challenge: Effective Strategies for Challenging Behaviours in Early Childhood Environments, by Barbara Kaiser and Judy Sklar Rasminsky (Ottawa: Ontario: Canadian Child Care Federation, 1999).

Constructive Guidance and Discipline: Preschool and Primary Education, by Marjorie Vannoy Fields and Cindy Boesser (Upper Saddle River, NJ: Prentice Hall, 1997).

REFERENCES

Beatty, J. J. (1999). Observing development of the young child. Upper Saddle River, NJ: Merrill/Prentice Hall.

Bhavnagri, N. P., & Samuels, B. G. (1996). Making and keeping friends: A thematic unit to promote understanding of peer relationships in young children. *Childhood Education, 72,* 219–225.

Bost, K. K. (1999). Social competence, social support, and attachment: Demarcation of construct domains, measurement, and paths of influence for preschool children attending Head Start. *Child Development, 69,* 192–218.

Burk, D. I. (1996). Understanding friendship and social interaction. *Childhood Education, 72,* 282–285.

California Tomorrow. (1999). *A place to begin.* Oakland, CA: Author.

Cohen, M. (1967). *Will I have a friend?* New York: Macmillan.

Crowley, A. L. (1999). Training family child care providers to work with children who have special needs. *Young Children, 54,* 58–62.

Derman-Sparks, L., & the A.B.C. Task Force. (1989). *Anti-bias curriculum: Tools for empowering young children.* Washington, DC: National Association for the Education of Young Children.

Dreikurs, R., Greenwalk, B., & Pepper, F. (1982). *Maintaining sanity in the classroom.* New York: Harper & Row.

Duncan, T. K., Kemple, K. M., & Smith, T. M. (2000). Reinforcement in developmentally appropriate early childhood classrooms. *Childhood Education, 76,* 194–203.

Eaton, M. (1997). Positive discipline fostering the self-esteem of young children. *Young Children, 52*(6), 43–47.

Froesch, M., & Sprung, B. (1999). On purpose: Addressing teasing and bullying in early childhood. *Young Children, 54*(2), 70–73.

Gartrell, D. (1997). Beyond discipline to guidance. *Young Children, 52*(6), 34–43.

Iwamura, K. (1984). *Tom and Pen.* New York: Bradbury Press.

Kaiser, B., & Rasminsky, J. K. (1999). *Meeting the challenge: Effective strategies for channeling behaviors in early childhood environments.* Ottawa: Canadian Child Care Federation.

Kemple, K. M. (1991). Preschool children's peer acceptance and social interaction. *Young Children, 45*(3), 70–75.

Ladd, G. (1996). Friendship quality as a predictor of young children's early school adjustment. *Child Development, 67,* 1103–1119.

Lowenthal, B. (1996). Teaching social skills to preschoolers with special needs. *Childhood Education, 72,* 137–141.

Marion, M. (1995). *Guidance of young children* (4th ed.). Englewood Cliffs, NJ: Prentice Hall.

Milne, A. A. (1961). *Now we are six.* New York: Dutton.

National Institute of Child Health and Human Development (2000). *The longitudinal cohort study of environmental effects on child development.* Washington, DC: Author.

Ramsey, P. G. (1991). *Making friends in school.* New York: Teachers College Press.

Reinsberg, J. (1999). Understanding young children's behavior. *Young Children, 54*(4), 54–58.

Rogers, C. (1951). *Client-centered therapy.* Boston: Houghton Mifflin.

Rogers, F. (1987). *Making friends.* New York: Putnam.

Seefeldt, C., & Barbour, N. (1998). *Early childhood education: An introduction* (4th ed.). Upper Saddle River, NJ: Merrill/Prentice Hall.

Seefeldt, C., & Galper, A. (1999). *Active experiences for active children: Social studies.* Upper Saddle River, NJ: Merrill/Prentice Hall.

Seefeldt, C., & Galper, A. (2000). *Active experiences for active children.* Upper Saddle River, NJ: Merrill/Prentice Hall.

Spivack, G., & Shure, M. B. (1978). *Social adjustment of young children.* San Francisco: Jossey-Bass.

Stromshak, E. A. (1999). The relation between behavior problems and peer preference in different classroom contexts. *Child Development, 70,* 169–182.

Thorndike, E. L. (1913). *Educational psychology: The psychology of learning.* New York: Teachers College Press.

Vygotsky, L. (1978). *Thought and language* (Rev. ed.). Cambridge: MIT Press.

PART III   The Integrated Curriculum

CHAPTER 7 Planning an Integrated Curriculum

When you enter Ms. Hope's classroom, you are immediately enthralled with children's drawings and paintings of cats and dogs on the walls. After admiring the artwork, you note that a group of children are building a larger-than-life-sized "dog" from empty boxes and found objects. They stop working to discuss what to use to make the dog's "eyes" and where they should be placed.

In the block area, fences are being constructed to corral plastic and wooden figurines of dogs and cats. Printing a sign, one child explains, "This one says CATS, this one DOGS."

In another area of the room the teacher is working with a group constructing a graph categorizing different kinds of dogs. Another group of children are "reading" to one another from picture books about animals in the library area. A mural decorating the library corner illustrates children's perceptions of Eugene Field's The Duel *(1927).*

It is obvious to anyone that the children in Ms. Hope's classroom are learning about animals, specifically cats and dogs. It is equally as obvious that the theme of dogs and cats is being integrated into the entire curriculum. You have noted Ms. Hope talk about and question mathematical concepts as she works with individuals and groups. You have listened to children reading about cats or dogs to one another, watched as they wrote signs, and marveled over their paintings of dogs and cats.

Ms. Hope's kindergarten illustrates the beauty and power of a unified curriculum, one that is organized around a theme and planned to involve children in project learning. This chapter describes how kindergarten teachers are able to implement meaningful, integrated learning experiences for four- and five-year-olds. The chapter defines an integrated, thematic, or project approach to teaching and learning; describes how to create an integrated curriculum; and illustrates how to implement the project, unit, or theme.

DEFINING AN INTEGRATED CURRICULUM

n an integrated curriculum many of the activities children engage in are related to a specific theme or topic (Jones & Nimmo, 1994). In Ms. Hope's classroom, the art, math, music, and movement activities the children engaged in, as well as the books they read, the stories they wrote, and the projects initiated and implemented, were centered around cats and dogs.

A number of terms—"project," "thematic," and "unit learning"—are used interchangeably to describe an integrated curriculum.

Units, Projects, and Thematic Learning Share Similarities

Thematic learning, projects, and units are related because each is solidly grounded in similar theories of learning. Dewey's theory that meaningful curriculum is not just the memorization of isolated facts but also a unified whole first led to implementing curricula planned around units (Dewey, 1900). Over the years, Piagetian and Vygotskian ideas of children constructing knowledge through their social, physical, and mental activity gave support to unit, thematic, and project learning (Seefeldt, 2000; Trepanier-Street, 2000).

Because each approach is grounded in similar theories of learning, each shares the belief that learning occurs through the process of constructing knowledge through physical, social, and mental activity. Projects, thematic learning, and units each do the following:

◆ Provide an integrated approach to the curriculum. Each of the approaches presents an integrated approach to the curriculum. When learning experiences in the kindergarten are integrated, revolving around a given theme, children are better able to make connections between facts and ideas, develop an understanding of abstract concepts, and develop higher-order thinking strategies (Bredekamp & Rosegrant, 1995).

◆ Provide relevance to the curriculum. Content that is a part of an organized whole and grounded in children's everyday lives makes sense to children. For example, when children count how many teachers and children in the school have a cat or dog, numbers, abstract symbols, and numerals have meaning. Counting by rote or counting circles on a duplicated sheet does not.

◆ Give children the opportunity to develop a sense of community, working cooperatively with one another. Working together to build a dog of boxes, paint a mural, or build corals with blocks, children have an opportunity to relate to and cooperate and share with one another. They have something in common to talk and share ideas about and a goal that can only be achieved by working together. Vygotsky saw this type of social activity as the generator of thought. He believed that thought was constructed through social interaction and the exchange of dialogue.

◆ Create opportunities for flexibility in teaching and learning, responding to the interests and experience of the children. Because thematic learning, units, and projects are flexible, they can be planned for varying lengths of time. A unit, theme, or project can last a few days or weeks, continuing until children have satisfied their curiosity and interest in the topic. Likewise, children may lose interest in a project or unit after a day or two. Other projects or themes can last for weeks as the children's interest evolves and takes them in different directions. One teacher continued a unit on trees throughout the fall, expanding it to include a study of wood, where wood came from, and how to purchase wood and work with it. Eventually, children began to study paper and even made their own out of wood pulp.

◆ Respond to the diverse needs of students. Children can pace themselves, staying longer with activities that satisfy their interests, or selecting tasks that permit them to practice skills or gain mastery over new skills.

Units, Projects, and Thematic Learning Are Subtly Different

Even though units, projects, and thematic learning are based on similar theories and the terms are often used interchangeably, there are subtle differences between the approaches.

The Project Approach.   The project approach is described by Chard (1998) as an "in-depth study of a topic or a theme" (p. 2). The key feature of the project approach is the focus on answering questions about a topic posed by either the children, the teacher, or the teacher working with the children (Gillespie, 2000; Helm & Katz, 2000; Katz, 1994).

Thematic Learning.   Thematic learning involves planning around a specific theme. Children can initiate the theme, or teachers can select a theme. Some teachers select a theme on the basis of children's interests or questions. Others select themes on the basis of a curriculum goal, parental concerns, current events or issues, or special community resources, such as a traveling exhibit of a space module, the birth of a new zoo baby, or something as common as a rainy day. When teachers plan around a theme, children, as in the project approach, can initiate questions about a topic that they are interested in and explore the question.

Other characteristics of the project approach are a part of thematic learning as well. Both provide opportunities for children to work independently, allowing the curriculum to be tailored to the individual needs of the children. As in the project approach, teachers begin by observing and interviewing children to find out what topics they are interested in studying, how much they know about a topic, and what misconceptions they have.

Units.   Units are also organized around a theme and include characteristics of project and thematic work. They differ subtly from project and thematic learning because a unit is planned and developed in advance by the teacher and is designed to last for a specific amount of time, perhaps several days, a week, or even a month. With units, however, there is still room for children to initiate, and teachers follow children's cues as the unit develops. One teacher, noting children's interests in worms on the sidewalk after a rain, initiated a unit on worms that she had planned and implemented the previous year. The children were enthusiastic about making a worm farm for the room, but after the farm was completed, they lost interest in worms. The teacher abandoned her extensive plans for children to study worms and instead followed the children's interests in parsley caterpillars devouring the parsley the children had planted to use in a salad.

CREATING AN INTEGRATED CURRICULUM

Each school system will specify the form of both long-term lesson plans, whether these are units, themes, or projects, and short-term lesson plans. Regardless of the forms a system uses, planning, both for short-term lesson planning and for long-term planning for units, themes, or projects, involves the following:

1. selecting a topic or theme
2. specifying goals and objectives
3. translating theoretical goals and objectives into practice
4. identifying developmentally appropriate activities to teach the content
5. how the lesson, unit, or theme will be evaluated

Selecting a Theme or Topic

Themes or topics for lessons can be selected to support children's current interests and knowledge and also broaden their knowledge in new areas. The actual selection of a theme or topic can stem from a variety of sources. Some topics are selected because of children's interests, others are chosen because they are related to events taking place in the children's lives, and still others are considered a part of the school's unified curriculum.

Before deciding on a theme, teachers do the following:

◆ Examine the system's goals and objectives. Before deciding on the topic of animals, Ms. Hope examined the school system's goals and benchmarks for kindergarten in her district. Reading these over, she found that the theme of animals could be used to fulfill any number of general goals. Animals could be observed, counted, graphed, and categorized. Then, too, because children could study many animals firsthand, the theme could lead to children being able to express themselves through language and the arts. Concepts, skills, and attitudes from the social studies, such as responsibility, careers, and community, could be fostered as well.

◆ Observe the children. Ms. Hope's class was particularly interested in the birth of a litter of kittens to one classmate's Siamese cat. Their interest in animals, specifically cats, seemed at an all-time high. Teachers also observe the develop-

ing skills of children and the information, content, and knowledge they already possess. Observing clarifies teachers' roles in scaffolding activities so that they are within the intellectual reach of children, yet challenging. By observing, teachers note how and when to create opportunities for children to learn new concepts and skills and how to enhance learning while maintaining children's experiences (Almy, 2000).

◆ Observe the environment. Teachers determine what is going on in the school, community, and physical environment. Children's everyday experiences and their questions and interest in their environment serve as a springboard for topics. If the newly planted grass is coming up in front of the school, growing may become the topic of a theme. A balloon race in one community led to a project about flight in one kindergarten. The opening of a new supermarket in another community led to a unit on how food gets from farms to stores.

◆ Make judgments about the age appropriateness of the topic. As Ms. Hope planned, she asked herself: Is this something children need to know now? How will they use the information now? Or is this something they'll be able to learn more efficiently when

Themes and projects can stem from community resources.

CRITERIA FOR SELECTING TOPICS FOR THEMATIC, PROJECT, OR UNIT LEARNING

1. Examine school system goals and objectives
2. Observe children to determine their interests, needs, and current knowledge/ understanding of the topic
3. Locate resources in the classroom, school, and community environments
4. Determine whether the topic is age-appropriate
5. Examine the cultural relevance of the topic

they are older. Is this concept, fact, or idea something children can actually experience? Can children feel, touch, observe, smell, take apart, and put something together again in order to experience the concept? For example, one classroom became interested in watching ice cubes melt (Bredekamp & Rosegrant, 1995). The children placed ice cubes in different areas of the play yard and room and waited to see which cubes would melt the fastest. Sensing the children's excitement, the teacher borrowed a model of a water molecule to bring to class the next day. She proceeded to explain how water was made of tiny molecules and how these changed because of the temperature of the water. As she proceeded to talk about molecules and the effects of heat, children began to squirm. Two children started a game with a piece of candy one had in her pocket, and two others began a game of pinching each other and the other children. While four- and five-year-olds are interested in physical phenomena and are ready to build experiential knowledge of the effects of heat on water, their cognitive maturity negates their being able to understand or be interested in the abstraction of molecules and their transformations.

♦ Determine the cultural relevance of the topic by asking: How culturally relevant is the topic? In the culture of the children, do rain clouds, animals, specific holidays and celebrations, or time have special meanings? A case in point is that for some Native Americans handling animal bones is considered inappropriate or the fact that in some cultures dogs and other animals are not considered pets.

Some topics or themes that kindergarten teachers have found fulfill children's interest and the goals of the system and are age and culturally appropriate are as follows:

Typical	Possible
Special Me	Wood/Woodworking
My Family	Fish
Community Helpers	Rocks
Transportation	The Herb Shop
My Senses	Clothing

Defining Objectives

Once the topic is selected, goals and objectives are determined. Ask yourself: What is it that children need to learn, experience, and do after the project, theme, or unit is finished? Jot down your answers to these questions.

Then ask the children what they know and want to learn about the topic. This gives children experience in setting goals and objectives and teaches them how to plan. It also strengthens children's feelings of autonomy, giving them ownership of the curriculum. When they are asked what they want to learn, they feel in control and motivated to learn.

Ms. Hope did this after she decided that the theme of animals would meet her criteria. During one group meeting, she asked children to talk about animals they knew. Children told about their pets, pretend animals, and zoo, circus, and wild animals. Focusing the discussion a bit more, she then asked which animals they would like to learn more about. The children named dozens of animals they wanted to learn about as Ms. Hope recorded their responses. That evening she categorized the animals into domestic, farm, and wild animals. The next morning she presented children with the list, asking them to vote on which type of animals they wanted to learn about. The children voted to study domestic animals. She narrowed their choice once again by asking them to vote for the specific domestic animals would like to learn about. Dogs and cats, which both received the same number of votes, were chosen.

Ms. Hope then asked the children to brainstorm about how they would go about their study of cats and dogs. Together the children said that they could learn by reading books, talking with people who knew a lot about dogs and cats, observing cats and dogs, and taking care of them.

She continued to involve the children in planning. She had them dictate a letter to a veterinarian, inviting her to come and tell them about cats and dogs. They called the local library and scheduled a visit so they could read about cats and dogs. "We're coming," the girl who was given the responsibility of calling the library told the librarian.

Organizing Objectives

Once the broad, overriding objectives have been determined, whether by the teacher or in collaboration with the children, teachers find that organizing the objectives into thematic and skill objectives is helpful.

Thematic Objectives.   Some objectives stem from the theme itself. Theme objectives direct the content from the unit, project, or thematic learning; how the information will be organized and presented; and how the experiences will be evaluated.

It is more important to select a limited number of well-thought-out objectives that can guide the unit or project than to list numerous, general objectives. Objectives should focus on the information, key concepts, or content you want the children to learn.

The process of webbing is helpful in planning theme objectives. Using this approach, a theme is selected, and then the teacher, with or without the children, brainstorms about what the desired learning outcomes are for the theme. Figure 7–1 is an example of a web for the topic "Cats and Dogs." Teachers obviously do not have to do everything they put in the web. It is only a planning step in identifying possible thematic objectives appropriate for children to learn.

FIGURE 7–1   **Learning Web: Cats and Dogs**

Art

Drawing/painting/constructing
   cats and dogs

Music/Movement

Singing songs,
   moving to music like cats and dogs

Language Art

Listening to sounds of cats and dogs
Reading about cats and dogs
Writing about cats and dogs
Discriminate listening to experts

Social Studies

Learning responsibility
Careers with animals
Community regulations

Life Sciences

How to sustain life of cats and dogs
Likeness and differences of breeds
   of cats and dogs
Likeness and differences in care
   of cats and dogs
Similarities in cats and dogs

Mathematics

Measuring and weighing cats and dogs
Sequencing breeds by size
Comparing sizes and shapes of cats and
   dogs

Skill Objectives.   Skill objectives are useful in guiding the selection of skills. Skills are goal-directed activities that require a certain amount of competency to perform (Wasik, 2001). In the field of early childhood, there is considerable variability in defining necessary skills for four- and five-year-olds. Often individual schools or systems define what skills four- and five-year-olds are to gain in kindergarten. These are not competencies that children are expected to master but rather behaviors that they should have opportunities to practice.

Some examples of skills are as follows:

1. Classifying: Sorting items into categories
2. Describing: Listing attributes of an item or giving an account of an event
3. Following directions: Performing an action in response to a command
4. Listening: Hearing with thoughtful attention
5. Matching: Grouping items on the basis of identical attributes
6. Predicting: Telling about a future on the basis of previous information
7. Sequencing: Determining and demonstrating the proper order of a series of
   items

Other skills are more specific, such as the following:

a. Letter recognition
b. Name recognition
c. Number recognition
d. Counting

Thematic and project planning includes opportunities to learn specific skills.

The challenge of teaching young children is to teach both the theme objectives and the skill and attitude objectives in an integrated way. The theme objectives help define the content, and the skill objectives are practiced in the theme-related activities. If the theme objective is that dogs and cats come in different shapes and sizes, the activities need to allow children to learn that dogs and cats are different sizes and shapes, and also to practice other skill objectives, such as listening, matching, sequencing, and counting. The goal is to provide activities that allow for the integration of theme and skill objectives. See Figure 7–2 for a chart of thematic and skill objectives.

Writing Objectives

Once the broad ideas of what you want children to learn and what they want to know have been determined, you need to very specifically define the exact knowledge, content, skill, and attitude objections you will want children to learn. To be effective, objectives must be stated in ways that are measurable.

For example, it is not very useful to state, "Children are to know, understand, increase knowledge of, appreciate, enjoy, or gain knowledge of content, a skill, or an attitude." These terms are broad and open to interpretation. The goal "children will know about animals" does not give enough information about what you will present to children or how you will know what they have learned. When you use

FIGURE 7–2 An Integrated Curriculum

Theme Objectives

Learning about Cats and Dogs

◆ Develop knowledge of the wide variety of cats and dogs
◆ Learn how to care for and be responsible for cats and dogs
◆ Be able to describe differences and similarities between cats and dogs, including how to care for them

Skill Objectives

School Performance Standards

1. READING
   a. Develop vocabulary
   b. Learn the names of three different cats and three different dogs
   c. Identify beginning letters of names of cats and dogs that are the same as those beginning children's names.

Sample Activities

◆ Read factual, fictional, and fantasy books about cats and dogs; consult reference books and Web sites.
◆ Make a chart from photos and pictures of familiar cats and dogs; label these with the name of the breed. Identify the beginning letter of names of breed.
◆ Give children pictures of cats and dogs cut from magazines or other print material. Children cut around the picture and mount on a 6- by 9-inch card. Label the picture with the name of breed and beginning initial. Children play card games they make up, matching breeds or matching names beginning with the same initial letter.
◆ Begin a class cat and dog book. You might make several books with children contributing pictures and stories. One book could be titled *Cats and Dogs We Know* and include those that children are acquainted with. Another could be *Cats and Dogs We've Never Seen* and could be devoted to fantasy ideas of cats and dogs.

2. WRITING
   a. Express ideas, feelings, and experiences about cats and dogs through drawings, paintings, and writing using invented spelling.
   b. Engage in group writing/dictation activities to communicate to others or for specific purposes.

Sample Activities

◆ Children have opportunities to draw, paint, or write each day. They may chose to use the computer, write at the writing center, or take writing materials to another area of the room.
◆ Begin a journal about the life of a pet cat or dog.
◆ As a group, write an invitation to a veterinarian to visit the class; a list of questions to ask the vet, and a thank-you note after the visit.
◆ Make lists of how to take care of a cat or dog.
◆ Create a fantasy story about the life of a cat or dog.

3. MATHEMATICS
   a. Create, read, and use graphs
   b. Seriate animals by size
   c. Use one-to-one correspondence in counting cats and dogs

Sample Activities

◆ Take a vote and count the number of children who prefer cats the best and those who like dogs better than cats. Record the vote.
◆ Create a pictorial graph of pets that children have in their homes. Ask children to read the graph, identifying the most frequent animal, the next frequent, and the least frequent.

◆ Create a set of photographs picturing a variety of breeds of cats and dogs. Have children seriate by size.

4. LIFE SCIENCES
   a. Observe physical similarities and differences in the anatomy of cats and dogs
   b. Learn to care for cats and dogs

Sample Activities

◆ Give children plastic hand mirrors or have them look in a class mirror to examine their eyes. Ask them what size, shape, and color their eyes are and determine the color of their pupils. Note and record children's eye and pupil colors, shape, and size of their eyes on a graph.
◆ Examine the eyes of cats and dogs. Note where cat's and dog's eyes are placed. What shape, color, and size are their eyes? Write and illustrate a story of how cat, dog, and human eyes differ and are the same.

5. MUSIC/MOVEMENT
   a. Observe how cats and dogs move
   b. Develop control over large muscles

Sample Activities

◆ Observe cats and dogs moving in their homes or neighborhoods or bring a cat or dog to school and observe how they move.
◆ Go to the zoo and watch the big cats move. Compare their movements with those of smaller cats.
◆ Show a video clip from the musical *Cats* and observe how people move like cats.
◆ Read "Stretching," a poem by Mary Britton Miller about a cat stretching. It begins "The black cat yawns, opens her jaws, stretches her legs."
◆ Have children pretend that they are large or small cats and move to music as a cat would. Strengthen children's imaginations by asking them to describe the type, color, size, and breed of cat they are pretending to be.

6. VISUAL ARTS
   a. To express ideas through symbols
   b. Use joining tools and materials to create a sculpture of a cat or dog

Sample Activities

◆ Sketch while observing a cat or dog at home, school, or the zoo.
◆ Create two or three teams of children. Each team is given the same instructions of using a collection of junk materials (empty boxes, bits of metal, plastic containers, and so on) and joining tools (staples, clips, nuts/bolts, and tape) and told to design and then construct a model of either a cat or a dog.

7. SOCIAL SCIENCES
   a. Develop knowledge of careers with animals
   b. Understand that veterinarians, like others in the service profession, are paid for their services

Sample Activities

◆ Read factual books about the career of veterinarian science.
◆ Visit a veterinarian's clinic and observe how she cares for cats and dogs. Also, ask her office staff to show the children how people pay for her services.
◆ Ask the veterinarian to discuss the common physical and other needs of cats, dogs, and humans.
◆ Set up a veterinarian office as a dramatic play center where children can have their toy animals cared for and treated and can pay for the services.

more specific terms like the following, you have a guide for planning and directions for evaluating children's learning:

- ◆ Define
- ◆ Describe
- ◆ Name
- ◆ Identify
- ◆ Observe
- ◆ Construct

- ◆ Solve
- ◆ Compare
- ◆ Differentiate
- ◆ Contrast
- ◆ Categorize
- ◆ Identify

As you plan and teach, you can focus on experiences that involve children in naming, categorizing, and comparing things and ideas. Then, to assess their learning, you observe or ask them to name, categorize, or compare things or ideas.

Identifying Developmentally Appropriate Content

Keeping in mind the thematic, content, and skill objectives, teachers begin developing their plan. The content consists of the information or knowledge that is to be presented. While the objectives guide *what* the children will learn, the content guides *how* the children learn the information.

Activities are selected on the basis of desired concepts to be taught, the goals and objectives to be met, the season of the year, and the needs and interests of the children. The activities, projects, field trips, and materials are selected on the basis of the theme and the concepts presented.

The content needs to do the following:

1. Be challenging enough to keep the children interested and to be able to scaffold learning
2. Be able to be implemented in the classroom
3. Be chosen to meet a learning, skill, or attitude objective
4. Stem from a concept key to the specific content discipline or the subject matter being studied

Learning Experiences.   Learning experiences are the core of the theme, unit, or project. The learning experiences are the vehicle through which the content is expressed. These experiences are planned to foster the goals and objectives of the unit. The following boxes illustrate how to plan learning experiences.

The following lists and describes key learning experiences for four- and five-year-olds.

PLANNING LEARNING EXPERIENCES

1. State overriding goals of the experience
2. State instructional objectives
3. List the materials you need
4. Describe the activities the children will do and the things you will do
5. List activities to extend and expand the learning activities
6. State how the learning experience will be evaluated

1. Language arts: Language is key to cognitive and literacy development (Snow, Burns, & Griffin, 1999). Creating opportunities for children to talk, engage in dialogue, and receive thoughtful feedback about what they say develops language and vocabulary skills. Other examples of activities in language arts

SAMPLE LESSON PLAN
MOVEMENT (FIVE-YEAR-OLDS)

Goals

To expand children's language usage to include movement terms

To develop an awareness of designated direction

Instructional Objectives

Children will demonstrate an ability to respond to instructions for moving forward, away from, and toward.

Children will demonstrate an ability to move objects backward, forward, away from, and toward.

Children will demonstrate an ability to move objects backward, forward, away from, and toward in response to instructions.

Children will use the correct terms to describe their movement (backward, forward, away from, and toward).

Materials

Two stuffed "astronaut" dolls

Markers and paper

Procedures

1. Ask children to find a space in the room that is all their own. Ask them to stand in a space and move their arms out around them. If they cannot touch anyone or anything else, they have found their own space.
2. Explore movement by posing problems for children to solve. Have children jump up and down, then jump up and land without making

a sound. Or ask them to hop on one foot as high as they can and land without making a sound.

3. Then ask children to jump forward, then backward, and then to hop forward and backward. Ask children to find other ways to use their feet and legs to move forward and backward. They might walk, march, slide, and glide.
4. Ask children to find a partner. If they have trouble doing so, assign partners. With the partner, ask children to move backward, forward, away from, and toward each other.
5. Have children in pairs take turns being the teacher and giving directions.
6. Have children practice jumping backward and forward once again. This time, ask them to focus on how their legs and feet move. What do they do with their arms when they jump? Their head and chest? Then children can sketch themselves jumping. Or ask a child to be a model, jumping backward and forward as the other children sketch her.

Evaluation

Play "Mother May I?" In groups of three or four, have children stand in a line. Instruct children to move so many steps forward, backward, away from, and toward you, but only after they say, "Mother May I?" Have children take turns being the leader. As they do so, note which children move appropriately.

Ask individual children to move the astronaut dolls forward, backward, toward, and away from them.

---

include storybook reading; Big Book activities; recording group ideas in writing; journal writing; storytelling; story development; oral discussion of the theme, units, or projects; and reporting to the group (Wasik, 2001).

2. Mathematics: Any topic or theme presents opportunities to develop math concepts. Children might match, count, measure, weigh, or classify similar objects as part of a unit. A unit on seeds may provide opportunities to count out seeds and make comparisons about the physical features of different seeds. Children can count the number of days it took the plant to sprout, chart the growth of the plant, and measure the amount of water necessary to keep the plant moist. Cooking activities also provide many opportunities to explore math concepts.

Story book reading is a part of project or thematic learning.

3. Social studies: Planning experiences for the children to know the environment around them is an important part of unit planning. Field trips through the school, neighborhood, or community are an important part of learning for four- and five-year-olds. Planning for visitors to come to the class and provide background information or additional firsthand experiences adds to children's learning.

4. Physical and life sciences: Content from both the physical and the life sciences provide additional learning experiences. Firsthand experiences, such as planting a seed and watching it grow, are more efficient and effective than having someone tell about seeds growing or reading about seeds.

5. Art: Art can take many forms. Painting, drawing, modeling with clay, papier-mâché, and many other arts-and-crafts activities can be integrated into the unit. Art is a wonderful way to provide children creative opportunities to express themselves. It is important to remember that the children's expression is more important than having a perfect end product. Have the children take primary responsibility for doing the projects.

6. Music: Music is an important way for children to express themselves. Making up songs, learning favorite tunes, and playing musical instruments contributes to children developing their good listening skills and an enjoyment of music (Hildebrandt, 1998).

7. Movement: Young children need to have opportunities to move around and develop large-muscle coordination through movement activities. Often, movement activities are combined with music activities. Children sing and dance or jump around while they play musical instruments.

8. Food/snack: Eating or snack time is an important part of the children's day, and many things can be taught during this activity. Math concepts can be reinforced as children count out napkins or juice. Also, the social aspect of snack time, where children gather together and learn to talk and listen to one another, is important.

9. Free play: Play is how young children learn. Although all activities should involve play, children also need time in which they are engaging in free play. This can take place on the playground or in a center in the classroom. Opportunities need to be provided where children can use their imagination and just play.

10. Technology: Technology should be integrated into the unit and enhance the concepts and topics being studied. Computer software that helps develop skills and unit concepts can be used. Filmstrips, books on tape, and CD players can all be used to make experiences more hands-on and real for young children.

Integration

As children engage in various activities, they are learning about the theme objective and other skills important for four- and five-year-olds as well as having fun. When a child is listening to *The Gingham Dog and Calico Cat*, he or she is also learning new vocabulary words, discussing information, and identifying types of cloth. In the art center where the children are building the larger-than-life-sized dog, they are comparing big and little, sorting on the basis of color and shape, making comparisons, and counting. Concepts and skill development are woven throughout the activities. Painting a picture is learning about colors, holding a paintbrush, expressing ideas, and discussing your picture with a friend or the teacher.

IMPLEMENTING AN INTEGRATED CURRICULUM

After the unit topic or theme has been decided, possible theme and skill objectives have been selected, and activities are planned, you need to plan how to carry out the activities in day-to-day experiences for the children. Developing a framework or a schedule of how the day will flow will be helpful in implementing the unit.

Developing a Framework or Schedule

Before you begin a unit, it is helpful to consider the amount of time that is spent on each activity. There are two general approaches that can be taken to organize the day: developing a general framework or developing a schedule. A general framework outlines what you want to accomplish during the day and the types of activities that you have planned for the children. Using this method, you determine movement from one activity to another by the children, who set the pace and determine the amount of time given to an activity. Using the schedule approach, the teacher determines the order and the amount of time spent on a given activity. In both approaches, the same activities can be done, but the amount of time spent on the activities and the way the day is organized can vary.

It is important to listen to the needs of the children to determine the length of an activity. If the majority of the children are engrossed in activities, some at the sand

and water table, some at the art center, and some at the dramatic play center, it is clear that the children are engaged. However, if during a circle time activity half the children are beginning to move around, talk to one another, and focus on activities throughout the room, it is clear that the activity is not engaging the children. The length of time of any activity should be determined by the attention span of the group.

The goal of both methods is to establish what is going to take place in the classroom on a given day. Planning is the key to good classroom organization. However, a schedule is a guide, not a rigid plan. If while making bread the children are fascinated with the dough rising, do not discourage them from talking about this process and observing just to keep a predetermined schedule.

Introducing a Theme, Unit, or Project

There are many ways to introduce a new unit. The purpose of the introduction is to arouse children's curiosity by stimulating their interests in a topic. This can be done through the following:

◆ A teacher-initiated question. The teacher can ask a specific question about a topic, raising the children's curiosity: How many different kinds of dinosaurs do you think there were? Why do leaves change colors in the fall? How big are your feet and hands?

◆ A book on a specific topic. Books are great springboards for introducing a unit. Reading *The Carrot Seed* by Ruth Krauss (1993) can be used to introduce a theme on seeds or plants. *Swimmy* by Leo Lionni (1992) or *The Rainbow Fish* by Marcus Pfister (1996) can be used to interest the children in sea life and fish.

SCHEDULING FOR PROJECT, THEMATIC, AND UNIT LEARNING

Planning Time (15 minutes)

Describe the activities of the day. Individuals and small groups decide on what they will do, how, and with whom.

Work Time (60 minutes or more, indoors and outdoors)

Carry out plans and circulate through centers, working alone, with another, in a small group, or with a teacher.

Snack and Rest Time (Individual choice)

Open snack, with children serving themselves, lets children make choices as to when they need snack.

A quiet place to read or just be alone also permits children to rest when they feel the need.

Special Activities (15–20 minutes)

Time to sing, read together, put on a puppet show, or listen to a visitor is planned. Other learning activities, such as counting or talking about why and where the rain formed puddles, take place.

Evaluation (15–20 minutes)

Some time for the group to come together to talk about what they did and how they did things during worktime and to evaluate their own learning is a part of thematic, project, or unit learning.

◆ A field trip. A field trip can be used to excite the children about a new topic. A trip to the zoo can begin the unit on zoo animals. Visiting the post office can peak children's interest in people in their community.

◆ An arranged experience. To call children's attention to a topic, you can display objects in the classroom that are related to that topic. Displaying large gears and objects that have wheels can stimulate questions that lead to a unit on gears.

Transitioning from One Unit to Another

Just as it is important to make day-to-day connections when implementing project or thematic learning, it is also important to make connections from one theme to another. In a child's world, what happens on one day is not considered separate from what happens on another day. One role of the teacher is to help children make connections. One can easily transition from a unit on fish to a unit on water. The transition from a unit on seeds to a unit on spring is also clear. The challenge, however, comes when the next unit or topic is not directly related to the previous topic. In these instances, it is helpful to do the following:

◆ Make it clear to the children that you are moving from one topic to another.
◆ Have a culminating activity to celebrate the completion of a unit.
◆ Try to make appropriate connections whenever possible.

Evaluating a Theme, Project, or Unit

The final stage of implementing a unit is to determine whether

◆ the goals and objectives of the unit have been met
◆ the activities were developmentally appropriate
◆ the skills presented were integrated into the unit
◆ the children had fun learning

After each theme, project, or unit, it is helpful to review these points in determining the effectiveness of the unit. As a natural part of teaching, teachers reflect on the experiences of the past day, week, or month.

Some evaluation is informal as teachers reflect on daily activities: "Today the activity on making drums went well; next time I will use glue sticks instead of liquid glue." "I need to allow more time for the children to cut out the paper flowers." "Next time we study plants, I think it would be better to plant lettuce seeds instead of flowers."

More formal evaluation includes observations of children during work and play over a period of time. A teacher who developed a unit on rainbows observed the children, weeks later, drawing rainbows in the art center. She noted how they used the vocabulary from the books that they read and how they were able to label the colors in a rainbow.

Structured activities can be implemented as well. For example, themes can be evaluated by asking children to draw, write, or dramatize some concepts presented in the unit. A learning center activity, game, or specific task can be designed to help you individually assess children's understanding of concepts presented in a unit.

IN SUMMARY

Developing an integrated curriculum is an essential component in teaching young children. This chapter presents a series of guidelines for planning an integrated curriculum. In summary, these are the essential steps in planning and developing an integrated curriculum:

1. Selecting a topic: Make sure that the topic is appropriate for the age and skill level of the children. Make sure that the topic is of interest and can be enjoyable for the children.

2. Selecting theme objectives: Once the topic has been decided on, what do you want the children to know about the topic or what things do they want to know about the topic? Use a web to outline potential theme objectives for the unit.

3. Coordinating theme and skill objectives: How can skills such as listening, matching, and learning letters be presented along with the theme objectives? Four- and five-year-olds will need to acquire certain skills and this skill development needs to be coordinated and integrated with the theme objectives.

4. Activities: The theme and skill objectives are translated into practice through activities. Children engage in activities in various content areas, including literacy, math, art, and music. It is through the activities that children learn the various concepts.

5. A daily plan: A daily plan takes the form of either a schedule or a framework guiding the daily activities. The daily plan is not a rigid schedule but a guide for planning the time constraints faced in a day.

6. Structuring activities: As part of planning, you will decide what activities will best work in small and large groups and in centers. There are benefits to both small- and large-group activities. In addition, centers allow young children to work on activities independently.

7. Evaluation: Evaluation is an important aspect of planning an integrated curriculum. Were the activities engaging, and did the children learn from them? Were the activities age and skill appropriate? What things would you change, and what things would you keep for next time? Did Sally play with others today? Was Ted able to count the number of seeds at center time? Determining the strengths and weaknesses of the unit will make you a better teacher.

EXTEND YOUR IDEAS

1. Interview four- and five-year-olds about what their interests are. Relate those interests to possible themes that could be implemented in your classroom.

2. Highlight several objectives from your theme and web how they will relate to the daily content areas and skill development.

3. Write a letter to parents that share the benefits of an integrated curriculum and prepares them for their involvement.

4. An important part of curriculum development is evaluation. Describe how you would evaluate what children learn from your sample theme.

5. Describe three activities that you would do with four- and five-year-olds for one of the unit topics that you have selected. Outline what skills are being addressed in those activities. 🖐

REFERENCES

Almy, M. (2000). An interview with Millie Almy. *Young Children, 55*(1), 6–10.

Barclay, K., Benelli, C., & Schoon, S. (1999). Making the connection: Science and literacy. *Childhood Education, 75,* 146–152.

Bredekamp, S., & Rosegrant, T. (1995). *Reaching potentials: Transforming early childhood curriculum and assessment* (Vol. 2). Washington, DC: National Association for the Education of Young Children.

Chard, S. C. (1998). *The project approach.* New York: Scholastic.

Dewey, J. (1900). *School and society.* New York: McClure Phillips and Company.

Field, E. (1927). *The duel.* New York: Saalfield Publishing Company.

Gillespie, C. W. (2000). Six Head Start classrooms begin to explore the Reggio Emilia Approach. *Young Children, 55*(1), 21–27.

Helm, J. H., & Katz, L. (2000). *Young investigators: The project approach in the early years.* Washington, DC: National Association for the Education of Young Children.

Hildebrandt, C. (1998). Creativity in music and early childhood. *Young Children, 53*(6), 68–71.

Jones, E., & Nimmo, J. (1994). *Emergent curriculum.* Washington, DC: National Association for the Education of Young Children.

Katz, L. (1994). *The project approach. ERIC/EECE Newsletter 6*(1): 1–2. Urbana, IL: ERIC Clearinghouse on Elementary and Early Childhood Education.

Krauss, R. (1993). *The carrot seed.* New York: Harper.

Lionni, L. (1992). *Swimmy.* New York: Knopf.

Pfister, M. J. (1996). *The rainbow fish.* New York: North South Books.

Seefeldt, C. (2000). *Active experiences for active children: Social studies.* Upper Saddle River, NJ: Prentice Hall.

Snow, C. E., Burns, M. S., & Griffin, P. (1999). *Language and literacy environments in preschools. ericece@uiuc.edu/http://ericeece.org.*

Trepanier-Street, M. (2000). Multiple forms of representation in long-term projects. *Childhood Education, 77,* 18–26.

Wasik, B. (2001). Teaching the alphabet to young children. *Young Children, 56*(1), 34–41.

CHAPTER 8

Assessing Kindergarten Children

"I'm the smartest kid in my class," five-year-old Christie Marie told her grandmother. "Oh," said her grandmother, "and how do you know this?" "Well," said Christie Marie, "the teacher gave us this test, and I finished the whole thing before she even handed it out to the rest of the kids."

While Christie Marie's conclusion that she is the smartest in her class could be questioned, there is no question that Christie Marie's growth, learning, and development in kindergarten will and should be assessed. Practically, teachers need to have some idea of what children already know. An idea of children's concepts, vocabulary, and understanding of mathematical and other ideas is necessary if teachers are to teach on the edge of children's existing knowledge, matching what they want children to learn to what children already know.

Schools also have the responsibility to assess children in order to identify potential learning problems and provide appropriate remediation for children in need. Diagnosis and screening to identify children who may need further evaluation and educational intervention, required by federal law, is a necessary step in planning an individual education plan (IEP).

Then, too, simply because children are in kindergarten, assessment and evaluation is essential. The information gained through assessment informs teachers about the effectiveness of the curriculum and program. With this information, teachers and schools have a better understanding of what and how they can change or improve the program and curriculum to increase their effectiveness.

Additionally, our society has placed great expectations on children's kindergarten experiences. The belief that early educational experiences can affect children's future academic achievement and success in school is strong (Kagan, 1999; Washington & Andrews, 1998). When hope is so great, the need to account through assessment and evaluation for the time, energy, and money invested in fulfilling that hope is enormous.

This chapter begins with a discussion of the use of, and issues surrounding, different methods of assessment, including standardized tests, and recommendations for assessing kindergarten children.

ASSESSMENT AND EVALUATION METHODS

While there is general agreement that kindergarten children's learning, progress, growth, and development in kindergarten should be assessed, how this assessment and evaluation should take place is a highly debated, emotionally loaded question.

First, young children, as Christie Marie's experience illustrates, are not good candidates for assessment, especially through standardized testing. With little knowledge of tests and testing, and even fewer test-taking skills, children have been observed randomly placing marks in each circle or box, as Christie Marie did, marking only the circles in the middle of a page or filling them in to create a pattern.

The nature of kindergarten children themselves poses other problems. Kindergarten children have a limited repertoire of behaviors that can be assessed. All young children, simply because they are young, have limited vocabulary skills, they are unable to think abstractly, and their understanding of the world is colored by their egocentric thinking. All of this limits not only the choice of assessment methods but also the validity and efficiency of methods.

Further, children's growth and development affects the reliability of any number of assessment techniques. Children's growth is characterized by spurts, leaps, and lags. One day they may not be able to recognize or print their name, whereas the next they can both recognize their name and name the letters while printing it. A single test or other assessment technique administered on one day may be a poor indicator of a child's growth, development, or learning.

Many assessment methods, like standardized testing, take time away from children's learning. The preparation and the time to administer the assessment intrude on the children's opportunity to learn (Bredekamp & Copple, 1997).

AUTHENTIC EVALUATION AND ASSESSMENTS

Recognizing the necessity of assessment and evaluation, the field of early childhood education has developed assessment methods and techniques designed to match children's developmental level. Many state departments of education and most school systems recommend methods that are ongoing and informal. That is, the evaluation and assessment of young children is related to the ongoing activities or the program and linked to the curriculum. These are called *authentic evaluation methods* (Adams, 1998; Cuthertson & Jalongo, 1999; Meisels, 2000).

Authentic methods add to, or complement, what is already going on. They do not detract from the daily program, nor are they divorced from the daily activities of the kindergarten (Anderson, 1998; National Association for the Education of Young Children [NAEYC], 1988). Authentic methods also give teachers a clear idea of children's growth, learning, and development. Authentic methods include (a) observations, (b) checklists and rating scales, (c) structured interviews, (d) work samples and portfolios, and (e) self-evaluations.

Observations

Daily, teachers spontaneously observe children, talk with them, and reflect on children's growth and learning, asking themselves, "How did Sasha do today?" or say, "Ashok is making good progress in learning letters. He pointed out that the letter 'A' in his name is the same as the letter 'A' that begins Alice's name." When these routine observations are formalized and conducted scientifically, the simple act of observing children can reveal a great deal about the nature of children.

Observing, however, is far from a singular or simple process. There are many techniques and methods available, from the spontaneous and simple to the formalized and sophisticated (Fassnacht, 1982). The methods selected will depend on the purpose of the observation (Beatty, 1998).

Informal observation methods are chosen when teachers want to find out how individual children are relating to others or using language and mathematics or other skills. For instance, a teacher wanting to know whether a child is gaining independence would informally observe what the child does with her coat when she enters the kindergarten. Does she wait until someone helps her? Does she drop it on the floor? Or does she hang it up? If teachers want to use observations as the basis of decision making, they will select more formal methods of observing children.

Narrative or Anecdotal Observations.   When the goal is to describe children, their dialogue, and what they are doing, as Vivian Paley does in *The Kindness of Children* (1999), narrative or anecdotal methods are useful. You simply note and record what children are doing and saying, as Fox and Tipps (1995) did when they wanted to describe children's behaviors on swings. Their notes included a record of events in the outdoor play area, descriptions of the swing sets and surrounding environment, and descriptions of the interactions between children and teachers.

Event Sampling.   Event sampling is another type of observation. Teachers who want to find out about a specific behavior or situation would observe children only when the event occurred. One teacher wanted to find out whether a program designed to teach children sharing and cooperative behaviors was working. She observed only when she noticed children cooperating or sharing. At the end of one day, she and her aide had notebooks full of anecdotes about children sharing toys, working together to solve problems, or stopping their play to include others.

Another teacher, concerned about a four-year-old who bit other children, decided to observe the event of biting. As she did so, she saw that the child bit others when he was frustrated or could not communicate his wants or needs to others. By observing when the child was becoming frustrated, the teacher was able to stop the biting before it began. After stopping the biting by not letting it happen, she focused on teaching the child skills to enable him to interact with others without biting to get his way.

Time Sampling.   Time sampling is valuable when teachers are interested in understanding how a child is adjusting or learning. By observing the child once every 10 or 15 minutes, noting what he or she is doing at the time, teachers are able to gain a good cross section of a child's behaviors in kindergarten. This helps teachers come to know each child as an individual, understanding how the child handles transitions, working with others or with teachers.

Checklists and Rating Scales

More structured observations can take place with the use of checklists and rating scales. Teachers can design these for a specific purpose, such as finding out what mapping skills children use spontaneously as they play, how they are using math materials placed in the housekeeping area, or which social skills are developing. Other checklists and rating scales may be provided by the school or district as guides to assessing individual children's growth and learning or to evaluate the total program.

Whatever kind of checklist or rating scale is used, teachers will first need to observe children's behavior. Teachers have set aside time to observe while the aide is in charge of the children. Placing the checklist on a clipboard, the teacher scans the room and, using the list, checks those behaviors being exhibited. Or teachers may observe during the day and, recalling their observations after the children have gone, complete the checklist.

Objectivity.   Whatever observational method you select, objectivity will be necessary. No two people will ever see the same thing. One teacher watching a kindergarten child splashing in the water while chanting "Splish, splash, take that" sees a child aimlessly splashing water while chanting a potentially violent song. Another teacher sees the child and notes her ability to make up a rhythmic chant that goes along with the child's actions.

One teacher reported Allan to her principal, saying, "This child is constantly angry. He just can't control his anger." The principal asked that she observe Allan, recording only his behaviors without using the word "angry." The teacher observed Allan the next morning and wrote, "Allan stomped into the classroom. He tossed his coat on a chair." "Allan laughed loudly when the blocks fell." "Allan yelled across the room asking Josh to play with him at recess." Over time the teacher found that Allan was not angry—he was simply loud and boisterous. Rather than needing a reprimand from the principal or the help of a psychologist, he needed to be taught different ways of behaving while inside.

A measure of objectivity can be achieved by examining your feelings and attitudes toward children. Ask yourself how you really feel about children splashing water or those who are loud and boisterous. Once you have identified your feelings, try to put them aside and focus only on children's actual behaviors (Seefeldt & Barbour, 1998).

Objectivity is also obtained by learning to observe and describe details. The details of the room, materials, and the things other children did or said and describing the child's behaviors in detail increase objectivity. Observe a child doing something as simple as walking into the room. Focus on the details. How does the child hold her shoulders? What is her facial expression? What is she wearing? How does she use her hands and arms as she walks? What does she say? Describe children's facial expressions and their nonverbal and verbal language (Beaty, 1998).

"Get a grip," a new teacher said when her principal asked her to observe Clifford during the morning as she supervised center time. "You must be kidding. How can I observe, interact with children working in centers, and teach at the same time?" True, observing may seem overwhelming to new teachers, but experienced teachers have developed a variety of techniques that enable them to observe and teach at the same time. Some keep sticky note pads with them, jotting down telegraphic notes as they observe a child. While getting ready to go on a field trip, one teacher noted Alisha helping Kim button her coat. Alisha said, "This button goes with this hole, watch. Now you do it." The teacher jotted down the date and noted on the card "A helped Kim w/ coat." She stuck the note in Alisha's portfolio, and later, while organizing portfolios, she used the note to jog her memory as she wrote a full description of the incident and its meaning.

To ensure that every child is observed, teachers keep a box of cards with each child's name at the top of the cards. Each day they select two or three cards from the file and several blank cards to carry with them during the day. Focusing on one or two children each day ascertains that all children are observed over time. The blank cards are useful for recording incidents that illustrate an aspect of children's learning. At the end of a unit or project or of a semester or year, these quick observational notes will provide teachers, children, and their parents with a fairly complete and accurate picture of children's growth, learning, and progress in kindergarten.

Experienced teachers observe children's skills on a continual basis.

Technology is useful in observing children. Instead of writing narratives or filling in checklists while observing, teachers have found that using digital cameras, videotapes, or audiotapes is useful. Teachers can use these later as the basis of completing a checklist or to illustrate a child's progress or needs to parents or other staff (Beatty, 1998). With others analyzing the same behavior episodes captured on tapes, a larger degree of objectivity is obtained.

Many teachers transfer their notes to a computer at the end of a day or week. This way they can search for key words or use other methods to organize their notes.

Structured Interviews

Piaget's life work was based on observing children. Observations of his own three children led him to develop the clinical method, which combined observations of children with questioning, probing, and observing again.

For example, to find out children's understanding of one-to-one correspondence, he would give a child six little bottles along with a tray of glasses and say, "Look at these bottles. What shall we need if we want to drink? (Glasses). Well there they are. Take off the tray just enough glasses, the same number as there are bottles, one for each bottle" (Piaget, 1952, p. 42). The child herself makes the correspondence, putting one glass in front of each bottle. If she takes too many or too few, she is asked, "Do you think they're the same?" until it is clear that the child can do no more. Once the correspondence is established, the six glasses are grouped together, and the child is again asked, "Are there as many bottles as glasses?" If the child says "No," she is asked, "Where are there more?" and "Why are there more here?"

Teachers can use the same type of structured interview to probe children's understanding of concepts, facts, their feelings, or social situations. Design the interview to relate to your goals and objectives. One teacher had focused on mapping skills throughout the month. To find out what knowledge of maps the children had gained, she drew a map of the school and neighborhood. She sat with each child and asked, "Show me our school." and "Show me how you would walk from the school to the gas station." Another teacher interviewed children to find out their understanding of story sequence. Showing children a picture, she asked them to tell the story of the picture using a flannel board and flannel cutouts. She recorded their stories in note form and later put them on the computer.

After a trip to a clothing store, a teacher wanted to find out something about children's understanding of economic concepts. Individually, she talked with each child, asking, "Where do the clothes come from?" "How do they get to the store?" "Where does the money come from?" "Who works at the store?" "Where do they live?" "What do they do?" and "Why do they work there?" When children told her that the people "make the clothes in the back of the store," she probed. "Why do you think that?" Or when they said that the clerks made money in the back of the store, she asked why they thought that.

When interviewing children, give them plenty of time to respond. Ask questions designed to prove their thinking, such as "Why does the sun come up?" "Tell me more." "Show me" or "That's interesting, another girl told me . . . what do you think of that?" This forces children to think again, clarify their thinking, and in the process give you a better idea of their thought processes.

Interviews can be conducted during activity time or any time you and a child can get together for a few moments. As you interview children, observe the following:

◆ How *consistent* are the child's responses? Does the child respond in the same way to the same types of questions?
◆ How *accurate* are the child's answers? How correct are they?
◆ Is the child's response *clear*? Is the reasoning clear, logical, and acceptable?
◆ How *complete* is the response? How many aspects of the concept were covered? How many were not? How many illustrations of the concepts were given?

Performance Standards or Benchmarks

The idea of assessing children's learning by asking them to perform a given task has been used to assess kindergarten children. Goals 2000 offers examples of how performance standards work. Goals 2000, which states what children are to know by the time they leave a specific grade, also includes what the child should be able to do or perform as an indication of achievement of the goal.

To assess what children have learned in kindergarten, they may be given specific tasks to perform. The tasks are directly related to the goals and objectives of the curriculum and program (Eisner, 1999). For example, the arts standards state that children should be able to perform eight basic locomotor movements: walk,

Asking children to perform a task is one method of assessment.

run, hop, jump, leap, gallop, slide, and skip. To determine whether a child has achieved this standard, you would ask the child to demonstrate these movements (Consortium of the National Arts Education Association [CNAEA], 1994). The geography standards state that the child should know and understand the location of places within the community. To find out whether the child has gained this knowledge, "They should be able to sketch a map from memory of the local community showing the route to and from school" (Geography Education Standards Project [GESP], 1994, p. 108).

Work Samples and Portfolios

"Portfolios are a purposeful collection of children's work that illustrates their efforts, progress, and achievements, and potentially provides a rich documentation of each child's experience throughout the year" (Meisels, 1989, p. 37).

Portfolio assessment, which has been found to accurately predict children's performance on standardized tests and overall performance in school (Meisels, Liaw, Dorfman, & Nelson, 1995), is highly valued by teachers, parents, and children. Teachers believe that they gain valuable information about children that leads to improved instruction and curriculum (Althanases, 1994; Hurst, Wilson, & Cramer, 1998). Children and parents enjoy portfolios as well. Both seem to take pride in selecting work to be included in the portfolio and enjoy reflecting on the work in the portfolios, and parents value the portfolio as a record of their children's history.

When portfolios are to be used as an assessment tool, a relatively structured approach to their creation is recommended (Meisels, 1989). Meisels (1989) suggests that core items and other items constitute a child's portfolio. The core items are pieces of work sampled from the domains of personal and social development, language and literacy, mathematical thinking, scientific thinking, social studies, art and music, and physical development. Other items are samples of work from all domains selected by the child or parent or by the teacher to illustrate a specific learning or task achievement.

All work is dated, and details about how, when, and under what conditions the work was completed are recorded. Growth charts, checklists, standardized test scores, and observations can also be included (Seefeldt & Galper, 1998). See the following for examples of other items included in portfolios.

EXAMPLES OF PORTFOLIO ITEMS

♦ Children's drawings, paintings, scribbles, or other artwork

♦ Logs of books read to or by children

♦ Photographs of children working on a special project or product

♦ Notes and comments from interviews or performance tasks

♦ Copies of pages from journals illustrating invented spelling

♦ Recordings of children telling or reading a story, reciting a poem, or recording some special event

♦ Videos of children

♦ Dictated or written stories

Teachers often use the portfolio as a part of parent-teacher conferences. Going over the portfolio with parents gives meaning to report cards (Weldin & Tumarkin, 1999). Some go over the portfolio with the child, entering into a dialogue about the work samples. This gives teachers insights into the child's ideas of his or her own growth and learning while giving children autonomy and control (Herbert, 1998). These teachers often invite the child to explain the portfolio to his or her parents as a part of the conference.

Although the portfolio is an accurate representation of one child's progress over time, the work in one portfolio cannot be compared to that in another. Rather, each child's work is analyzed and evaluated for progress toward a standard of performance (Seefeldt & Barbour, 1998), one that is consistent with the goals and objectives of the kindergarten (Grace & Shores, 1992).

Self-Evaluations

Children who know themselves know what they can do well and what they need to learn, have strong self-identities, and can exercise control over their behaviors and learning (Bandura, 1997). Involving children in their own evaluation is one way to foster children's feelings of efficacy or control. Teaching children to evaluate themselves also enables them to develop memory and to begin the lifelong process of monitoring and reflecting on their own thinking and learning.

Four-year-olds can begin to think of how they have grown and what they have learned over a week, month, or semester. You might ask four-year-olds to tell what they liked best about the day and why, what materials they enjoyed, and which they had problems with or to describe their progress in a specific area.

Five-year-olds can answer the questions of what they learned, their best subject, what they need to learn, what they think is their hardest subject and how they will learn it, and what they can do now that they could not when they first came to kindergarten. Their answers can be recorded through drawings, writing, dictation, or orally on a tape or video recorder.

After completing a science project, one teacher made a list of the concepts that he believed children had learned and then posted these. He asked children to write what they remembered of the project in their journals, listing the skills they had learned and those they thought they could improve on. Their responses were used by the teacher in planning follow-up lessons and conferencing with parents (Seefeldt & Barbour, 1998).

STANDARDIZED TESTS

Authentic assessment techniques are a necessary part of the kindergarten program and curriculum. On the spot, teachers can use an observation of children interacting to teach social skills, or the results of an interview can be immediately used to extend, expand, or clarify and refine children's thinking and ideas.

School systems and state departments of education sometimes require a different type of evaluation. To account for children's learning, schools need to have some indication of how groups of children are achieving. Despite the problems associated with the use of standardized tests, many school systems select these as a means of summing up the overall worth of a kindergarten program and accounting for children's achievement.

As the name suggests, standardized tests are designed to be standard. Developed around a pattern, standardized tests assess a specific domain, content area, attitude, knowledge, or skill. They must be given under the same conditions, with the same directions, and within the same specified time period. They usually have a manual that contains instructions for administering, scoring, and interpreting the test results. If there is any variation in the methods or timing of the administration, the test is no longer considered standardized.

There is a norming sample on which the test was developed. This sample should be representative of the children taking the test. If a test was normed on children who are very different from those in your class or school, then the test would not be a very good judge of what your children know and can do. For instance, middle-class suburban children are raised in a culture that differs from that of children living in rural or poor urban areas of the country. Most existing tests, even though some are translated into Spanish, seem inadequate to assess bilingual children or those from diverse cultural backgrounds (Gullo, 1994).

The results of standardized tests are interpreted on the basis of the normal curve. By using the normal curve, one can identify how an individual deviates from the standard. Within the normal curve and the normative standards derived from the curve, it is possible to make meaningful evaluations about an individual child or school. Kindergarten children may be administered several different types of standardized tests, including (a) readiness tests, (b) achievement tests, (c) screening and diagnostic tests, and (d) intelligence tests.

Readiness Tests

One group of standardized tests is designed to predict readiness to learn or the probable degree to which success in some specific subject, segment of education, or area of the curriculum can be achieved. Kindergarten readiness tests are developed to assess the children's ability to profit from instruction in the near future, kindergarten, or first grade rather than later elementary school.

Tests designed to measure children's readiness to learn to read are called reading readiness tests. Reading readiness tests and general readiness tests are similar in a number of ways. Both are designed to measure the specific academic skills and knowledge children have mastered. Kindergarten readiness tests assess whether a child has the appropriate sensory motor, cognitive, language, and social-emotional skills and knowledge necessary to be successful in kindergarten or first grade. Reading readiness tests emphasize the skills required for the early stages of reading. These skills might include oral vocabulary; rhyming or matching words; visual matching of figures, letters, or words; visual perceiving of figures, letters, or words; or naming letters and reading words.

General readiness tests include the Gesell School Readiness Tests: Complete Battery (Ilg & Ames, 1972) and the (Ireton Thwing, 1974). The Peabody Picture Vocabulary Test: Revised (Dunn & Dunn, 1991), a test of receptive language, is sometimes used as a reading readiness test.

Achievement Tests

Achievement tests are designed to assess what a child has been taught or learned in a given area of instruction or at least a sample of what a child is able to do at the time. A wide range of achievement tests are available and widely used in kindergarten. With an achievement test, the standing of an individual child or children in different programs or schools can be compared using the common base of an achievement test. Children's progress over time can also be compared.

Some achievement tests are norm-referenced tests. This means that the test results tell you how the child's performance on that test compares with that of other children of the same age and grade. Other tests are criterion-referenced tests that inform teachers how well the child has mastered a set of instructional goals and objectives with the criteria specified. These are usually designed by a school system and inform teachers how well a child has mastered specific material, not how well the child is doing in comparison with other children of the same age.

Examples of norm-referenced tests used in kindergarten are the Boehm Test of Basic Concepts (Boehm, 1986), California Achievement Test (CTB/McGraw-Hill, 1985), and the Woodcock-Johnson Tests of Achievement: Revised (Woodcock & Johnson, 1990).

Screening and Diagnostic Tests

Under law, schools are responsible for identifying potential learning problems and to provide remediation for young children at risk. Diagnosis and screening consist of a brief assessment procedure designed to identify children who may need further evaluation and educational intervention (Meisels, 1989). Standardized tests of

Often state laws require diagnostic screening.

achievement may be used to diagnosis children, but these are not used to assess children's achievement but rather to "identify the existence of a disability or specific area of academic weakness in a child. Test results are used to suggest possible causes for the disability or academic weakness as well as suggest potential remediation strategies" (Gullo, 1994, p. 40).

According to Meisels (1989), screening measures can be grouped into three areas. The first is visual-motor and adaptive skills. This involves control of fine motor movements, eye-hand coordination, and the ability to recall sequences and reproduce forms. The second area is related to language skills, comprehension, and thinking, and the third includes gross motor skills.

Frequently used screening and diagnostic tests include the Denver Developmental Screening Test (DDST; Frankenburg, Dodds, Famdal, Kazuk, & Cohrs, 1975) and the Developmental Indicators for Assessment of Learning (Revised) (DIAL-R; Mardell-Czudnowski & Goldenberg, 1983).

Intelligence Tests

Intelligence tests differ from achievement, readiness, or diagnostic tests. Although they may be used as a part of a diagnostic or readiness battery, intelligence tests purport to assess a child's general ability, not what a child has learned. Typically, this means that they measure abstract intelligence—the ability to see relations, make generalizations, and relate and organize ideas represented in symbolic form. Children's scores are expressed as a mental age. This describes the level at which the child is performing.

Intelligence tests can be administered individually or to groups of children. The Stanford-Binet Intelligence Scale (Fourth Edition) (Thorndike, Hagen, & Sattler, 1986) and the Wechsler Preschool and Primary Scale of Intelligence (Revised) (Wechsler, 1989) are two prevalently used intelligence tests that are individually administered.

ISSUES OF ASSESSMENT

Early childhood educators have followed Rousseau's admonition to "Study your children, for assuredly you do not know them" (Rousseau, 1947). They study kindergarten children using a variety of assessment methods and techniques. The methods of authentic evaluation and assessment, which includes observations of children, structured interviews, and portfolios, is used to monitor the growth and learning of individual children. Standardized tests, which do offer some information about how an individual child is doing, are usually used to describe groups of children.

Neither authentic evaluation methods nor standardized tests are perfect. The field has a long way to go in increasing the reliability and validity of authentic assessment techniques. The objectivity of authentic assessment is also a problem. No matter how objective teachers attempt to be in selecting work samples to place in a portfolio, their prior experiences, values, and attitudes continue to influence their judgment. Decisions about what behaviors to observe, what the work in the portfolio actually means, or what questions to ask in an interview are not considered fully valid because they are affected by the teacher's personal belief systems, attitudes, and values. Whether the samples of work or observations really do measure or assess what the teacher thinks they do can be questioned.

Sabrina's parents were told by the kindergarten teacher that Sabrina would not be ready for first grade. The teacher said that she has observed Sabrina who not once sat still and never listened but rather talked all the time. Further, she said, she asked her to perform several tasks, and Sabrina failed each. She did not know the ABCs when asked to recite them and failed to correctly complete assigned work sheets. Her parents, thinking Sabrina was an especially verbal child, sought help from the school counselor, who gave Sabrina the Peabody Picture Vocabulary Test. Sabrina's score indicated that she had the reflective vocabulary typical of a seven-year-old, rather than a five-year-old. With this information, Sabrina was permitted to progress to first grade where she excelled in reading.

Authentic assessment techniques, in addition to being subjective, lack reliability. They often fail to reproduce the same results if used again with the same child. What a teacher observes one day may not be present the next. Moreover, the findings obtained from authentic assessment

WHY STANDARDIZED TESTING IS INAPPROPRIATE

The National Association for the Education of Young Children's (1988) Position Statement

◆ Young children are not good test takers

◆ Young children are growing and learning rapidly—what they do not know one day they may the next

◆ There is no such thing as a culture-free test.

techniques conducted on individual children cannot be generalized to other children. This means that the results or findings cannot be applied to the total group of children, nor can comparisons between children or groups of children be made.

Standardized tests are considered another good source of information that can be used diagnostically or to provide insights into children's development and learning. Although standardized tests purport to be objective, reliable (producing the same score each time given to a specific child), and valid (measuring what they purport to measure), they too are influenced by the culture in which they were constructed and by their administration. Because every test is developed within some culture, no test is culture free. Each reflects the values and attitudes of the culture. There are tests that purport to be culture fair, however. These, like the Goodenough-Harris Draw a Person Test (Goodenough & Harris, 1969), have been developed in multiple cultures and require no or little language for administration.

Teachers' administration of tests affects their validity and reliability. Glidden (1996) discusses how teachers interpret test items—"Look at the picture again, you know, it's the fluffy dog"—or fail to follow standardized procedures because of a lack of training and the failure of school systems to monitor consistent procedures. Children's performance on standardized tests depends on their background of experiences. Designers of standardized tests recognize this and have tried to base the selection of test items on experiences common to the group for whom the test will be used. But sometimes this view is narrow and limited and, many critics claim, based on an urban middle-class American culture. And it is true that standardized tests of readiness, achievement, and intelligence, reflecting middle-class culture, are highly verbal and abstract and emphasize speed, competition, and doing "one's best."

Standardized tests, unlike authentic assessment (which is ongoing and related to the curriculum), provide information only about what a given child can do at a given moment in time. Just as most of us can recall a "bad hair day," each of us remembers taking a test when we were not feeling our best, were upset about a personal problem, or were just tired. Some college professors, recognizing this, permit students to remove one test score or grade or an assignment, by replacing it with some other task as a means of accommodating these bad test days.

Standardized tests also are limited in informing teachers about individual children's needs. They give teachers a score on a test and a percentile ranking that tells them only how this individual child stands in relation to the children in the norming group. This is not very useful in helping teachers plan to meet the needs of an individual child.

Thus, no one form of assessment can stand alone in making decisions about a child's learning, strengths, or weaknesses (Genishi, 1992; Gullo, 1994; Haladyna, Haas, & Wilson, 1998; Mitchell, 1992). No one standardized test score or one set of observations offers sufficient information for teachers, their principals, or the school system to determine the following:

◆ Children's access to kindergarten
◆ Placement in remedial, developmental, transitional, or special classes
◆ Retention in kindergarten

◆ Placement in a homogeneous group on the basis of a single test score or any other form of assessment

Given the detrimental effects of denying children access to kindergarten or placing them in developmental or other transitional classrooms before or following kindergarten to ready children for the next grade placement (Bredekamp & Shepard, 1989; Shepard, 1992) have a major impact on children's lives and can never be made on the basis of any one assessment or evaluation alone (Bredekamp & Copple, 1997, p. 133).

For this reason and for general ethical concerns, parents must be informed before their children are assessed or evaluated in any way. When authentic evaluation and assessment is linked to the curriculum, informed consent is not necessary. Because they are tied to the curriculum, the findings from authentic evaluation are usually shared with parents. However, if the findings of authentic evaluation are to be placed in children's permanent records or used in making life-altering decisions, then the parents should be informed.

Claiming that standardized tests and other assessments are necessary tools of accountability, school systems usually do not require informed consent in order to use the findings of assessments. Regardless, parents must be informed of the type of evaluation or assessment and when it is to take place and given copies of the test results.

Most school systems accommodate the individual needs of young children, ensuring that all children succeed at their own pace. Thus, it is rare that placement decisions will take place. Even so, there are special cases when decisions must be made about children's grade placement. When this occurs, multiple sources of information must be considered. This includes, but is not limited to, that obtained from observations by teachers, standardized test results, school specialists, other authorities, and most of all children's parents and other family members.

IN SUMMARY

Kindergarten assessment is necessary. The results of assessment inform teachers about children's progress and needs and how they can improve their curriculum and kindergarten program. Regardless, assessing young children is problematic. Multiple techniques, methods, and sources of information must constitute kindergarten assessment.

Authentic assessment techniques are most useful in informing teachers on a continual basis about children's progress, their strengths, and their needs. Teachers observe children and note their progress, needs, and strengths. Periodically, they collect samples of children's work, take photos of them completing a task or engaged in some activity, or write anecdotes about how children mastered a specific task or skill. These are placed in the child's portfolio and, when analyzed together, offer an accurate picture of children's growth and learning in kindergarten.

School systems also need to know how groups of children are achieving and progressing in kindergarten. To do so, systems may administer standardized tests, including readiness, achievement, diagnostic, and intelligence tests.

Neither authentic assessment techniques nor standardized tests are perfect. Neither can be used alone to make decisions about children's grade placement, retention, or placement in a special group. Making life-altering decisions such as these requires much more than a single test score or findings from authentic assessment and must be made in consultation with teachers, resource personnel, and parents.

EXTEND YOUR IDEAS

1. Obtain copies of readiness, achievement, diagnostic, and intelligence tests from a school counselor or the testing department of your college or university. Compare these. List how they are alike and different. You could share your findings in class.

2. Talk with parents of kindergarten children. Ask them how their children are assessed, how useful and fair they think the assessment is, and how they would improve assessment.

3. Review a child's portfolio with a teacher. Note core and other items. Ask the teacher who makes the decision about which items are placed in the portfolio and how he or she uses these to analyze the child's progress and needs. ✋

RESOURCES

The Building Tool Room offers an Assessment Terminology: A Glossary of Useful Terms, prepared by the Assessing Learning Conference (Washington, DC, 1995). Access the glossary at *http://www.newhorizons.org/assmtterms*.

The Integrated Classroom: The Assessment-Curriculum Link in Early Childhood Education, by Sue C. Wortham. Upper Saddle River, NJ: Merrill/Prentice Hall. (1996).

This book prepares future teachers of young children for the challenges of integrating assessment and the curriculum.

Developmentally Appropriate Assessment: The DLM Early Childhood Professional Library 1, by Elizabeth F. Shore. Dallas, TX: DLM Professional Library. (1996). This book demonstrates how to assess kindergarten children appropriately.

REFERENCES

Adams, T. L. (1998). Alternative assessment in elementary school mathematics. *Childhood Education, 74*, 226–229.

Althanases, S. Z. (1994). Teachers' report of the effects of preparing portfolios of literacy instruction. *The Elementary School Journal, 94*, 421–439.

Anderson, S. R. (1998). The trouble with testing. *Young Children, 53*(4), 25–30.

Bandura, A. (1997). *Self efficacy: The exercise of control.* New York: Freeman Press.

Beaty, J. (1998). *Observing development of the young children* (4th ed.). Upper Saddle River, NJ: Merrill/Prentice Hall.

Bredekamp, S., & Copple, C. (1997). *Developmentally appropriate practice in early childhood programs* (Rev. ed.). Washington, DC: National Association for the Education of Young Children.

Bredekamp, S., & Shepard, L. (1989). How best to protect children from inappropriate school expectations, practices, and policies. *Young Children, 44*(3), 13–23.

Consortium of the National Arts Education Association. (1994). *Dance, music, theatre, visual arts: What every young American should know and be able to do in the arts.* Reston, VA: Author.

CTB/McGraw-Hill (1985). *The California Achievement Test.* New York: Garland Publishing Co.

Cuthertson, L. D., & Jalongo, M. E. (1999). But what's wrong with letter grades? *Childhood Education, 75,* 130–136.

Dunn, L., & Dunn, L. (1991). *The Peabody picture vocabulary test.* Circle Pines, MN: American Guidance Service.

Eisner, E. (1999). The uses and limits of performance assessment. *Phi Delta Kappan, 80,* 658–662.

Fassnacht, G. (1982). *Theory and practice of observing behavior.* London: Academic Press.

Fox, J., & Tipps, R. S. (1995). Young children's development of swinging behaviors. *Early Childhood Research Quarterly, 10,* 475–505.

Frankenburg, W. F., Dodds, J., Fandal, A., Kazuk, E. & Cohrs, M. (1975). *Denver Developmental Screening Test (DDST).* Denver: Denver Development Materials.

Genishi, C. (1992). *Ways of assessing children and curriculum.* New York: Teachers College Press.

Geography Education Standards Project. (1994). *Geography for life: National geography standards.* Washington, DC: Author.

Glidden, G. (1996). *Assessment irregularities: A discussion guide for current issues in test administration.* Wichita, KS: Wichita Public Schools.

Grace, F., & Shores, E. F. (1992). *The portfolio and its use: Developmentally appropriate assessment of young children.* Little Rock, AR: Southern Association for the Education of Young Children.

Gullo, D. F. (1994). *Understanding assessment and evaluation in early childhood education.* New York: Teachers College Press.

Haladyna, T., Haas, N., & Wilson, J. (1998). Continuing tensions in standardized testing. *Childhood Education, 74,* 262–274.

Herbert, E. A. (1998). Lessons learned about student portfolios. *Phi Delta Kappan, 79,* 583–586.

Hurst, B., Wilson, C., & Cramer, G. (1998). Professional teaching portfolios: Tools for reflection, growth, and advancement. *Phi Delta Kappan, 79,* 578–583.

Ilg, F. L., & Ames, L. B. (1972). *Gesell school readiness tests: Complete battery.* New York: Harper & Row.

Ireton, H., & Thwing, E. (1974). *Minnesota child development inventory.* Minneapolis, MN: Behavioral Science Systems.

Kagan, S. L. (1999). Cracking the readiness mystique. *Young Children, 54*(4), 2–3.

Mardell-Czudnowski, D. D., & Goldenberg, D. S. (1988). *Developmental Indicators for Assessment of Learning (Revised).* New York: Childcraft Education Corporation.

Meisels, S. J. (1989). High stakes testing in kindergarten. *Educational Leadership, 46*(7), 16–22.

Meisels, S. J. (2000). On the side of the child: Personal reflections on testing. *Young Children, 55*(6), 16–20.

Meisels, S., Liaw, F., Dorfman, A., & Nelson, R. F. (1995). The work sampling systems: Reliability and validity of a performance assessment for young children. *Early Childhood Research Quarterly, 10,* 277–296.

Mitchell, R. (1992). *Testing for learning.* New York: The Free Press.

National Association for the Education of Young Children. (1988). *Testing of young children: Concerns and cautions.* Washington, DC: Author.

Paley, V. (1999). *The kindness of children.* Cambridge, MA: Harvard University Press.

Piaget, J. (1952). *The child's conception of number.* New York: Norton Library.

Rousseau, J. J. (1947). *L'Emile ou l'education.* In O. E. Tellows & N. R. Tarry (Eds.), *The age of enlightenment* (pp. 416–513). New York: F. S. Crofts.

Seefeldt, C. (1998). Assessing Young Children. In C. Seefeldt & A. Galper (Eds.) *Continuing Issues in Early Childhood Education.* 317–347. Upper Saddle River, NJ: Merrill/Prentice Hall.

Seefeldt, C., & Barbour, N. (1998). *Early childhood education: An introduction* (4th ed.). Upper Saddle River, NJ: Merrill/Prentice Hall.

Shepard, L. (1992). Retention and redshirting. In L. Williams & D. Fromberg (Eds.), *Encyclopedia of early childhood education* (pp. 278–280). New York: Garland Publishing.

Thorndike, R. L., Hagen, E. P., & Sattler, J. M. (1986). *Stanford-Binet Intelligence Scale-Fourth Edition.* Riverside, CA: Riverside Publishing Co.

Washington, V., & Andrews, J. D. (Eds.). (1998). *Children of 2010.* Washington, DC: National Association for the Education of Young Children.

Wechsler, D. (1989). *Wechsler Preschool and Primary Scale of Intelligence*—Revised Edition. New York: The Psychological Corporation.

Weldin, D. J., & Tumarkin, S. R. (1999). Parent involvement: More power in the portfolio process. *Childhood Education, 75,* 90–94.

Woodcock, R. W., & Woodcock, M. B. (1989). *W J–R Test of Achievement*. Chicago: Riverside Publishing.

CHAPTER 9

Art in the Kindergarten

"I just love art time, I really do," Bryan told his uncle, who asked him how kindergarten was going. Bryan, like most kindergarten children, find creating visual art a most rewarding, pleasant activity (Seefeldt, Galper, & Denton, 1997).

Perhaps it is the brightness and fluidity of the paints, the satisfying feel of clay and wood, and the colors of markers on paper that appeal to kindergarten children. Or it could be the beauty that results from their work that is so pleasurable. "Once I made the most beautiful butterflies in kindergarten. I painted them blue and yellow and pink and they were so, so beautiful," explained one child.

Dewey (1944), however, would give a different reason making art appeals to kindergarten children. The fact that art materials are open-ended mandates that children, as Dewey said, "bring mind to them" is probably the real reason kindergarten children love art.

Given open-ended materials—paints, paper, markers and crayons, wood, clay, and cloth and yarn—children are the ones who have to figure out not only what to do with the materials but also how they will do it. They are the ones who set goals for themselves and monitor their own thinking and doing as they try to achieve their goals. When children are failing to achieve their goals, they are the ones who adjust their actions and change their plans. And when they have reached their goals—determined only by them, not by others—they are the ones who experience the joy of achievement and the satisfaction.

This does not happen when children are asked to follow the will and directions of another. Children do not feel in control, experience the thrill of autonomy, or discover the job of achieving a goal when asked to complete worksheets, workbooks, or participate in some group project that has been chosen and directed by the teacher.

A group of four-year-olds were given rocks, pieces of felt, and paints and instructed to make turtles by pasting the felt to the bottom of the rocks and painting the tops. Watching the children randomly trying to paste the pieces of felt to the rocks, a visitor asked, "What are you doing?" "I don't know," replied one child and, shrugging her shoulders, added, "the teacher told us to make turtles" (Seefeldt, 1993).

This chapter is based on the assumption that kindergarten teachers know that the power to perceive, imagine, explore, and invent belongs to the children. This chapter presents a discussion on the value of art for developing children's thinking, how artistic expression develops, how to foster kindergarten children's progress in creating and appreciating art, and techniques for evaluating and assessing children's progress in the visual arts.

THE VALUE OF ART

rt is basic. Of course, every subject area is important, but no kindergarten program could succeed without emphasizing art. Through making, looking at, and talking about their own artwork and the art of others, four- and five-year-old children are doing the following:

◆ Expressing their feelings and emotions in a safe way. They learn to control their emotions and recognize that they can express and handle negative as well as joyous feelings through positive action.
◆ Practicing and gaining fine muscle control and strengthening eye-hand motor coordination. Holding paintbrushes and learning how to control paint, crayons,

scissors, and other art tools, children gain skills necessary for later writing activities as well as a feeling of control over themselves and their world.

◆ Developing perceptual abilities. Awareness of colors, shapes, forms, lines, and textures result as children observe these and try to replicate them through art.

◆ Being given the opportunity to make choices and solve problems. How do you get the legs to stick on a clay figure? What color should I use? Making art offers children a multitude of choices and many decisions to make.

◆ Seeing that others have differing points of view and ways of expressing these than they do. Comparing children's drawings, paintings, or models gives children concrete, dramatic examples of how different people express the same thing in different ways. While learning that their way is not the only way, they learn to value diversity.

◆ Becoming aware of the idea that, through art, culture is transmitted. Becoming acquainted with the art of the past, children are involved in learning something of their origins and themselves.

◆ Experiencing success. Because art leaves the end open to the creator, all children experience a measure of success. This is why art activities are appropriate for children with special needs. Regardless of the physical or mental need of the child, there is some art media and activity through which they can experience success.

◆ Making connections between the visual arts and other disciplines. Art integrates the curriculum. Content from every subject matter can find form through art.

Mathematics: Children become aware of different sizes, shapes, and parallel lines and use every mathematical concept as they discuss their art and the art of others.

Science: Paint changes texture as it dries, powdered paint and chalk dissolve in water, and chalk produces bubbles when dipped in water. The physical sciences are ever present as children produce art.

Economics: This and other concepts from the social studies develop. Children become producers by making art and consumers by using the materials of art.

Language: Children learn to talk about their art and the art of others and develop the vocabulary of art (Manning & Manning, 1996).

Beginning reading: Children make and read symbols that represent reality.

Social skills: Sharing paints and paper, cooperating to create a group mural or other project, and assuming responsibility for cleaning up, children gain valuable social skills through making art.

ARTISTIC EXPRESSION DEVELOPS

Most important perhaps, art is a symbol-making activity. Four- and five-year-olds, because they are in the preoperational stage of thought, are the true symbol makers. This makes art a powerful tool for developing children's thought, the oral and written language, and their ways of knowing and understanding themselves and their world (Golumb, 1992; Raines & Canady, 1990).

Four- and five-year-olds are in the process of becoming aware of and developing the use of symbol systems. They use oral language proficiently and know that they can take meaning from pictures. Some four-year-olds and most five-year-olds can differentiate written words from pictures, not only in books but in their own artwork as well. Making and talking about art builds on children's developing awareness of, and use of, symbols. Thus, art is essential in the kindergarten; not just because children love it so, but because the curriculum must match and build on children's developmental needs.

The Power of Scribbles

"Sure," says a parent, "when you describe the power of art in children's symbolic learning, you can talk a good game, but all my child does is scribble. What kind of power is in a scribble?" True, four- and five-year-olds, because they are in the preschematic stage of art, scribble. But these scribbles serve as powerful symbolic representations of their thoughts, concepts, and emotions. They contain the seeds that will later sprout into reading and writing (Dyson, 1990).

When children draw, paint, model, sew, or construct, they first mentally create an image or thought in their mind. Holding this thought, they then make a mental search for the symbols they could use to express it. Finally, they find a way to transfer these symbols onto a piece of paper using markers, crayons, or paint or using any other media to express their ideas or feelings through symbols (Eisner, 1997; Gardner, 1987).

Piaget (Piaget & Inhelder, 1965) related the process of making art to the development of thought. He believed that art began in children's development of object permanence, or the ability to understand the permanent existence of objects, and to think of these even though they are not physically present. This evocation requires a symbol to stand for what is not in the here-and-now. To be able to represent, in symbolic form, something that is not in children's here-and-now world is the means by which children organize their experiences of the world and further come to understand it. Imagery and the use of symbols is one way of symbolizing the world, while language is another way.

Children's abilities to represent their images parallels their cognitive development (Piaget & Inhelder, 1965; Wolfe & Perry, 1998). During the sensorimotor period of development, from birth through age two, children scribble. These scribbles are uncontrolled and are more like physical acts related to children's sensory experiences than expressions of children's thinking (Lowenfeld, 1947; Wolfe & Perry, 1998).

During the preoperational stage of thought, from around four through seven years of age, children learn that they can control their scribbles, and they use and repeat lines, circles, squares, and other marks to represent objects and things in their world.

Four-Year-Olds Scribble.   If four-year-olds have had plenty of prior experiences scribbling, they can hold a brush or drawing tool the same way that adults hold pens or pencils, although some may still grasp the crayon full fisted when they begin kindergarten. Hand preference is usually firmly established, and drawing materials are thought of and treated as tools, not as toys or objects to be played with, as children under four years of age often do.

Four-year-olds can use a variety of techniques as they scribble. They are able to produce shapes at will and use these to represent things in their world. The first shape that appears stands for a human being and is roughly oval or circular. Four-year-olds gradually elaborate on the symbol, adding eyes, arms, and legs. Other symbols are used to depict buildings, animals, trees, flowers, and objects. These are represented through crude marks that are practiced over and over and become increasingly embellished and elaborate. The shapes and marks are dispersed all over the paper. There is no baseline.

Four-year-olds, as opposed to younger children, start to demonstrate an interest in their scribbles. They may say, "Look what I made," or talk as they scribble, "Horsie, horsie, horsie, up and down, up and down." According to Lowenfeld (1947) and Wolfe and Perry (1998), this naming of scribbles indicates that children are now thinking in terms of images, not just engaging in muscular activity as they did at three.

Still, four-year-olds approach scribbling without a plan in mind. Chances are, if you ask a four-year-old what he or she is drawing or painting, the response will be "I don't know yet, I'm not finished." One four-year-old drew a long "S"-like line on a sheet of paper. She said, "Oh now I know," and adding an oval shape at the end of the "S" line, continued, "It's a duck—here's the neck, and here's the head," she said pointing to the "S" line and oval. Others, if asked what they made, may make something up to please the adult. When Andrea's aunt asked what she was drawing, she replied, "It's a house."

STAGES OF ART

Lowenfeld's Stages of Art

1. Scribbling—ages 2–4. The first stage of self-expression.
2. Preschematic—ages 4–7. Representational attempts.
3. Schematic—ages 7–9. Achievement of a concept of form.
4. Gang stage—ages 9–11. The dawning age of realism.
5. Stage of reasoning—11–13. Pseudo-realistic stage.

Wolfe and Perry's Stages of Art

1. Object-based representation—12–14 months. Children treat art and art materials as they do other objects.
2. Gestural representation—14 months–2 years. Children focus on the representation of motions and movements.
3. Point-plot representation—2–3 years. Children attempt to give meaning to their graphic expressions. The scribble may be named.
4. Visual-spatial information systems—3–5 years. The use of relative size and shapes to depict a geometric reality begins to appear.
5. Rule-given visual spatial systems—5–7 years. A schematic and highly conventional attempt to give geometric reality dominates children's drawing.

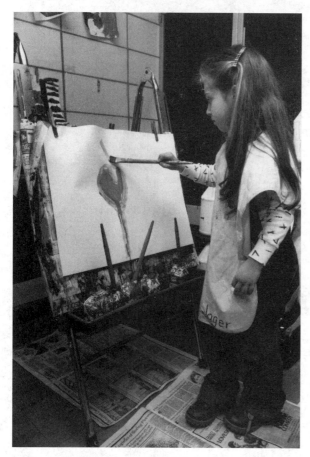

Four- and five-year-olds will want to name their products.

Five-Year-Olds Scribble. By five, children who have had plenty of opportunity to scribble and develop control over the drawing tools will begin painting or drawing with a plan in mind. They will even select drawing tools—paints, crayons, and paper—that they think are best suited to permit them to fulfil their plan. "Do you have any gold paint?" asked five-year-old Kim. "I want to paint Wynken, Blynken, and Nod's nets of silver and gold," he informed his teacher, who had often read Eugene Field's poem "Wynken, Blynken and Nod" before rest time.

Most five-year-olds are able to represent what they know in their drawings and paintings. Their scribbles are becoming increasingly realistic. Even though their drawings in no way resemble those of a child in Piaget's concrete operational stage of development (ages 7 to 11), they are schematic and realistically illustrate personal concepts and generalizations. An adult can easily see and understand what the child has drawn.

The drawings of five-year-olds show attention to relationships in their environment, such as spatial arrangements. Many begin to use a baseline and skyline in their drawings. Children will progress from placing objects randomly above the baseline to placing objects and things on the baseline with the skyline at the top of the paper. They begin to rely on geometric lines and shapes to represent reality. Because they draw what they know, not what they see, they may draw transparencies, or x-ray pictures, to indicate what they know to exist, even though it is not logically visible.

Products become more important to five-year-olds. They will want to name them, ask you to write the story of their painting on it, or have their name printed on their drawings. They may want you to keep their painting, but most often they want to take them home to share them with their parents, relatives, or friends.

FOSTERING KINDERGARTEN CHILDREN'S PROGRESS IN CREATING AND APPRECIATING ART

Fostering and appreciating art includes the following:

◆ Knowledge of national standards in order to select appropriate goals and objectives for art in the kindergarten

◆ Skill in motivating children's artistic expression
◆ Knowledge of how to select art media and guide children as they learn to use a variety of media

National Standards

Goals for art in the kindergarten stem from the National Visual Arts Standards (National Art Educators Association [NAEA], 1994). Although these fail to specify how the kindergarten art curriculum might differ from that in any other grade, the standards state that younger children should engage in "experimenting enthusiastically with art materials" (NAEA, 1994, p. 33) and other developmentally appropriate practices that will prepare them to achieve the standards when in the elementary grades.

Kindergarten children can begin to develop the following:

◆ An awareness of different visual arts media, techniques, and processes
◆ A knowledge of visual art structures and functions by using these in their creations
◆ The use of a wide range of subject matter, symbols, and ideas
◆ The ability to think about and reflect on the characteristics of their work and the work of others
◆ The connections between the visual arts and other disciplines

These standards guide teachers in determining how they will motivate children's artistic expression, select materials, and guide children in their use so that children can appreciate art.

Motivating Children's Artistic Expression

Kindergarten teachers, who want children to be able to use a wide range of subject matter, symbols, and ideas in their art do not (1) tell children what to create, (2) give them patterns to copy or trace, or (3) show them how to draw or paint. Rather, on the basis of constructionist theories of learning, they motivate children's art by providing them with

◆ continual and meaningful experiences
◆ psychological safety
◆ selected teaching strategies

Continual and Meaningful Experiences. "I don't know what to draw, show me," whines one child while another busily draws a stereotypic rainbow. What are children to draw if they have little to think about, few ideas, and no feelings or emotions to express? Children cannot produce art without a store of ideas, feelings, or imaginations. Rather than asking children to copy teachers' ideas, or showing them how to draw, kindergarten teachers arrange for children to have firsthand and vicarious experiences that push for expression.

Teachers in Reggio Emilia, like many in the United States, do this. They make certain that children think, ponder, and reflect on their experiences. They talk with children, engaging them in dialogues to foster awareness of an event. Teaching children to be aware of and to focus on their environment may be the most productive motivation, however. When children are asked to really look at the bark of a tree, to feel it, to see the branches and how they are joined to the trunk, to examine the ways the leaves are attached to the branches, and to feel and smell the leaves, they are able to draw on stored images to create art (Engle, 1996).

We all walk in the rain at some time or another. But a walk in the rain is not a real experience unless children are mentally involved. Teachers ask children to look at a raindrop as it falls on them, then look another way, using a magnifying glass. They ask them to catch a raindrop in their hands or on their tongues or watch as the rain falls on windowpanes, sand, or the sidewalk (Seefeldt, 1993).

Involve five-year-olds in recording their experiences. Give each a throw-away camera, perhaps purchased by the Parent Teachers Association, or ask parents to bring inexpensive cameras to school one day. By photographing their experiences, five-year-olds are learning to focus and look at the world around them in another way as well as learning the skills of the photographer.

How a simple rain puddle becomes an experience is described in *The Hundred Languages of Children* (Commune de Reggio Emilia, 1987). Children's interest in a banal puddle led to splashing in the puddle, feeling the mud at the bottom, and observing how the surface acted as a reflector. The game of mirroring motivated children to draw representational, as well as surrealistic and imaginative, worlds that might be found in puddles.

Occasionally, you might suggest a theme. Perhaps you might ask children to contribute a picture for a class booklet of "Stories We Like," "Things We Wear," or "Shoes." No child is forced to do so, but the theme could serve to stimulate thought. Around Mother's Day, teachers have suggested that children make a portrait of their mothers, their families, or themselves. Other themes might be drawing and writing about animals they have seen, things they have learned to do in kindergarten, when they were babies, what they will do when they are teens, and so on.

Not all experiences need to be firsthand. Imaginations empower humans to create and engage in works of art (Greene, 1997) and can be called into play. Eagan (1997) claimed that imagination and fantasy stories, which "most powerfully engage children" (p. 343), are other sources of motivation for art. He suggested teachers read fantasy stories to children and provide them with the art materials that would enable them to represent these or their own fantasies through art. "Just Pretend" ways in which children use their imaginations (at the top of the next page).

Awareness of the art of others offers another form of motivation for children's artwork. It also fulfills a major goal of the art standards, that of being able to think and reflect on art, relating the art of others to their own work.

The art found in children's literature is a familiar starting place to introduce children to the art of others. When you read books, name the author and artist. Talk about the pictures and how the artist might have executed the drawings. The collages of Eric Carle in *Brown Bear, Brown Bear* (Martin, 1969) are good examples. Then provide colored tissue paper and other pieces of paper along with scissors and glue so that children can make their own collages.

Or look at and examine ceramic sculptures and discuss how the artist created the work or the story they were telling by making the object, stimulating children's

JUST PRETEND

Ask children to use their imaginations. Reading a poem about the fog creeping in on a cat's feet or about the moon provides children with images they can express through art. After reading the poem or story or singing a rhyme, talk about it. You might begin the discussion by asking the children to think about the poem and recall parts or phrases they like the best or to talk about the character they thought the bravest, silliest, or most beautiful. You might ask them to relate the poem or story to their own experiences: "Did you see the moon last night?" Then ask them to use their imaginations to paint, draw, model, or construct their ideas of the poem or story.

You could read the following:

◆ *The Sugar Plum Tree* by Eugene Field and ask children to paint their idea of the Sugar Plum Tree.

◆ *The Three Billy Goats Gruff* and have children construct the wickedest troll they can imagine.

◆ Christina G. Rosetti's poem "What Is Pink?" and, providing all shades of pink paints and markers, ask children to paint or draw all the pink things they know and like.

◆ Maurice Sendack's *Where the Wild Things Are* and ask children to create the land where the wild things went after Max banished them from his dreams.

◆ *Rain, Rain, Go Away* and ask children to draw what they could do when they go out to play on another day.

◆ "Wynken, Blynken and Nod" (Field, 1927), who sailed off in a wooden shoe to catch all the beautiful fish that lived in a sea of dew and ask children to paint all the beautiful fish that lived in the sea.

◆ Read any story, but do not show children the illustrations. Then have them illustrate the book, drawing or painting the parts they liked the best or remembered.

◆ Ask children to illustrate a story they have written.

own ideas about what they could make with clay. Show pictures of Calder's mobiles, or go to a museum to see them and create mobiles when you return to the classroom.

One teacher purchased a number of postcards of paintings of flowers by different artists. She placed these on a table and listened as the children sorted through them, picking out their favorites or just looking at them. She then talked about how the different artists looked at flowers in different ways. Georgia O'Keeffe, for instance, looked at one part of a flower. Van Gogh looked at an entire field of sunflowers. The teacher asked children what art media the different artists used. Then the class went on a walk to a local field, and the teacher took instant photos of the children in the field of flowers. Returning to the class, the children painted, sculpted, and drew detailed, lovely and diverse flowers.

Psychological Safety.　In order to give free reign to their ideas or feelings, children must have a measure of psychological safety. It is not possible to express yourself when you are feeling insecure, frightened, or inadequate.

Coloring sheets, patterns to trace or copy, or being told to make a face out of a paper plate just the way the teacher did destroys children's beliefs in their own capability and abilities. Giving an outline of a dog and asking to color in the lines is telling children that their idea of a dog is inadequate and inappropriate. Children

**HAVE YOU
EVER THOUGHT . . .**

that when an adult

♦ shows a child what to draw;

♦ gives them a paper plate, some triangles, and some circles and directs them to make a face; and

♦ asks them to color in an outline of a dog on a worksheet,

the adult is limiting the child of

♦ the opportunity to think for him- or herself,

♦ thinking and finding a way to express these thoughts in symbolic form, and

♦ communicating his or her ideas to others?

who have experienced coloring and worksheets, when asked to draw or create, doubt themselves and are unable to do so.

How teachers praise and recognize children's work can provide a measure of psychological safety. When a child showed his painting to a teacher, the teacher said, "Oh, I just love it!" "But you say that to everyone," the child replied. Instead of teachers responding that they like the product or saying that it is lovely, teachers can give positive feedback by actually describing the painting or talking about the way the child created it. "You used yellow, blue, and red all over the paper." "You joined the box here and here and then added this long, curved strip of paper." Instead of making judgments about the product, talk about what the child was doing as she created the product ("Your whole body moved"); (Sparling & Sparling, 1973), describe the details in the painting ("You used red lines all over"), or talk about how it makes you feel ("These circles make me feel happy inside").

Talking to children recognizes their work and enriches their immediate experience, expanding their understanding of the nature of visual forms and their own activity as artist (Thompson, 1995). When teachers sensitively engage children in a conversation about their art, they lead children to name and then ponder, initiate, and pursue the process of creating visual forms.

Walking through a museum viewing paintings of flowers by Georgia O'Keeffe, Monet, Manet, Rembrandt, Cezanne, and Picasso, you realize that there is no right or wrong way of expressing the idea of flowers. Children, too, have different ways of expressing themselves through art. Each child, regardless of his or her capabilities or special needs, can experience a measure of success through art. Treat each product with deep respect. This does not mean that you praise each and every scribble. A teacher, meaning well, told a child who was randomly playing with paints, mixing them and dashing them onto a piece of paper, "Oh how lovely. You're a great artist!" The child shook her head, frowned at the teacher, and said, "But I was just messing around." It does mean, however, that the work of all children is recognized and displayed, not just the work of those who have special talents. From time to time a painting or drawing can be placed in a construction paper frame or mounted on a mat.

Selected Teaching Strategies.   Teachers do not dictate what children will produce, nor do they direct the process of producing art. But children do need "interested adults and other children to listen to their plans, respond to their ideas, and offer assistance and support for their explorations of visual forms and meanings" (Thompson, 1995, p. 82).

Recalling Vygotsky's theory that there are two kinds of development—what the child can do unaided and what the child can do with the guidance of an adult or older peer (Vygotsky, 1986)—teachers do teach children skills necessary for them to produce art. For example, children need to be taught to use a slip to join two pieces of clay, to use needle and thread to stitch a design, or to join pieces of wood to create a collage.

Giving children time to develop techniques and master the media is another effective teaching strategy. By limiting media to things that children can (a) paint and draw with, (b) stitch, (c) construct, and (d) model, you give children the opportunity to develop skills in handling and controlling the media. Children will not be bored using the same media over and over again if they have new, interesting, exciting ideas, thoughts, and feelings to express. When there is a new thought or feeling pushing to be expressed, children will continually be challenged to find new and different ways of using the same paints, clay, paper, yarn, and markers to give form to their ideas.

SELECTING ART MEDIA AND GUIDING CHILDREN'S ART PRODUCTION

A variety of media, arranged so that children can see the choices available and readily and easily access them, is necessary. Sensitive motivation, teaching, and guidance lead children to developing an awareness of different techniques and processes that are possible through a variety of media as well as gaining knowledge of visual art structures and functions by using these in their creations.

A variety of media can be chosen.

Drawing

"You don't understand," a student teacher said, "I'm teaching in a *public* school kindergarten; there's no money for all the art materials you're asking us to use." Well, if there is not, there must at least be paper for children to draw on and drawing tools—crayons, markers, chalk, and pencils.

Because kindergarten children are in the symbol-making stage of art and thought, drawing is the single most critical kindergarten art activity. Every day, children should be able to draw. Of course, children first need something to draw about, and this is easy. Everywhere there are things to observe, see, and focus on that children can draw. One kindergarten class in a northern industrial city became engaged with the lowly pigeons that roosted on their windowsills during the winter. Yes, the adults thought the pigeons were a mess, but as children observed them over the year, their drawings of pigeons became more detailed. Children noticed and drew pigeon eyes, beaks, feathers, and feet. They compared pigeon characteristics to those of other birds. Both their drawings and the learning that took place were stunning.

Four-year-olds need large, chunky crayons because they are perfecting their grasp of drawing tools, and the fine, thin crayons may break. They do not need the full range of colors, only a few colors at a time. And because four-year-olds are learning to control their scribbles and will scribble for the fun of it and to gain eye-hand-muscle control, they will need plenty of newsprint or other kinds of large paper to color on. Younger four-year-olds, in the stage of exploring what they can do with the media, are probably not all that interested in the product that results from their scribbles.

Five-year-olds, even though many still need the large, chunky crayons when they begin kindergarten, enjoy drawing with the thinner crayons, which enable them to include more details in their drawings. The full range of colors and types of drawing tools—markers, pencils, and fabric markers—can be made available. Markers of all types are especially suited for children whose muscle development is not as fully developed as others or who have special physical needs. Some sets of crayons or markers might be stored in their original boxes for individuals to take to a table or corner of the room and draw by themselves. Others could be stored in color-coded tins or clear boxes, with red in one, deep rose in another, and so on. Another box of crayon scraps or chunky crayons that can be taken outside is also useful.

Large sheets of paper, of many different textures, shapes, and sizes, should be available for the children. If children's interest in drawing lags, add pieces of sandpaper, thin sheets of wood, cardboard, box tops, or Styrofoam trays to motivate them. Colored construction paper, wax paper, and aluminum foil are also interesting to draw on and will add variety to children's drawing.

Chalk is an additional drawing tool. The bright colors, softness, and ease of application make chalk a favorite. In addition to white chalk, both large, chunky sticks and regular-sized pieces of colored chalk can be provided. White chalk is best with colored construction paper or other dark surfaces, and colored chalk is best on light paper or surfaces. Chalk drawings can be preserved by spraying them either with cheap, pump hair spray or with a special fixative that can be purchased from school supply stores. You can teach children to dip a piece of chalk into a small container of liquid starch or a mixture of water and liquid glue before drawing. This gives a paintlike drawing, and the chalk, because it has been moistened with liquid, will adhere to the paper.

Crayons and drawing tools can be combined with other materials. Children may draw a figure on one kind of paper and then cut it out and mount it onto a sheet of contrasting paper, or crayon drawings can include bits of fabric glued onto the drawing. One group of children, having drawn portraits of their mothers, used scraps of material from the collage area and cut these out and pasted them onto their portraits to represent clothing.

These young symbol makers can use the symbol-making machine, the computer, as another drawing tool. Any program that enables children to draw and then print out copies of their drawings will do. KIDPIX by Broderbund, available for IBM or Macintosh, is a fun-filled art exploration program. With KIDCUTS, also by Broderbund, children can create paper planes, hats, and other creations that they can actually play with.

Painting

In the scribbling stage, four- and five-year-olds will first paint as they scribble, filling page after page with paint. So entranced with the paint itself, they will continue painting until the paper is completely saturated. After they have developed control over the paint, children will paint in much the same way as they draw. They will use the same ovoid symbols to represent people and animals and the same shapes for buildings and other objects. Because they are working with fluid paints and brushes, these symbols will be less detailed than those they can draw.

Painting can take place anywhere—at easels, on tables, or on the floor (Greenberg, 1999). You can prepare six-packs of paints in discarded yogurt containers for children to use when not painting at the easel. Paints must be bright and strong and the mixture thick. Watery paints and weak colors hold little attraction to children. Mixing small amounts of paint daily ensures freshness. Mix colors that permit children to represent their experiences. One group visited a local beekeeper. The next day the teacher mixed a variety of yellow and black paints so that they could paint the bees they had observed. Another class took a walk around the neighborhood to look at all the fruit trees in bloom on a spring day. The teacher provided all kinds of pink, lavender, and shades of white paper and paints. She did not ask children to draw their ideas of the trees they had observed, but the paintings that resulted illustrated children's focus on the trees and their ability to use media in a variety of ways to reflect on their experience.

Easel, paints, brushes, paper, and smocks should be easily accessible to children and arranged in ways so that the child will need little adult assistance in order to paint. Paper can be stored near the easel, which is equipped with clips, clip clothespins, large thumbtacks that children can handle, and a variety of brushes, including small narrow ones, stored point up in a can.

Sometimes cleaning up is nearly as much fun and as valuable a learning experience as is painting. Children should also be able to clean up after their painting without the assistance of an adult. A can of water at the easel can be used for soaking and washing brushes, or, if there is a sink in a room, children can carry the can to the sink and wash brushes there. Wet paintings, which children may need a bit of help with, can be clipped to a clothesline to dry or placed in a hallway or some out-of-the-way area for floor drying.

Most watercolors, especially those that come in small tin boxes, are inadequate for children. If watercolors are of good quality and purchased with each color in a separate tin or cake, they can produce colors strong enough for children to enjoy. Textured watercolor paper and large watercolor brushes should be used.

Finger painting is not recommended in the kindergarten. However, it may be fun once in a while and could be useful for children who need to vent strong emotions or feelings or who have the need to develop specific large or fine motor skills. Nevertheless, the major task of four- and five-year-old children is that of symbol making, and finger painting does not permit them to develop symbol making or to develop control over the tools used to make symbols.

Fabric Stitching and Sewing

Stitching, sewing, and weaving are easy for four- and five-year-olds; that is, if they are taught the skills necessary to create with fabric. It is worth taking the time to do so, for sewing helps develop children's eye-hand-muscle coordination, necessary for later writing. Then too, developing skill with the media is necessary, for it is only after children have mastered the basic skills of cutting, stitching, and weaving that they will be able to create with fabric.

Start with cutting. Four-year-olds and some five-year-olds may be unfamiliar with scissors. Have them practice cutting a coiled roll of soft clay or plasticine, then move to cutting different kinds of paper. Children will cut paper just like they scribble, cutting and cutting with no purpose in mind. Only after children have mastered cutting, through perseverance and practice and with a good pair of well-made blunt-end but sharp scissors, can they cut cloth.

Next obtain blunt-end yarn needles and wild, bright yarns to lure, catch, and hold children's interest. You will have to thread the needles and knot the yarn for both four- and five-year-olds. Stick the threaded needles in a block of Styrofoam, ready for children's use. And all children, especially those who are left-handed, need a lot of practice and guidance before they will become independent with needles and thread.

You can show children how to stitch. Punch holes in Styrofoam meat trays or around the edges of paper plates or obtain plastic screening cut into small squares or rectangles with masking tape around the edges or cut apart plastic berry baskets. Then show children how to stitch. Five-year-olds who have experienced stitching as four-year-olds or who have developed skills over the kindergarten year can be taught how to use a running, cross, or chain stitch to make designs or pictures. With these skills, kindergarten children can use fabric and stitchery as another means of symbol making.

In five-year-old kindergartens, keep a sewing box for children's use. This box holds blunt needles, a variety of threads and buttons, scissors that cut cloth, and pieces of fabric. In one kindergarten, children who had been taught how to sew used this box to make cloths for their dolls, puppets, and stitch pictures as gifts for their parents.

Modeling

There really is nothing like working with real clay. Punching, poking, and pulling clay and creating three-dimensional objects is satisfying and rewarding. But it also gives all children, especially those in need of strengthening their muscles, valuable experience. While many kindergarten teachers make or purchase all kinds of play clay, "gak," or other substitutes, these really do not serve the same purpose as real clay (Koster, 1999).

Clay does take some special care. It must be stored properly. It must be kept moist enough to be pliable. An old garbage can or a diaper pail with a tight-fitting lid is a good container. Make small fist-size wads of clay and poke through them so that the moisture permeates the entire ball of clay. Cover the clay with moistened terry cloth towels. Keep masonite boards or pieces of oilcloth near the clay container. Children can take a piece of clay and a board or the cloth to a table or desk and begin working with clay.

Take some clay and find out what you can do with it. Punch it, poke it, and shape it into some object. You can make eyes or ears on an animal by poking into the clay with a pointed object, and you can make legs by pulling out pieces of clay. Make a ball out of the clay, put your thumbs in the middle, and stretch it out to form a bowl or pot. If you want a handle on a bowl you have made, you need to roughen both the edges that you want to join and moisten both with slip, which will act like glue. Slip is a bit of clay softened and dissolved in a bit of water.

Kindergarten children need time to experiment with and explore what they can do with clay before being taught the techniques of working with coils, decorating clay objects, or joining pieces. At first, children make balls or snakes with the clay. Eventually, they will try to make an object.

What can you do with clay?

Five-year-olds can be shown how to make a pot or bowl from a ball of clay, or you can demonstrate how to use the snake coils they make to form a pot and how to pull out pieces for legs or arms for the people or animals they make. Using tools, combs, sticks, or other objects, show children how they can decorate their products and use slip.

Clay products will harden as they dry. They are, however, very fragile unless fired in a kiln, which is not often found in an elementary school. Even if there is a kiln in the school, it probably will not be possible to actually fire more than one or two pieces per child during a year.

Constructing, Collage, and the Computer

"Where's that junk box?" asked Joyelle as she toured the classroom during the kindergarten roundup designed to ease children's transition from Head Start to five-year-old kindergarten. "In Head Start," she explained, "we had a big, big junk box. It was filled with lots of stuff for us kids, and we could make anything we wanted to."

A junk box—filled with boxes, the plastic dividers in boxes of cookie, soft plastic-coated wire, pipe cleaners, beads, and other recycled "junk"—permits children to express themselves by building three-dimensional objects. Materials can be organized in clear plastic containers and cookie tins, with each holding a different kind of material—beads, buttons, pieces of wood, dried flowers, or seeds. Categorizing the materials facilitates children finding just the right thing for their construction or collage and gives them one more experience with ordering their world.

In Reggio Emilia, children have access to more than a junk box to make their selections as they construct three-dimensional projects. In the child care centers of Reggio, every possible kind of material that children can use in their construction are attractively displayed. Buttons, feathers, fancy papers, paper cupcake holders, pieces of wood, plastic glasses, wires, boxes, and pieces of plastic and metal pipes are displayed in clear plastic containers on open shelves, along with masking and duct tape, staples, glue, hammer and nails, and an assortment of glues and other tools that can be used to join materials together.

One five-year-old group used the materials found on the shelf to construct a large 5- by 8-foot dinosaur. Another group glued many clear plastic glasses together to construct a glass sky scraper they had seen on a field trip.

You can ask parents to recycle materials that can be used in construction. And you can obtain hundreds of empty boxes, paper cans, and other containers from local factories and packaging plants. Empty rejected cleanser cans, cracker and toothpaste boxes, and plenty of tape and glue motivated one kindergarten class to construct huge forts, castles, airports, and houses.

Mobiles and Stabiles. Showing children how to make mobiles and stabiles opens up another avenue for construction. A stable is a fixed mobile, with a base made of clay, wood, or Styrofoam. Clay is usually easiest for children to use. Toothpicks, straws, wires, pipe cleaners, or even weeds, twigs, pieces of bark, or seed pops are stuck into the clay base and decorated as children desire. At first children will randomly arrange the materials, but once they master the technique, they can create interesting, thoughtful structures.

Mobiles, which hang from the ceiling and move in the wind, are a bit more difficult to construct. Five-year-olds, however, can understand the concept of a mobile—that it should hang freely for the air to breeze through it and move its parts—and can be helped to construct one. Mobile bases can be coat hangers. Strings with ribbons, paper, cutouts, beads, or other things are attached to the hanger. Because five-year-olds may not be able to tie, adults have to attach the things to the hanger. Group mobiles can be successful. Children could draw and cut out a picture of something that lives in a pond, an item of clothing they do not wear, or something that Mother Hubbard might find in her cupboard if it were full.

Collage.　Collage, with its immediate product and textured, three-dimensional effect, is a favorite of kindergarten children. It is a form of art in which bits of objects are attached to a flat surface to communicate an idea or feeling or organize an experience. Lightweight materials like papers and fabrics can be pasted on ordinary construction paper or cardboard, but heavier objects need a plywood or wood backing.

Anything can be used for a collage. Children can choose from the "junk box" or a "magic box" of scrap materials freshened by removing unused objects with new, interesting ones. When children begin making collages, as with any other media, they will scribble, randomly pasting objects on paper. Collages take on more meaning if children gather the materials themselves. Go for a walk with the object of collecting materials to make a nature collage. A classroom or play yard collage can be made from scrap materials found in the room or yard.

Food is never appropriate for use in making collages or any other artwork. Four- and five-year-olds are trying to make sense and order out of their world. Taught not to play with food, four- and five-year-olds find it disorienting to then be told to make a collage using food. Then too, other art materials have more potential for fostering children's expression than do food products. Finally, it is unconscionable to play with and waste food. Children who come to school hungry will find it difficult to understand why food is being used to play with.

Constructing on the Computer.　There are a few programs that allow children to construct three-dimensional objects (Char & Forman, 1994). "Smart Blocks," from the Massachusetts Institute of Technology, has computers in the blocks themselves.

EVALUATING AND ASSESSING CHILDREN'S PROGRESS

The National Goals, along with a knowledge of child development, offers teachers the guidelines for evaluating children's progress in the visual arts. You will want to observe and chart children's developmental progress in the following:

◆ Developing an awareness of different visual arts media, techniques, and processes. You might observe each individual's ability to do the following:
  • Choose from a variety of media to represent their ideas and emotions, using all the media available
  • Control the media in order to obtain special effects

- Combine media, such as paints and construction and collage and drawing, to express him- or herself
◆ Knowledge of visual art structures and functions by using these in their creations. Does the child:
  - draw simple geometric shapes and figures that become increasingly elaborate and complex?
  - exaggerate important parts?
  - increasingly use details (eyelashes, nostrils, and fingernails) in drawings and paintings?
  - employ decoration in the products?
  - use colors and forms to represent ideas?
◆ Use a wide range of subject matter, symbols, and ideas. Are children's products:
  - becoming increasingly original?
  - reflecting a variety of subject matter and ideas?
◆ The ability to think about and reflect on the characteristics of their work and the work of others. Are children:
  - talking spontaneously about their work to one another, discussing how they obtained a certain effect or what they like about their own and others' work?
  - pointing out the shapes, colors, and designs they and others use in their work to represent their world?
  - able to recognize the work of artists familiar to them such as Eric Carle's collages or the drawings of Maurice Sendak?
◆ Making connections between the visual arts and other disciplines. Are children using:
  - concepts of mathematics as they draw (shapes, sizes, and numbers) or counting as they mix paints or construct an object?
  - art to represent their experiences with the social studies and subject matter from the sciences?
  - ideas that stem from poetry and literature, incorporating the written language in their drawings?

Keep track of children's artistic progress in a number of ways. From time to time, ask each to draw a man, a woman, or themselves for you to keep. Date these, and at the end of the year assemble them into a booklet titled "Rachel's Drawings of a Man," or woman, or self. This gives you and the parents a clear indication of the progress each child has made in using and gaining control over the tools of art and their ability to move from scribbling to early symbolic representation.

Arrange to keep a portfolio for each child. Think carefully about what to include in the portfolio (Meisels, Liaw, Dorfman, & Nelson, 1995). Label the work with the date and a narrative describing its importance. "Caleb talked all the while he was completing this painting. He described and talked about the colors he used and why." Each month you might select a drawing or painting to include in the portfolio or a photograph of a three-dimensional object to have a record of the child's progress throughout the year. You can also ask children to select the work they value to include in the portfolio. Again, date this and include a note describing its importance.

The work in the portfolio is not compared with the work of other children; rather, the child's work is analyzed and evaluated for the progress the child has made. Several times a year, you can go over the portfolio with each child, entering into a dialogue with the child about the work sampled. This enables you to gain insights about the child's perceptions and perspective about his or her work and progress (Seefeldt & Barbour, 1998).

In Summary

Put your trust in four- and five-year-old kindergarten children, and they will reward you with glorious works of art. By understanding and respecting the stages of art and offering children experiential and vicarious motivation, the right materials, guidance, and sensitive teaching strategies, they will produce art that is stunningly beautiful.

Begin by recognizing the values of art in the kindergarten curriculum and consider the national standards to guide you in planning art for kindergarten children. Kindergarten children do not need a plethora of media but rather the time to develop control over drawing and painting tools, sewing, modeling, and constructing. Once they develop skills and techniques in using these materials and have ideas, feelings, or thoughts to express, they will create works of art fitting for a museum.

Kindergarten children will not do so, however, if asked to follow an adult's idea of how to make a turtle or a spaceman or asked to color in trite worksheets. These destroy children's psychological confidence, their ability to trust themselves and their ideas and ways of knowing, and their willingness to take a risk and express themselves fully and freely.

Extend Your Ideas

1. Collect scribbles of four- and five-year-old children over time. Identify the differences in those executed by each age-group. Chart children's progress from undifferentiated scribbles to elaboration, and finally representation.

2. Observe in a kindergarten. Focus your observations on two children. Record which art media they choose most frequently. Time how long each paints, draws, or constructs. What art media would you say children enjoy the most on the basis of your findings?

3. Make a list of children's books with outstanding illustrations that could be used to introduce children to the concept of an artist and to develop different techniques with the media.

4. Write a letter to parents explaining the power of art in the kindergarten curriculum and children's lives.

RESOURCES

Contact your local art museum to find prints, postcards, slides, or CDs of the work of famous artists. The National Gallery of Art, Department of Extension Programs, and the Smithsonian Institution, both in Washington, DC, are also excellent sources of free and inexpensive art reproductions. Both have Web sites that can be accessed by conducting a search with their names. Art & Museum Links is another Web site that has excellent resources for teachers. The Crayola Web site and the National Art Educators Association offer teachers numerous resources in the visual arts.

Considering Children's Art: Why and How to Value Their Works, by B. S. Engle (Washington, DC: National Association for the Education of Young Children, 1999).

REFERENCES

Char, C., & Forman, G. (1994). Interactive technology and young children: A look to the future. In J. Wright & D. D. Shade (Eds.), *Young children: Active learners in a technological age* (pp. 167–178). Washington, DC: National Association for the Education of Young Children.

Commune de Reggio Emilia. (1987). *The hundred languages of children.* Reggio Emilia, Italy: Commune de Reggio Emilia.

Dewey, J. (1944). *Democracy and education.* New York: The Free Press.

Dyson, A. (1990). Symbol makers, symbol weavers: How children link play, pictures and print. *Young Children, 45*(2), 50–57.

Eagan, K. (1997). The arts as the basics of education. *Childhood Education, 73,* 346–349.

Eisner, E. (1997). Cognition and representation: A way to pursue the American dream? *Phi Delta Kappan, 78,* 348–354.

Engle, B. S. (1996). Learning to look: Appreciating child art. *Young Children, 51*(3), 74–79.

Field, E. (1927). *Child verses.* New York: Saalfied Publishing.

Gardner, H. (1987). Zero based arts education: An introduction to ARTS PROPEL. *Studies in Art Education, 30*(2), 71–83.

Golumb, C. (1992). *The child's creation of a pictorial world.* Berkeley and Los Angeles: University of California Press.

Greene, M. (1997). Metaphors and multiples: Representation, the arts and history. *Phi Delta Kappan, 78,* 387–394.

Greenberg, P. (1999). Painting every day. *Young Children, 54*(5), 81.

Koster, J. B. (1999). Clay for little fingers. *Young Children, 54*(2), 18–22.

Lowenfeld, V. (1947). *Creative and mental growth.* New York: Macmillan.

Manning, M., & Manning, G. (1996). Arts in reading and writing. *Teaching PreK–8, 26*(6), 90–91.

Martin, B. (1969). *Brown bear, brown bear.* New York: Holt, Rinehart & Winston.

Meisels, S. J., Liaw, F., Dorfman, A., & Nelson, R. (1995). The work sampling system: Reliability and validity of a performance assessment of young children. *Early Childhood Research Quarterly, 10,* 227–296.

National Art Educators Association. (1994). *Suggested policy perspectives on art content and student learning.* Reston, VA: Author.

Piaget, J., & Inhelder, B. (1965). *Play, dreams and imitation in childhood.* New York: Norton.

Raines, S., & Canady, R. J. (1990). *The whole language kindergarten.* New York: Teachers College Press.

Seefeldt, C. (1993). Art: A serious work. *Young Children, 50*(3), 39–54.

Seefeldt, C., Galper, A., & Denton, K. (1997). Head Start children's conceptions of and expectations for their future schooling. *Early Childhood Research Quarterly, 12,* 387–406.

Seefeldt, C., & Barbour, N. (1998). *Early childhood education: An introduction.* Upper Saddle River, NJ: Merrill/Prentice-Hall.

Sparling, J., & Sparling, M. (1973). How to talk to a scribbler. *Young Children, 28*(3), 333–342.

Thompson, C. M. (1995). Transforming curriculum in the visual arts. In S. Bredekamp & T. Rosegrant (Eds.), *Reaching potentials: Transforming early childhood curriculum and assessment* *(Vol. 2)* (pp. 81–93). Washington, DC: National Association for the Education of Young Children.

Vygotsky, L. (1986). *Thought and language.* Cambridge: MIT Press.

Wolfe, D., & Perry, M. D. (1998). From endpoints to repertories. *Journal of Aesthetic Education, 22,* 17–34.

CHAPTER 10 Music and Movement

"I am here, I am here," sings Andrew, announcing his presence as he dashes into the kindergarten room. Life is filled with music! So is the kindergarten! From the moment children enter the room and are greeted with a welcoming hello song or chant to the moment they leave, music is intricately woven throughout every fiber of the day, filling children and teachers alike with delight and pleasure (Moravicik, 2000).

This chapter begins by presenting the concept that music is integral in the kindergarten classroom. It describes the values of music and how musical abilities develop in young children. The role of the national standards in designing musical activities in moving, listening, and singing that promote children's musical skills, knowledge, and attitudes concludes the chapter.

Music Is Integral

hroughout the day, the joy and wonder of music is experienced spontaneously by individuals, small groups, or teacher and children together (Hildebrandt, 1998). In the morning, children or teachers break into song, singing "Oh what a beautiful morning" or "zip-a-dee-doo-dah, zip-a-dee-ay, my oh my, what a wonderful day," setting the tone for the rest of the day.

Songs and music are a big part of the opening meeting. Name songs are sung as children greet one another. A birthday is celebrated by singing "Happy Birthday," the song Patty Smith Hill wrote for children in one of the nation's first kindergarten programs. Songs in observance of Flag Day, President's Day, and other holidays are sung. Musical instruments are played, and music is introduced to stimulate children's imaginations, motivate ideas for thematic and project work, and spur creative thought.

Music continues during center time. Teachers knew even before research confirmed the fact that kindergarten children frequently break into extemporaneous, original, and standard songs while engaged in center work. Children may chant the sounds of animals as they put puzzles together or make a scrapbook, depict the sounds of machines as they build with blocks, or sing a familiar song. Playing house or just moving through the room, children spontaneously engage in rhythmic movements, moving themselves and objects in rhythmic ways (Tarnowski & Leclerc, 1994).

Teachers sing during center time as well. At times they may sing a refrain, "Sing, sing and be happy," or chant, "Everybody, everywhere, soft and slow." A few chords on the piano or autoharp can give children and teachers alike a chance to relax and calm themselves. Teachers may use center time to introduce a new song or sing a refrain of a familiar song.

Center choices make music available in other ways. In the music center, children can make and listen to music or play with musical instruments. They may make up a play or opera using felt figures and a flannel board (Andress, 1995b). And outdoors, rhythm instruments, drums, and circle games that involve rhymes and song are indispensable.

Transition times are eased with the sound of music. During cleanup time, teachers sing "Picking up blocks, putting on a shelf" instead of "Picking up paw paws, putting in a basket." A couple of songs, chants, or finger plays smooth those in-between times—between a snack and going outside or waiting for a resource teacher.

The day closes with song. Singing "Today was Wednesday, what did we do to-day?" helps teachers and children reflect on and summarize the activities of the day. And when children are ready to leave, good-bye songs are sung—"Good-bye everybody, yes indeed, yes indeed! Good-bye Trisha, good-bye Dimintri, good-bye everybody," letting each child know that they are valued, respected members of the kindergarten.

Just because music surrounds children throughout their day does not mean that music is not given a special place in the curriculum (Wolf, 2000). Each day, time is set aside for music. During this time, the goals and objectives of the music program—those of increasing children's musical skills and understanding and extending their interest in music and their ability to create, make, and enjoy music—are fostered.

THE VALUES OF MUSIC

Music's prominent place in the kindergarten is based on the value of music to children's growth and learning. The values of music are many and varied. Research and theory document the following:

◆ Music has intrinsic and instrumental value in and of itself. Music is critical to human development and to creative thought.

◆ Music can also be used to present ideas and build concepts, teach or persuade, entertain, design, plan, beautify, and create (Consortium of National Arts Education Associations [CNAEA], 1994).

◆ Music plays a valued role in creating cultures and building civilizations. Music awakens children to folk arts and their influence on their own lives and the lives of others (CNAEA, 1994).

◆ Music is a social activity. Listening to music and singing or dancing together unites children. Individuals come to feel a part of the community when singing together.

◆ Music is another way of knowing, another symbolic mode of thought and expression. From the enactive and iconic mode of knowing and learning about the world through action, perception, and imagery, music grows to become a symbolic mode of learning.

MUSIC AND READING READINESS SKILLS

Learning to Read Through the Arts (O'Brien, 1999) demonstrates that music fosters many of the skills necessary for learning to read, including the following:

◆ Auditory discrimination—hearing the differences in sounds, rhythms, and words.

◆ Auditory memory—remembering melodies and songs.

◆ Vocabulary development—introducing new musical as well as other vocabulary words.

◆ Understanding syntax and grammar—songs may begin in one tense and end in another.

◆ Story sequence—stories, songs, operas, and symphonies have a beginning, a middle, and an end.

◆ Phonemic awareness—recognizing beginning and ending sounds and rhyming words.

◆ Word segmentation—learning that words are segmented from sentences and that these may be segmented for effect.

◆ Music gives children unique opportunities to create and be fluent in their thinking. They can respond in unique ways to listening or moving to music and create new songs and rhymes.

◆ Music gives children the opportunity to express their feelings and ideas freely as they dance in the light of a sunbeam, pound a drum, or sing a song of joy.

◆ Music is mathematical. The rhythmic quality of music fosters children's ability to keep time and count sequences.

◆ Music is physical. Children sway, clap, dance, or stomp to music, gaining control over their bodies. Even singing is a physical activity that requires the ability to control muscles, vocal chords, and breathing.

◆ Music benefits children with special needs. Because music is a pleasurable, non-threatening experience, it can be used to help a special needs child feel more comfortable within the group.

◆ Music develops the skills necessary for learning to read and write (Andress, 1995a). The Music and Reading Readiness Skills box on page 185 describes how and why music is necessary for the development of reading readiness skills.

MUSIC DEVELOPS

Because aptitude for music seems to stabilize around age nine (Gordon, 1990), the early years are considered critical to the development of the child's potential for comprehending and producing music. In a rich musical environment with appropriate guidance from adults, four- and five-year-old children learn to perceive, initiate, and discriminate among rhythm and tonal patterns with increasing precision. They form concepts of musical syntax while assimilating music concepts into personal music making, beginning a lifetime of understanding, performing, and enjoying music (Gordon, 1990).

Rhythm and Movement Develop

From the random movements of the infant and the spontaneous swaying and bouncing to music of the toddler develop the fairly complex dancelike movements of four- and five-year-olds.

Four- and five-year-olds are motivated to move to music, but their movements are not always synchronized to music in response to a steady beat, rhythmic qualities, or overall musical effect (Stellaccio & McCarthy, 1999). They can move fast or slow and stop and turn with some smoothness and control over their bodies, but they still have difficulty understanding that a relationship exists between the sounds they hear and what their muscles do. When left on their own, children tend to limit their movements, repeating a few patterns.

Four-year-olds can manage to keep a beat with clapping or rhythm sticks but still have difficulty with simple motor rhythmic tasks at a fast tempo, or with simultaneous tasks, such as moving and singing (Holohan, 1987; Rainbow & Owen, 1979).

Five-year-olds have learned to move to music with more smoothness, refinement, and rhythm. They have a greater understanding of height, weight, distance, and depth and can skip, run, and catch a ball or even something as delicate as a soap bubble without breaking it.

Four-year-olds can begin to keep time to music.

Expressively, five-year-olds are able to use movement in symbolic ways. They can express an idea, a feeling, or an emotion through a movement. They can create a dance, a skit, or a play to symbolize their feelings and experiences. Together the imagination and thinking involved in moving creatively, along with control of motor skills, permit symbolic expression (Seefeldt & Barbour, 1998).

Listening to Music Develops

Everyone, at any age, can enjoy listening to music. All they need to do is attend, perceive, relax, and enjoy (McGirr, 1995). If four-year-olds have had sufficient background experiences with music, they can listen attentively, picking out sounds of specific instruments from a recording if they have been introduced to the instrument. They enjoy making their own sounds as they listen to music, applying concepts of loud, soft, happy, sad, light, heavy, fast, or slow (Louks, 1974).

Five-year-olds advance from making gross discriminations in sounds to making fine discriminations. They are able to listen to a story song, piano selection, or recording of an orchestra and can discuss the performance and their listening experience as well (Music Educators National Conference [MENC], 1994).

Kindergarten children seem to enjoy listening to all musical styles (Sims, 1986). Some have found that five-year-olds prefer popular music to classical (Greer, Dorrow, Wachhaus, & White, 1973). This preference has been related to social learning theory (Stellaccio & McCarthy, 1999). Repeated exposure to music, social learning, and the qualities of music seem to affect children's preference for music. Just hearing a specific type of music over and over does not seem to affect children's listening preferences (Schuckert & McDonald, 1968), but the approval and support of adults and teachers does seem to have a positive influence on children's musical preferences (Callihan & Commings, 1985).

Singing Develops

Singing seems natural for four- and five-year-olds who, skipping along, break into song, chanting, "Skip, skip skip, up, down, up down," or digging in the sand, accompanying the activity with "Sandy cup, sandy cup, filling up, up, up!" These chants are not true songs but consist of a repeated tone or begin with a repeated tone and end with a descending third. The rhythm begins in 2/4 time and ends in 6/8. Their chants are generally accompanied by physical, rhythmic movement, such as walking, hopping, pounding, rocking, or splashing water, and are reminiscent of those of Native American dance rituals, Haitian voodoo chants, or the early litanies of the Christian Church (Moorehead & Pond, 1941).

Even though they break into spontaneous chants, kindergarten children still have difficulty carrying a tune. Generally, they are midrange singers and will be able to match some of the pitches. Some do so with ease, whereas others need further experiences and sometimes hard work to "find" themselves in terms of singing. Some can sing alone and seem to carry a pitch better when singing alone than with a group.

Fostering Kindergarten Children's Progress in Creating and Making Music

Fostering and making music includes the following:

◆ Knowledge of national standards in order to select appropriate goals and objectives for music in the kindergarten
◆ Designing music activities in moving, listening, and singing that promote children's skills, knowledge, and attitudes toward music

NATIONAL STANDARDS AND GOALS OF MUSIC EDUCATION

The standards for music education established by the Consortium of National Arts Education Associations (1994) describe in operational terms the value and importance of music for the educational well-being of children and our nation. The standards, which are stated for kindergarten through grade 4, offer kindergarten teachers a framework for designing their movement, listening to music, and singing curriculum.

At the end of kindergarten, all children should be able to do the following:

◆ Identify and demonstrate eight basic locomotor movements: run, walk, hop, jump, leap, gallop, slide, and skip
◆ Be able to travel forward, backward, and turn at high, low, and middle levels

◆ Understand that dance is a way to create and communicate meaning
◆ Use critical thinking skills as they explore, discover, and realize the multiple ways dance can be used to express themselves
◆ Enjoy listening to a variety of music forms
◆ Be able to identify simple music forms
◆ Identify the sounds of different instruments from various cultures as well as children's voices from male and female adult voices
◆ Sing a varied musical repertoire alone and with others
◆ Improvise melodies, variations, and accompaniments
◆ Understand that songs are written as well as sung

Movement

Movement seems a part of the very being of four- and five-year-olds. Four-year-olds dart and dash about the room and playyard; five-year-olds seem to skip, hop, and twirl rather than walk. Do these perpetual motion machines really need instruction in learning to move? Obviously, they need space in which to move and the freedom to do so, but in kindergarten, children can learn to control their movements, connecting them to music, and to use movement to express their feelings, thoughts, and ideas.

Begin by following the natural movements of four-year-olds. Rather than asking them to move to music or to move across the room as bears or ducks, teachers begin by building on the child's own natural movements. They may follow a child's walk with a drumbeat, saying, "This is how your feet sounded when you ran across the floor, listen" or "This is the way your body went when you rolled over and over," repeating the sounds with a drum or other rhythm instrument.

Talk about the way children move. Observe and think about how the child moved. General comments such as "Good" or "Nice" do not help children understand their movements or name them. You might use words to describe the movements, such as "heavy," "strong," "light," "fast," or "slow"—"Your toes go so lightly over the floor"—or talk about the direction of the movement (up, down, or low) or how the child used the space; for example, did he or she travel throughout the space or stand in the same spot moving only his or her body?

Introduce music gradually, beginning by using the children's own ideas and letting them establish their own pace. With four-year-olds, you can start by introducing them to the sound of one instrument at a time. Children might be asked to move to the sound of a drum, tonal block, or triangle. One teacher, sitting on the floor with a small group of children, began to shake a maraca. She asked, "How does this sound make you want to move?" "Wiggle, wiggle," the children said, and they wiggled as they sat. Then she asked them to stand up and, pretending that they were glued to the floor, wiggle different parts of their bodies. Changing rhythms and the intensity of the sounds, she asked them to wiggle or move to the sound using the entire room. Then she asked them to stop when the maraca did. Over time other instruments were introduced in the same way so that children would become familiar with making their bodies move to different sounds. Throughout, the teacher named the sounds of the instruments and children's movements, introducing the words "loud," "soft," "fast," "slow," "staccato," "gentle," "legato," and so on.

Connect children's enactive experiences to the symbolic by asking them to draw themselves as they move to different sounds. You might shoot videos so that individual children can observe their own movements and have a base for representing these in their drawing and painting.

This introduction to moving to sounds is necessary before asking children to move to music, which is a complex process. Children must first have knowledge of different sounds and the ability to distinguish between them and to name and conceptualize their movements (Schoon, 1998).

Props may be useful. One teacher of four-year-olds gave the children a ball to roll. Sitting in a circle on the floor, the children rolled a ball back and forth while the teacher followed the rhythm of the rolling and the stopping of the ball with a drum. Five-year-olds might be given balls to bounce to the rhythm of a song, holding the balls on certain phases, bouncing them for others, or bouncing them steadily to the beat of a drum.

Five-year-olds enjoy shadow movement play. With a strong light, perhaps using a slide projector light to highlight a wall in a semidarkened room, children can move in front of the light, observing their shadows on the wall. Children can move by themselves, or with partners, to music, or to the beat of a drum while the others watch.

Moving symbolically grows from children's iconic and enactive experiences of moving to sounds or the beat of an instrument. For children to dance or move symbolically as if they were an animal or a sailboat or to dance as if they were birds, they must first have observed and experienced these things. Children have visited the zoo and observed animals moving, have watched vehicles move in the traffic stream, or have had vicarious experiences observing animals or other things in their world on television, in the movies, or on the computer.

Supporting children's moving from the enactive to symbolic, teachers may suggest ideas. They might ask children to pick an animal they saw at the zoo and move as if they were that animal or to move as if they were happy, sad, or walking underwater. Finally, five-year-olds could be asked to dance or move to a story, perhaps a musical one, such as *Peter and the Wolf*, or to create a dance that will tell a story of their own.

Listening

Listening, a part of every musical experience, is far from a passive experience. Listening to music means being able to attend, perceive, think, and reason. Research suggests that most four- and five-year-olds are ready to listen to music. They are able to:

◆ attend to music, but not to more than one element at a time
◆ learn to make and label single discriminations and be receptive to learning and using language to describe music
◆ make discriminations on the basis of their own performance before they are able to make discriminations in listening situations (Sims, 1986)

What sounds do you hear? In the room, on the playyard, or during a walk through the neighborhood, take time to listen. Stop and ask children what they hear. Do they hear a cricket singing in their room? What song does it sing? What does it mean? Stop to listen to the songs of cicadas in the trees in early fall or the sound of crows cawing to each other.

Five-year-olds might keep a sound journal. Through sketching or writing, they could keep a record of the sounds they heard during the day and what the sounds reminded them of and a drawing of what made the sound. Some may even use their imaginations to draw the sounds they heard (Rubin & Merrion, 1995).

Four-year-olds, with their love of the sounds of silly language, enjoy listening to silly songs, nursery rhymes, and expandable songs like "Wheels on the Bus," "There Was an Old Lady," or "The Ants Go Marching."

With an extensive background in listening to music, most five-year-olds are able to enjoy listening to short story music, such as *Peter and the Wolf, The Sorcerer's Apprentice*, or parts of *Swan Lake*.

Because you want children to be active listeners, the use of background music during activity or rest time should be carefully considered. Some say that background music teaches children to tune out music rather than to learn to listen to and enjoy music.

Rhythm instruments were developed for use in the kindergarten by Patty Smith Hill and Anna Bryan, who believed that through the use of found objects, such as rhythm instruments, children would learn to explore a variety of sounds, learn to discriminate between these sounds, and develop the skills of listening to music.

To effectively utilize rhythm bands to increase children's listening skills, you will need at least a few good rhythm band instruments. Purchased tone blocks, a step xylophone, bells, and good drums offer children quality sounds and are probably necessary if children are to distinguish between sounds. Rhythm band instruments can be constructed by the children, and often, when they participate in making these, their interest increases. The music resource teacher in the school or system office may be able to provide professional instruments and help you and the children make others.

The instruments, whether purchased or made, are used to create music, not just to make noise. Children are introduced to one instrument at a time and for a specific purpose. For instance, children may take turns accompanying a song with the beat of a drum or rhythm sticks. Add bells, sand blocks, and other instruments and practice these until children are familiar with all the instruments and the sounds they make. You might ask children which instruments they would choose to accompany parts of songs. For instance, children might suggest using sand blocks to accompany singing the song "Scraping Up Sand, Shiloh, Shiloh" or bells to accompany singing "Twinkle, Twinkle, Little Star." As children explore the instruments, ask them the following:

◆ How many of the instruments make a striking sound?
◆ Which produce ringing sounds?
◆ Which make scraping sounds?
◆ How can the instruments be used to produce long, short, or smooth sounds?

A full band, with each child playing an instrument, is the end result. Shoot a video of the children's band. Listening to and viewing the video will help children evaluate their playing and gain skills in listening.

Having created their own band, children will be ready to listen to CDs or tapes and records of performances by musicians. Taping just a segment of a popular opera, musical, or symphony, perhaps one conducted by Billy McFarren, will offer children an appropriate listening experience. Visits from musicians, professionals, or older children who play a violin, viola, trumpet, or other instrument expand children's interest in listening to music and knowledge of how music is made.

Throughout all of children's experiences with listening to music, the vocabulary of music should be used. Talk about the sounds that are made using the vocabulary of music. Children are first able to understand the concept of loudness and distinguish loud from soft sounds. Next they are able to distinguish duration from pitch. Even five-year-olds, however, will still confuse the terms "high," "loud," and "fast" and "low," "soft," and "slow."

Singing

"This little cup of mine, I'm going fill it up, fill it up, all the time," five-year-old Tonja sings to the tune of "This Little Light of Mine" as she plays in the sand. In the same sandbox, Alberto sings, "Oh beautiful, for spacious skies, for amber waves of grain," demonstrating that all kinds of songs and every type of music are sung and enjoyed by young children.

Singing gives children pleasure. Perhaps it is the joy of the sounds or making them, or perhaps it is something deeper, rooted in culture and the need to be become one with a group. For whatever reason, kindergarten children fill their day with song.

Singing together gives children great pleasure.

Children enjoy nearly every kind of song, especially those about themselves and their day. "Mary Wore a Red Dress," "What Should We Do When We All Go Out?," "Here Is a Friend," and "Get on Board Little Children" are favorites, as are other songs about themselves, their parents, their homes, and their neighborhoods.

Folk tunes and nursery rhymes such as "Skip to My Lou," "If You're Happy," and "Johnny Works With One Hammer" are enjoyed. Lullabies, humorous songs ("There Was an Old Lady Who Swallowed a Fly" and "The Ants Go Marching"), and action songs that children can dance, stomp to, or act out are all enjoyed. Counting and alphabet songs ("A You're Adorable") and the familiar ABC song are all a part of kindergarten children's repertoires.

Four- and five-year-olds especially enjoy singing baby songs. When families or teachers have a new baby, it is fun to make a book of "baby songs" to give to the new baby. While experiencing the continuity of life, children feel grown up and important giving this gift to the new baby.

Also part of children's repertoires are patriotic songs ("America," "America the Beautiful," "This Land Is Your Land," and "Yankee Doodle") and traditional folk songs ("Hokey Pokey," "Row, Row, Row Your Boat," "Paw Paw Patch," "Skip to My Lou," and "She'll Be Coming 'Round the Mountain"). Ballads ("Go Tell Aunt Rhody," "On Top of Old Smoky," and "Down in the Valley") and many others are equally as popular with kindergarten children (Silbert, 1998).

Every culture has its own traditional folk songs. By introducing these to children, teachers not only show their respect and value for the culture of others but also demonstrate to children that all cultures are united through song and music (Kendall, 1996). One teacher introduced children to Chinese folk songs by inviting a new mother and baby to the class. The mother sang traditional Chinese lullabies to her new baby. Later the sibling taught some of these to the entire kindergarten class. Another asked a father from the Ukraine to sing and dance traditional Ukrainian songs to the children. He attempted to teach the boys how to do the traditional dances.

Teaching New Songs.   A new song can be introduced in a number of ways. Some songs lend themselves to being introduced or sung spontaneously. As children arrive, it is natural to sing, "Here is Martena, here is Martena! How are you today?" or on a rainy day to sing, "Rain, rain, go away, what should we do today?" When children leave, teachers sing, "Good-bye everybody, yes indeed, yes indeed. Good-bye Sasha, good-bye Vanessa, good-bye Fredis, good-bye everybody."

Songs are sung spontaneously during center time as well. During February, which was designated in one kindergarten as the "Songs of Love Month," the teacher introduced children to the song "Love Somebody" by singing it during center time. She sang the whole song to the children during music time and asked them to listen to the song again as she sang and played it on the piano and to think about whom they loved.

Then she had them participate in an echo game, singing a phrase of the song, "Love somebody, yes I do," and asking the children to be her echo by singing the phrase back to her. The next day at center time, she sang "Love Somebody" again while the children were working. A number joined in, and all giggled and smiled, knowing that she was singing about them. That morning during singing time, she had the children play a "your turn, my turn" game. She sang the first phrase, "Love somebody, yes I do, love somebody, yes I do," then, pausing, had the children sing the next phrase, "Love somebody, won't say who!" The following day, the children joined her in singing the entire song while she played the piano.

"But I can't sing! I can't teach children to sing," a new teacher says. Observe in a kindergarten for a moment. Ms. Ramos sits on a low chair next to the piano, calling children to come and sit with her using the same chanting style that children sing—"Anna, Anna, come and sit with me" or "Jose, Jose, come and sit with me." As the children join her, using an autoharp, Ms. Ramos plays a chord and sings children's names, again in a chanting voice. "Here comes Aletha, here is Alberto, how are you today?"

Today she is introducing a new song. She has been singing it to herself for several days, and last night she sang it to her roommate. Now she sings it again. Instead of playing the autoharp, she uses the tone blocks to help keep her voice in range. She sings the song all the way through, then repeats it once more. The children begin singing with her—some that is. Tomorrow she will sing the song again during center time and at singing time.

Even teachers who are unsure of their singing voice have found that they are more than able to sing with children. As Montessori suggested, they "sing with them, and they'll sing with you and you'll sing together as you march along."

Among the techniques teachers have used to help them develop confidence in their own singing are the following:

- Introducing the song using a CD or other recording.
- Making sure that they practice the song before presenting it to the children, learning it thoroughly. One teacher asked the music resource teacher to work with her as she learned new songs.
- Teaching the song to a few of the children who are able to carry a tune. Children who are natural singers can lead the teacher.
- Using some sort of instrument—an autoharp or a tonal block—to help keep the voice in range.
- Using hand motions; that is, moving the hand up or down following the melody of the song.

As you and the children sing together, introduce them to reading and writing music. At times you might show children music in the book or write a couple of stanzas of a favorite song on a chart and follow the notes as you sing the song. Other times you might chart children's spontaneous chants such as saying, "This is the way your song looks when it's written. Now others can read and sing it too." When children sing the song or chant, follow them by placing your hand under the note on the chart.

Making class books of children's favorite songs is another way to introduce kindergarten children to the idea that music is written. One teacher copied a few children's favorite songs and made booklets for each child to take home. A letter about the songs and how parents could use them at home was included in the booklet.

EVALUATING AND ASSESSING CHILDREN'S MUSICAL DEVELOPMENT

The national standards for music education offer a framework for evaluating and assessing children's growth in moving and listening to and singing music. A combination of observing children and asking them to perform specific musical skills can be designed.

At the beginning, during the middle, and at the end of the kindergarten year, ask individual children to demonstrate the following skills identified by the National Council of Music Educators. Here is an example of a chart you might use to record your observations of children's performance.

Name	Date	Skill	Level		
			High	Medium	Low
		Run			
		Walk			
		Hop			
		Jump			
		Leap			
		Gallop			
		Slide			
		Skip			
	Traveling forward				
	backward				
	turning at high, low, and middle levels				

On another day, select a recording of a familiar song or piece of music and ask individual children whether they can identify the sounds of different instruments. At the same time, you might also ask them to identify different types of songs and music. Playing a nursery rhyme, a folk tune, and a classical piece of music, ask them to tell you what kind of music is being played.

Observing children's spontaneous use of music will be necessary as well. You will want to observe and record the following:

◆ How individual children approach music. Do they choose to play with musical instruments, or do they listen to songs during center time?
◆ Whether they sing and chant alone as they work and play together.
◆ Which children improvise melodies, variations, and accompaniments to music.
◆ How children are using movement and dance to communicate their feelings and ideas.
◆ The critical thinking skills that individual children use as they explore, discover, and realize the multiple ways that music and dance can be used to express themselves.

Observe how children approach music.

◆ Whether children are demonstrating their understanding that songs are written as well as sung by writing their own songs or pointing to musical notes on a chart or in a book.
◆ Which children are expanding their ability to attend to, enjoy, and listen to music.

Find ways to include your observations in children's portfolios. You might videotape children's movements and dance or a song or chant they have sung and include a copy in their portfolio. Digital photos of individuals dancing, performing, or creating music or playing musical instruments could be included.

With each photograph or video recording, add some form of written explanation of the skill or ability the child is demonstrating. Record the date and time along with a narrative describing the importance of the observation: "This photograph shows Elisa playing the autoharp during center time. It is the first time she approached a musical instrument on her own. After experimenting for a while, she found the two notes corresponding to the tune of the name song we sing each morning. She then sang the names of several children."

IN SUMMARY

You do not have to be a musician or an artist yourself to enjoy music with children. Closely tied to children's growth and development, music is a joy! Music serves to lighten the day, lift spirits, and bring pleasure. Music is an integral part of children's growth and development but also an integral part of the kindergarten curriculum.

Music takes place spontaneously throughout the day as children and teachers sing and chant songs to one another or to themselves. A center where children can play, listen to, or make music is central. Finally, time each day is set aside for children to sing together and gain specific listening, moving, and singing skills.

Music, valuable in and of itself, is critical for the development of symbolic and creative problem-solving skills, reading readiness, social skills, and motor development and other skills, attitudes, and knowledge.

The early years are considered critical for the development of children's musical abilities and attitudes. In the kindergarten, teachers focus on teaching children to move to music, to listen, and to sing. Moving seems natural to kindergarten children, but through planned activities children will learn to coordinate their movements with music and sound.

Everyone at any age can enjoy listening to music. In the kindergarten, listening activities expand to asking children to pick out the sounds of specific instruments and to listen to the music they make. By the end of five-year-old kindergarten, children will be able to listen to short musical stories or other music.

Singing takes place throughout the day. During music time, however, children's musical knowledge is expanded with the introduction of new songs, songs from other cultures, and songs they themselves have created.

Even though they are not musicians themselves, kindergarten teachers find ways of introducing new songs to children and singing with children. They study and sing the songs to themselves or their roommates before introducing them to children and use the support of music resource people in the school.

EXTEND YOUR IDEAS

1. Find out what the goals for kindergarten music education are in your district or state. Obtain a copy of the standards and compare and contrast the goal statements. Which of the goals would be appropriate for guiding four- and five-year-old kindergarten curricula?

2. With a partner, select two songs from cultures other than your own. Each of you learn one of the songs and then teach it to the other. Can you draw conclusions that would be useful in teaching these and other songs to kindergarten children?

3. Begin a collection of songs that kindergarten children love. Talk to kindergarten teachers to find out their favorite songs and consult songbooks and other resources. Collect CDs or other recordings of songs that children would enjoy listening to. Include songs from diverse cultures.

4. Develop your own musical abilities. Attend a concert, opera, or dance or musical recital at your university.

Resources

Contact the National Endowment for the Arts, *http://www.arts.endow.gov/pub* for free or inexpensive resources used for teaching the arts.

The National Association for Music Education, *http://www.menc.org/,* offers a wide range of resources for teachers.

The National Standards for Arts Education are found at *http://www.artsedge.kennedy-center.org.*

References

Andress, B. (1995a). Music is beginning. In M. E. Ramsey (Ed.), *It's music* (pp. 15–18). Washington, DC: National Association for the Education of Young Children.

Andress, B. (1995b). Transforming curriculum in music. In S. Bredekamp & T. Rosegrant (Eds.), *Reaching potentials: Transforming the early childhood curriculum* (Vol. 2, pp. 99–108). Washington, DC: National Association for the Education of Young Children.

Callihan, D. J., & Commings, D. (1985). Expanding the music listening preferences of 3–4-year-olds. In J. Boswell (Ed.), *The young child and music* (pp. 79–82). Reston, VA: Music Educators National Conference.

Cohen, M. D., & Hoot, J. L. (1998). Educating through the arts: An introduction. *Childhood Education, 73,* 338–341.

Consortium of National Arts Education Associations. (1994). *National standards for arts education: What every young American should know and be able to do in the arts.* Reston, VA: Author.

Gordon, E. E. (1990). *A music learning theory for newborn and young children.* Chicago: G.I.A. Publications.

Greer, R. D., Dorrow, L., Wachhaus, G., & White, E. R. (1973). Adult approval of elementary school children. *Journal of Research in Music Education, 21*(1), 26–32.

Hildebrandt, C. (1998). Creativity in music and early childhood. *Young Children, 53*(6), 68–74.

Holohan, J. (1987). Toward a theory of music syntax: Some observations of music babble in young children. In I. W. Perry, J. C. Perry, & T. W. Draper

(Eds.), *Music and child development* (pp. 142–155). Reston, VA: Music Educators National Conference.

Kendall, F. E. (1996). *Diversity in the classroom.* New York: Teachers College Press.

Louks, D. G. (1974). *The development of an instrument to measure instrumental timbre concepts of four-year-old and five-year-old children: A feasibility study.* Unpublished doctoral dissertation, Ohio State University.

McGirr. (1995). Verdi invades the kindergarten. *Childhood Education, 71,* 74–80.

Moorehead, G., & Pond, D. (1941). *Music for young children.* Santa Barbara, CA: Pillsbury Foundation for the Advancement of Music Education.

Moravicik, E. W. (2000). Music all the livelong day. *Young Children, 55*(4), 27–32.

Music Educators National Conference. (1994). *MENC position statement on early childhood education.* Reston, VA: Author.

O'Brien, B. (1999). *Learning to read through the arts.* Glenn Rock, NJ: Learning to Read Through the Arts.

Rainbow, E. L., & Owen, D. (1979). A progress report on a three-year investigation of the rhythmic ability of preschool age children. *Bulletin of the Council for Research in Music Education, 59,* 84–86.

Rubin, J., & Merrion, M. (1995). *Drama and music: Creative activities for young children.* Atlanta: Humanics.

Schoon, S. (1998). Using dance experience and drama in the classroom. *Childhood Education, 74,* 78–82.

Schuckert, R. F., & McDonald, R. L. (1968). An attempt to modify the musical preferences of preschool children. *Journal of Research in Music Education, 16*(1), 39–44.

Seefeldt, C., & Barbour, N. (1998). *Early childhood education: An introduction* (4th ed.). Upper Saddle River, NJ: Merrill/Prentice Hall.

Silbert, J. (1998). *I can't sing book.* Beltsville, MD: Gryphon Publishing House.

Sims, W. L. (1986). The effects of high versus low teacher affect and passive versus active student activity during music listening on preschool children's attention. *Journal of Research in Music Education, 34*(3), 173–191.

Stellaccio, C. K., & McCarthy, M. (1999). Research in early childhood music and movement education. In C. Seefeldt (Ed.), *The early childhood curriculum: Current findings in theory and practice* (3rd ed, pp. 179–201). New York: Teachers College Press.

Tarnowski, S. M., & Leclerc, J. (1994). Musical play of preschoolers and teacher-child interaction. *Update: Applications of Research in Music Education, 13*(1), 9–16.

Wolf, J. (2000). Sharing songs with children. *Young Children, 55*(2), 28–32.

CHAPTER 11

Literacy Learning for Four- and Five-Year-Olds

"Do you want me to read you a story?" four-year-old Tim asks Kelly as he settles into a beanbag chair in the library corner. "You can't read, and besides, that book only has pictures," says Kelly. "Yes, I can read it," says Tim as he opens the wordless book and begins, "Once upon a time, there was a dog, and he was very big."

Although neither Tim nor Kelly can actually "read" these books, this exchange between Tim and Kelly demonstrates the different understandings that young children have of literacy as they grow and interact with books. Tim clearly understands that books are for reading and that people talk and say things when they are looking at a book. "Once upon a time" is a common beginning to stories that he has heard. Kelly has a more sophisticated understanding of literacy. She understands that words and not pictures are read. She also is beginning to understand that the words on the page represent specific messages and not what the reader wants it to say. Like these young emergent readers, children who have many opportunities to "read" and have books read to them develop the necessary literacy skills to learn to read and write.

This chapter includes (1) a discussion of the important aspects of literacy, (2) a discussion of the importance of language development in literacy development, (3) a description of the experiences and knowledge children need in order to develop literacy skills, (4) a presentation of the literacy expectations for four- and five-year-olds, and (5) a discussion of whole language and phonics instruction in relation to early literacy development. In Chapter 12, on language arts, we will discuss how literacy and literacy experiences are integrated in the early learning classroom.

UNDERSTANDING LITERACY

For teachers of young children, there are some important aspects to literacy that need to be explained. First, literacy encompasses more than just reading. Literacy is the development of reading and writing skills as well as the creative and analytic acts involved in producing and comprehending text (Burns, Griffin, & Snow, 1998). Children learn to read by writing and learn to write through reading.

Second, literacy development begins long before children begin formal instruction in reading. As we will discuss in detail in this chapter, children bring with them to school many concepts about literacy and certain competencies in oral language, writing, and reading (Burns et al., 1998). All these experiences contribute to literacy development. Although it is not the role of early childhood teachers to formally teach reading, the literacy experiences provided to four- and five-year-olds will affect how ready they are to benefit from formal reading instruction.

Third, learning to read and write is critical to children's success in school (Bowman, Donovan, & Burns, Bowman, Donovan, & Burns, 2001). One of the best predictors of whether a child will function competently in school is the level to which the child progresses in reading and writing. Although reading and writing abilities continue to develop throughout the life span, the literacy experiences for four- and five-year-olds set a critical foundation for future literacy development. Because of the importance of reading in children's development, it is necessary to understand the important factors that affect children's reading.

THE DEVELOPMENT OF LITERACY

Before a child learns to walk, she learns to crawl, cruises around furniture, and pulls to stand. Before a child speaks her first word, she babbles, coos, and plays with sounds. Similarly, before a child learns to read and write, she must develop certain abilities that set the foundation for literacy acquisition. One of the most important precursors to the development of literacy is language development (Snow & Tabors, 1993). Language sets the stage for literacy development. As four- and five-year-olds become more adept with language and have access to language and literacy experiences, they develop other abilities that are directly related to learning to read and write. Phonemic awareness, the development of letter knowledge, and an understanding of print are three other essential abilities that children need to acquire in order for them to be ready to benefit from formal reading instruction (Snow, Burns, & Griffin, 1998; Whitehurst & Lonigan, 1998).

As teachers of young children, it is important to understand that the development of all these abilities—language, phonemic awareness, and an understanding of print and letter knowledge—are not mutually exclusive and that a causal relationship may exist among these abilities (Dickinson & Snow, 1987). As children grow and develop, these abilities become interrelated to form the basis of literacy.

LANGUAGE DEVELOPMENT AS THE FOUNDATION FOR LITERACY

Literacy begins with the development of language (Dickinson & Snow, 1987; Dickinson & Tabors, 2001). From the first months of life, children begin to experiment with language. Babies coo, squeal, and babble. By the time children reach three years of age, they typically have 2,000 to 4,000 words in their vocabulary and begin to understand the structure of language. Four- and five-year-olds are speaking in three- to four-word sentences and making their wants and needs known through language. In order for language and literacy skills to be cultivated in young children, two essential experiences need to occur. Children need to talk with and listen to others, and they need to read with others.

Language is a social construct. Children learn language from interacting with the others around them (Neuman & Rosko, 1997). Four-year-old Sally points to the finger puppets in her classroom and says, "What's that?" Her teacher, Ms. Fast, says, "What does it look like to you?" "They look like mittens with heads," replied Sally. "Yes, they do!" says Ms. Fast, validating Sally's understanding of the puppets. "They are finger puppets, and you can play with them in this puppet theater. Watch Jason and Leah use these finger puppets to put on their show." "Finger puppets," repeated Sally. "I like them."

Through this brief conversation with Sally, Ms. Fast is helping Sally learn new words. Ms. Fast did not simply provide Sally with a label for the finger puppets and end the interchange there. Instead, she engaged Sally in a conversation about the finger puppets, allowing Sally's understanding of the puppets to evolve from her experience. Learning vocabulary and understanding the structure of natural language occurs as a result of conversations such as the one between Sally and Ms. Fast.

Teachers can interact with children in the following ways to provide opportunities to develop language skills:

◆ Respond to children's questions beyond yes/no answers.
◆ Rephrase and elaborate on your children's words. For example, the child says, "That's a kitty," and the adult responds, "Yes, that's a Siamese kitty. Look at its beautiful stripes."
◆ Model more complex vocabulary or sentence structures.
◆ Ask questions that allow children to clarify their statements.

These strategies often take time and patience, yet they will allow children to use language and receive feedback on the things that they say.

Reading with children is an essential component to developing language and literacy skills with young children. In particular, reading stories to young children provides opportunities to develop *decontextualized language* (Dickinson & Snow, 1987). Decontextualized language is language that conveys information distinct from content. For example, reading the book *The Little Engine Who Could* teaches children who would never have the opportunity to see or hear about a train to do so as well as learn words such as "engine," "tracks," and "steam." Books bring aspects to a child's world that they may not otherwise have the opportunity to experience. Reading books also provides opportunities for children to learn new vocabulary words and to hear language in a form other than the spoken word.

When reading books to young children, teachers do the following things to facilitate language and literacy development:

◆ Provide explanations and examples of new vocabulary words
◆ Ask open-ended questions to facilitate comprehension of the book
◆ Make connections between what happened in the book to what is happening in the lives of four- and five-year-olds
◆ Reread and retell books to reinforce comprehension and vocabulary development

PHONEMIC AWARENESS

According to a position statement by the International Reading Association, phonemic awareness is typically described as "insight about oral language and in particular about the segmentation of sounds that are used in speech communication" (International Reading Association [IRA], 1999). A child who possesses phonemic awareness understands that words are made up of sounds and that they can manipulate the sounds in words. A child with phonemic awareness skills can segment sounds in words. For example, he can pronounce the first sound in the word "top" or produce a word that rhymes with "man."

The word "phonemic" is derived from the word "phoneme," which is the smallest unit of speech. In the word "cat," for example, there are three phonemes: /k/, /a/, and /t/. The other letters within a word determine the specific sound that a letter makes. By themselves, letters do not make specific sounds. For example, the letter /a/ makes a different sound in the word "cat" than it does in the word "late." Even consonant sounds change with the context, as with the difference in the /t/ sound in "cat" and "butter."

The "awareness" part of phonemic awareness is important because it implies the level of knowledge that children, especially four- and five-year-olds, should have of phonemes. Phonemic awareness is not the mastery of sounds in words but the awareness of those sounds in words (Yopp, 1992). Children can be aware of the sounds words make without knowing the letter or label for the sounds in words that rhyme. Understanding that two words sound the same, rhyme, or begin with the same letter sound is phonemic awareness.

Over the past 10 years, increasing emphasis has been placed on phonemic awareness and its relationship to reading (Hecht, Burgess, Torgesen, Wagner, & Rashotte, 2000; Torgesen & Davis, 1996; Wasik 2000, 2001). Research has demonstrated important findings about phonemic awareness:

◆ Phonemic awareness is highly predictive of success in learning to read and, in particular, in learning to decode words. Children who can hear the various sounds in words and who are able to manipulate sounds in words are more successful in learning to read.
◆ Children as young as three years old have been shown to possess phonemic awareness skills (Maclean, Bryant, & Bradley, 1987). Typically, four- and five-year-olds develop these skills.

Understanding that words sound the same, rhyme, or begin with the same letter, is phonemic awareness.

◆ Opportunities to play with language result in the development of phonemic awareness skills. Playing with language in the context of natural play can encourage children to attend to the sounds in words (Yopp, 1992).

As teachers of four- and five-year-olds, one of the most important facts about phonemic awareness that you need to understand is that *phonemic awareness is not phonics.* Phonemic awareness is a precursor to understanding letter sounds in words (Wasik, 2001). It is not the systematic presentation of phonics. Regardless of the method used to instruct children to read (whole language, systematic phonics, or a combination of the two approaches), children need a strong base in phonemic awareness.

How can children develop phonemic awareness skills? Providing children with countless opportunities to play with language and to hear the sounds in words will develop phonemic awareness skills. Nursery rhymes, poems, tongue twisters, and silly word games promote the development of phonemic awareness. Children need to have the chance to hear sounds and produce sounds that are familiar to them as well as to learn new sounds in words. Activities that support phonemic awareness will be presented in Chapter 12.

UNDERSTANDING PRINT

Children learn about print by interacting with books and other written material. The children described in the beginning of this chapter clearly have experience with print. Although they are at different stages in the development of their understanding of literacy, they are both *emergent readers* (Morrow, 1997). An emergent reader exhibits reading-related behaviors, especially prior to a child's achieving the capacity to read fluently and conventionally. A child who is pretending to read, although he or she cannot recognize or decode words, is a good example of an emergent reader. Being an emergent reader is an important step in the long complex process of learning how to read. Tim can "read" with expression and tell a story about the pictures by using expression and inflection as he reads. As an emergent reader, Kelly understands that print carries the message that you read and that books without words cannot be read in the traditional sense. Both children, through repeated experiences with print, are figuring out the function of print as it relates to reading.

One of the skills that emergent readers develop is *concepts about print.* This terminology was coined by Marie Clay (1993), a well-known expert on early literacy. Outlined in the following are the characteristics possessed by a child who has developed a good understanding of concepts about print or concepts about a book:

◆ Understands that a book is for reading
◆ Can identify the back from the front of a book as well as the top from the bottom
◆ Understands that print and not pictures carry the message
◆ Understands that you read print
◆ Understands that you read print from left to right

◆ Knows where one begins to read on a page
◆ Can identify what a title, author, and illustrator are

As children are read to and have opportunities to interact with print, they learn how print works before they actually learn to read. Tim held the book he was going to read in the correct position and knew to turn the pages as he read. What he had not yet acquired was an understanding that print carries the message. Kelly did understand this aspect of print. As children learn more about the concepts of print and understand that the print is what is read, they actually stop "pretend" reading and will say that they cannot read. Instead, they will ask an adult or an older child to read the book. Their understanding of reading has become very complex, and they are beginning to figure out what they know and what their skills are.

Environmental Print

"I'll give you my Toys Я Us coupon for your McDonald's coupon," Jeanne says to Leah as they play grocery in the dramatic play area. "I'll take the McDonald's coupon, and I want the Cherrios one, too," Leah said. Neither Leah nor Jeanne can actually "read" the words on the coupons. Instead, they are "reading" the symbols or logos that are commonly associated with these common places and products (Harste, Woodward, & Burke, 1984). In making the association between a concept and a familiar logo, children are learning that a group of letters makes up a word that can be read and provide information. This is called *environmental print.* When children are exposed to printed materials and made aware that print communicates a message, they begin to make associations between the logos and symbols and the words (Kuby & Aldridge, 1997).

The environmental print that children tend to know best appears on food containers, especially cereal, soup, milk, and cookies, and on detergent boxes and bottles. Among signs, they recognize fast-food restaurant logos, road signs, traffic signals, and popular store chains, supermarkets, and service stations (Orellana & Hernandez, 1999). Making children aware of print in their environment by labeling common classroom objects, such as blocks and crayons, and labeling the different classroom areas, such as dramatic play and art center, creates a print-rich environment. Opportunities to experience environmental print allow children to have access to literacy experiences and facilitate building the foundation for literacy.

LEARNING THE ALPHABET

Learning the alphabet is another aspect of learning about print. As children begin to attend to the print on a page, they also become interested in letters that make up words. Learning the alphabet is an essential component of literacy development (Ehri & McCormick, 1998). Although some children can read some words and recognize environmental print before they know the alphabet, children need to know the alphabet in order to eventually become an independent and fluent reader and writer. As research in the area of early literacy has repeatedly shown, children who can recognize and name the letters in the alphabet learn to read with less difficulty than children who do not know the alphabet (Wasik, 2001).

As adults, we recognize the letters of the alphabet instantaneously. However, to appreciate the difficulty of this task, think about trying to learn an alphabet, such as Greek or Roman, that we are not familiar with or trying to learn the numerous characters that are in the Japanese or Chinese language.

Young children are faced with a similar challenge when they first begin to learn the letters of the alphabet. How do children begin to figure out the differences between letters? Research suggests that children begin by identifying *distinctive features* of letters. The distinctive features of our alphabet are characteristics such as whether a line is straight or curved (as in the "I" or "C") or whether curves are opened or closed (as in the "C" or "O") (Gibson, 1969).

When young children begin to focus on letters, they often consider letters to be the same that share the same features. Areal was playing with the magnetic letters on the board, and her teacher asked her to describe what she was doing. Areal proudly responded, "I'm putting all the letters that look alike together. Do you see? I put the 'D' and 'O' together, and in this pile I put the 'M,' 'N,' and 'I'." Because children frequently focus on the features of letters that are the same, they often confuse one letter for another (Ehri & McCormick, 1998). It is very common for children to confuse an "E" with an "F" or a "T" or to confuse an "N" with an "M". Distinguishing letters from one another requires that the child pay close attention not only to how the letters are the same but also to how they are different. Thinking about how things are different is not typically how children view the world.

Not only is it difficult for children learning letters to distinguish among the features of the letters, but it is also difficult to sort out how the letter is oriented in space. This is why children confuse "W" and "M," "p" and "q," and "b" and "d." As children have multiple opportunities to experience letters, they begin to identify the fine distinctions between letters. They also are able to accurately make associations between the shape of the letter and its name.

As children learn the names of letters, they also learn the sounds of letters (Wasik, 2001a). Knowing the letter name provides an anchor for the children to learn the letter sounds. Letter names do not change; an "a" is always an "a." Letter sounds do change. The /a/ sound in "bat" is different from the /a/ sound in "bait." Letter sounds are based on the letters that are associated within a word. Making connections between letters and letter sounds is called *sound-symbol correspondence*. As children become more facile with letter names, they become more interested in understanding the sounds that letters make. Beth is listening to *Brown Bear, Brown Bear,* and she comments to the teacher, "My name begins with the same letter as 'brown' and 'bear,' and it sounds the same, too." It is this sounds-symbol correspondence that will help later when children are taught formal reading instruction (Schickendanz, 1999).

In learning letters, children typically follow this developmental sequence:

◆ Recognizing letters
◆ Producing letters
◆ Learning letter-sound associations

Children need to develop knowledge about the alphabet in order to use letter and letter-sound skills for reading.

Knowing letter names provides an anchor for learning letter sounds.

CREATING PRINT

As children become interested in books and print, they begin to understand that print, like language, carries a message (Sulzby, 1986). Young children are motivated to write in order to express their ideas and thoughts through print. Four-year-old Mary heard the story of *The Three Bears* and said that she wanted to write her own story about three dogs because she liked dogs better than bears. At the writing center in her classroom, she was able to write her own version and read it to her class.

Writing, like reading, develops over time as children have repeated experiences with print (Sulzby, 1986). It is important to recognize early on that children are writing or attempting to express themselves in print even though what they produce does not look like conventional print. A picture that tells a story, small squiggles on a page, or wavy lines across paper are all symbols of expression of the emergent writer. *Emergent writing* consists of writing-related activities and behaviors, especially those prior to a child's achieving the capacity to write fluently and conventionally (Fang, 1999).

Development of Writing

From Pictures to Letters.   Many children will write—represent a message using marks—long before they can form or even recognize letters. Research on emergent writing has shown that there is a developmental pattern that children

Many children write long before they can form or write letters.

frequently follow in learning to write (Sulzby, 1985). Young children typically begin to communicate through pictures and will then "read" what the picture says. As children become more aware of print, "picture writing" is followed by scribble writing or zigzags or loops across the page. It is almost as if this is what children think that adults are doing as they are writing with speed and accuracy.

Libby is figuring out this process of writing. Her writing is a combination of scribble writing, mock letters, and conventional letters. In her story about her trip to the zoo, she is not yet using letters to represent individual words. Instead, her mix of some conventional and nonconventional writing is used to communicate her story about the lions and how loud they roared. As Libby's knowledge of literacy develops, she will begin to understand that letters make up individual words. At this point, her writing will begin to reflect this understanding as she begins to transition to using letters to represent sounds in words. A simple capital "L" may represent the word "lion," or an "R" may represent the lion's roar.

For teachers of young children, it is important to understand the different stages that occur in learning to write so that each stage can be reinforced and encouraged.

Organizing Print on the Page.   As well as learning how letters are formed and how to write conventionally, children are also learning how print is organized on a page. Does it go from left to right, from right to left, or both, sweeping back and forth like a computer printer? Does it start at the top of the page and go down or does it start in the middle and go down and back up to the top? Almost all the print that young children have contact with in our culture reads left to right and begins at the top of the page and goes to the bottom (Fox & Saracho, 1990).

Even though most four- and five-year-olds understand how print is organized on a page, they do not translate these conventions of print when they are writing. Young children's writing often appears quite disorganized, and it is. Most four-year-olds do not write on paper in any systematic order. One explanation for this is that young children lack the concepts of space that would allow them to stick to one specific orientation even if they knew the conventions (Piaget & Inhelder, 1967). Often in writing their name, children will begin in the middle of the paper, perhaps writing the first three letters of their name, and then turn the paper to write the remaining letters on the other side or write the remaining letters on the top of the page. Through repeated experience with print and writing, children do begin to incorporate the conventions of print orientation into their writing.

Using lined paper is often seen as a way to help children orient their print. Advocates of using lined paper argue that by providing lines and boundaries for writing, children can begin to control the direction of the writing, where the writing falls in space, and the size of the print. The research on this issue is inconclusive. An equally compelling argument is for providing unlined paper and allowing the children to express themselves in whatever way they can. The conventions of writing will naturally develop as the children's ability to write becomes more sophisticated.

Invented Spelling.   Maggie gave her teacher a note that read, "I wus vry hpy at scol." What Maggie's note suggests to the teacher is that Maggie has a very sophisticated understanding of the relationship between sounds and letters and how they play out in words. What Maggie has done is use the sounds that she hears in the words to write the words. This strategy is often called *invented, creative,* or *sound spelling* (Sulzby, 1986).

Maggie's teacher had her read her own note to ensure the accuracy of the message. Then she praised her for her wonderful message and that she was very good at writing. Not once did Maggie's teacher correct her spelling or tell her that she did something incorrect. One of the major goals of emergent writing is to provide children with the opportunities to express their feelings and ideas. By focusing on the mechanics and not the message, children will become discouraged because they do not want to be wrong or make mistakes.

WHAT FOUR- AND FIVE-YEAR-OLDS NEED TO KNOW ABOUT LITERACY

The National Association for the Education of Young Children (NAEYC) and the International Reading Association (IRA) (Neuman, Copple, & Bredekamp, 1998) developed a position statement addressing the literacy goals for young children. This statement was to clarify what was appropriate for young children to know and how it should best be taught.

For four-year-olds, the goal is to provide opportunities that allow them to "explore their environment and build the foundations for learning to read and write" (Neuman et al., 1998). In order to accomplish this, children can:

◆ enjoy listening to and discussing storybooks
◆ understand that print carries a message

◆ engage in reading and writing attempts
◆ identify labels and signs in their environment
◆ participate in rhyming games
◆ identify some letter and some letter-sound matches
◆ use known letters or approximations of letters to represent written language (especially meaningful words like their name, and phrases such as "I love you")

For five-year-olds, the literacy goals are to "develop basic concepts of print and begin to engage in and experiment with reading and writing" (Neuman et al., 1998). In order to accomplish this, children can:

◆ enjoy being read to and retell simple narrative stories or informational text
◆ use descriptive language to explain and explore
◆ recognize letters and letter sounds
◆ show familiarity with rhyming and beginning sounds
◆ understand left-to-right and top-to-bottom orientation and familiar concepts of print
◆ match spoken words with written words
◆ begin to write letters of the alphabet and some high-frequency words

Each child is unique and has unique experiences. However, in laying a sound foundation for literacy, four- and five-year-olds should have access to the opportunities described by the NAEYC/IRA.

WHAT LITERACY KNOWLEDGE YOUNG CHILDREN SHOULD ACQUIRE BEFORE THE FIRST GRADE

To prepare four- and five-year-olds for the challenge of learning to read, they need to acquire certain knowledge about literacy. In order to qualify these abilities and skills, the National Academy of Sciences published a research-based report titled *Preventing Reading Difficulties in Young Children* (Snow et al., 1998). In this document, a list of accomplishments that successful learners should exhibit by the end of kindergarten is presented. As with any list of accomplishments, it is neither exhaustive nor all-inclusive, but it does capture some of the essential aspects of literacy acquisition. The timing of these accomplishments will vary among children. However, these abilities are important because they provide teachers of four- and five-year-olds with an understanding of what children need to learn before they embark on formal reading instruction. Children should have accomplished the following by the end of kindergarten:

◆ Know the parts of a book and its functions
◆ Begin to track print when listening to a familiar text being read or when rereading one's own writing.
◆ "Read" familiar text emergently, that is, not necessarily verbatim but from the print alone
◆ Recognize and name all upper- and lowercase letters

◆ Understand that the sequence of letters in a written word represents the sequence of sounds (phonemes) in a spoken word (alphabetic principle)
◆ Learn many, though not all, one-to-one letter-sound correspondences
◆ Recognize some words by sight, including a few very common ones ("the," "I," "my," "you," "is," and "are")
◆ Use new vocabulary and grammatical constructions in one's own speech
◆ Make appropriate switches from oral to written language styles
◆ Notice when simple sentences fail to make sense
◆ Connect information and events in texts to life and life experiences
◆ Retell, reenact, or dramatize stories or parts of stories
◆ Listen attentively to books the teacher reads to class
◆ Name some book titles and authors
◆ Demonstrate familiarity with a number of types or genres of text (e.g., storybooks, expository texts, poems, newspapers, and everyday print, such as signs, notices, and labels)
◆ Correctly answer questions about stories read aloud
◆ Make predictions on the basis of illustrations or portions of stories
◆ Demonstrate understanding that spoken words consist of sequences of phonemes
◆ Given spoken sets like "dan, dan, den," identify the first two as the same and the third as different
◆ Given spoken sets like "dak, pat, zen," identify the first two as sharing one same sound
◆ Given spoken segments, merge them into a meaningful target word
◆ Given a spoken word, produce another word that rhymes with it
◆ Independently write many upper- and lowercase letters
◆ Use phonemic awareness and letter knowledge to spell independently (invented or creative spelling)
◆ Write (unconventionally) to express own meaning
◆ Build a repertoire of some conventionally spelled words
◆ Show awareness of distinction between "kid writing" and conventional orthography
◆ Write own name (first and last) and the first names of some friends and classmates
◆ Write most letters and some words when they are dictated

METHODS OF TEACHING READING

Although most teachers of four- and five-year-olds will not teach formal reading instruction to their children, it is important to have an understanding of the methods used. Reading instruction is divided into two main approaches: the whole language approach and phonics. Although the goal of both approaches is to teach children how to read individual words and comprehend what is read, the differences between the approaches are marked by the methods used to "read" individual words, the type of reading materials, and the strategies that children are taught in approaching text (Bruck, Treiman, Caravolas, Genesee, & Cassar, 1998; Stahl, Detpy-Hester & Stahl, 1998).

Whole Language Approach

The whole language approach is based on a philosophy of learning that emphasizes the importance of the development of language skills as it relates to reading and writing (Goodman, 1986). The whole language approach emphasizes two main premises: (a) The purpose of reading is to extract meaning, and (b) the skills needed to acquire reading are developed through repeated experiences of reading and not explicit instruction. The goal of whole language instruction is to give children numerous experiences with reading and the written word so that they will, through this experience, extract the necessary understanding of print to identify individual words and extract meaning.

As the name "whole language" suggests, reading instruction is taught in a way that keeps language whole, or undivided. Words are not analyzed into parts but instead are learned as whole units as part of the entire text. In this respect, whole language is similar to the "see and say" method of the 1950s in which children would memorize whole words related to stories such as in the Dick and Jane series. In pure whole language classes, children receive minimal instruction in the alphabetic principle that emphasizes the sound-symbol correspondence. Instead, the assumption is that children figure out the rules of language through their experiences with print. Learning to read is viewed as parallel with learning to speak. Learning to understand the "code" or words occurs through the process of induction. Children infer the sound-symbol correspondence from exposure to print and rely heavily on the context to learn the meaning of the word. They then apply this knowledge to figure out new words in stories. When a child comes to a word they do not know, they are encouraged to guess at the words on the basis of context and picture clues. The teacher may encourage the child to read the entire sentence for meaning rather than stop to analyze an unknown word (Morrow, 1997).

In a whole language curriculum, reading centers on children's literature. Typically, children do not use a basal series or books with phonetically controlled vocabulary. Children are taught to look at the whole word in the context of the meaning of the sentence rather than focus on the individual letters and sounds in a word.

Phonics Approach

The phonics approach to reading emphasizes (1) the understanding of the relation of letters and sounds in words, and (2) the application of these relations to analyze and decode unknown words. In a phonics approach to reading, children are explicitly taught how the alphabetic letters and letter groups apply to sounds in words. This is referred to as code-emphasis or code-based instruction. The underlying philosophy is to teach children strategies to figure out the parts of a word on the basis of the sounds that are found in that word. Sight words—words that are difficult to sound out because they do not follow the sound rules—are also taught using the phonics method.

In a classroom using the phonics approach, the letter-sound correspondence is taught early in the reading curriculum and applied to simple words that contain those patterns. Teachers instruct children in how the letter sounds as well as blending the sounds together to make words. Literature is read to children but they are not expected, at first, to read this literature. Instead, as they are practicing their analysis of sound-symbol correspondence in words, they often read books with "controlled vocabulary," vocabulary words that fit the patterns of sounds that they are learning. Thus, if children are learning about the short /a/ sounds, they will read books that contain this sound.

The emphasis on phonics is helping children develop strategies so that they can decode unfamiliar words. The context is used to help children understand the meaning of the text. Knowing individual sounds in words will help children figure out the words, and understanding the context will help bring meaning to the words and the sentence.

Writing and spelling are an important part of phonics instruction. Writing words to express ideas and attitudes requires one to focus on the individual sounds in words. Invented spelling or sound spelling allows the teacher to understand the children's knowledge of sounds in words.

The Reading Wars

In the field of reading research and, recently, in the popular press, much attention has been given to the controversy over which method of teaching reading is more effective: whole language or phonics. The irony of this war is that the battlefield is not in the classrooms. Most teachers who teach reading understand and agree that in order to teach young children to read, some combination of each method is most effective (Joyce, 1999). The fact remains that neither whole word nor phonics strategies alone can help children when they are learning to read. Instead, a combination of these strategies can teach a child about the importance of sounds in words and help him or her understand words from the context, and exposure to many rich language and literacy experiences can contribute to young children learning how to read (Adams, 1990).

Motivation and Reading

"It's your chance to vote on a free choice activity," Ms. Hope announces to her class. "Do you want to read this new book on dragons that I just got from our book club, or do you want to finish our collage on fall?" All but one hand went up for the vote to read the new book on dragons. One of the most important factors in teaching young children to read, one that is frequently overlooked, is motivation (Guthrie & Wigfield, 1997).

Many factors play a part in children's motivation or interest in reading. Frequent exposure to books and the association of reading as a pleasurable experience are important factors in developing children's motivation to read. If reading means curling up with a parent and sharing special time or learning about interesting and fun places and things, then reading is an experience that a child wants to keep coming back to. Also, if young children are around an older sibling who can read, young children often want to emulate the behaviors of older children, especially if these behaviors are valued. If value is placed on reading in a child's home, they will be motivated to be interested in books and read.

Experiences that children have at school can also facilitate their motivation to read. Making reading fun and interesting is an important part of the teachers' role in creating a motivating reading environment. Allowing children to have input in book selection, having them select books on topics that they are interested in, and making reading a special time can help elevate children's desires and interests in reading. The "at least one book a day" idea is a good classroom rule to follow.

ESL Children and Reading

Because of the importance that language plays in learning to read, children who do not speak English present an additional challenge to teachers of young children (Tabors & Snow, 2001). Although there is still significant controversy in the research literature regarding the most effective ways to teach ESL children reading, for four- and five-year-olds the goal should be developing language skills that allow children to take advantage of reading instruction (August & Hakuta, 1997). All the preliteracy skills, such as the development of concepts about print, alphabet knowledge, phonemic awareness, writing, and environmental print, are important for ESL children to be exposed to and to learn (Tabors, 1997).

The important aspect for teachers to keep in mind is to value the diversity that children who speak a language other than English contribute to the classroom. Although additional time may be needed to work on the meaning of vocabulary words and the pronunciation of words, this can help ESL students as well as native English speakers develop a better understanding of the language. Have the other, English-speaking children guide you. At times they will be better equipped to help explain words that may appear complex to you but can easily be explained by young children in a way that is delightfully simple and accurate.

Precocious Readers

In your tenure of teaching four- and five-year-olds, you will surely encounter the young child who comes to school reading. A child in a class of five-year-olds walked over to the bookshelf and selected an all-time favorite, *Where the Wild Things Are.* As he was reading, the teacher observed that what she heard was exactly what was written on the page. It was clear that this child was actually reading the words and not recalling them from memory. The teacher, without calling undue attention to the child, quietly patted the child on the shoulder and said, "Good job, I like the way you are reading the story." Although this is not a frequent occurrence, there are children who learn to read at a very young age. Although this child will stand out from the rest of your four- and five-year-olds on this skill, be careful not to change the focus of your classroom literacy experience or the level of expectations for the other children on the basis of one child's advanced skills.

Research on children who are precocious readers suggests that these children typically have well-developed vocabulary and language skills and typically had frequent exposure to print in their home experiences (Juel, 1988). In addition, these children are motivated to read and enjoy the processes. Although typically precocious readers continue to exhibit strong reading skills as they progress through school, it is not uncommon for all children, by the time that they reach the third grade, to be reading somewhat at the same level. Children who started out as late bloomers with regard to reading can be at the same skill level as the precocious reader by the third grade. Teachers need to understand that reading is a skill that is acquired at different rates by different children. These rates are not necessarily predictive of where some children will be after they leave kindergarten. Teachers should have high expectations for all children and provide the preliteracy experiences that motivate and interest all children to be successful readers.

The following chapter will outline how to put the preliteracy experiences in this chapter into everyday practice in your classroom.

IN SUMMARY

The development of literacy skills begins long before children enter school. Many important abilities must be developed in young children in order for them to develop literacy skills. Language development is a critical aspect in the development of literacy skills. Through book reading, children learn decontextualized language, which contributes to the development of language skills.

Children need to acquire other abilities in order to develop literacy skills. The development of phonological awareness contributes to children's ability to understand sounds in words. In addition, understanding print, developing knowledge of the alphabet, and learning to write helps build a solid literacy foundation in young children.

The National Academy of Science's report on *Prevention of Early Reading Failure* and the IRA/NAEYC's position statement on early literacy outlined key accomplishments for four- and five-year-olds. These reports show consensus in the field of early childhood regarding the literacy expectations for four- and five-year-olds.

Although the reading wars have been fought in journals and professional magazines, in the classroom teachers are practicing a combination of whole language and phonics. Children need a rich language base as well as skills to decode words.

Motivation is key to children being successful with literacy development. Children who are interested in literacy, are eager to learn, and feel that they can be successful are successful. Both ESL and learning disabled children need to find an appropriate place in the early childhood curriculum so that all children can be successful.

EXTEND YOUR IDEAS

1. Obtain copies of your school and district's kindergarten literacy goals and objectives. Compare them to the National Academy of Science's and the IRA/NAEYC's suggested accomplishments. Where are they in agreement, and where are there differences?

2. Review the National Academy of Science's recommendations for early literacy accomplishments. Do you think that they are developmentally appropriate for four- and five-year-olds? What would you change, and what would you add?

3. Observe a kindergarten class. Identify the opportunities the children have to learn language and vocabulary. How could you improve on the activities that you observed? Do the same for phonemic awareness activities. How would you improve them?

4. Have a class of four- and five-year-olds "write" their reaction to a story that you have read to them. Explore the different stages of writing that the children use. Try to identify, according to the stages of writing provided in this chapter, at what stage each child is writing.

5. Conduct a simple assessment with four- and five-year-olds. Have them hold a book and identify the various aspects of the concepts of print. Can they identify that you read left to write? Can they tell you that you read pictures and not words?

RESOURCES

These illustrate how children learn to read through play and real life experiences.

Start Early, Finish Strong: How to Make Every Child a Reader, by the U.S. Department of Education (Washington, DC: Author, 1999). This is a user-friendly, literacy guide for parents, teachers, and educators. It oulines the developmental milestones to be achieved at each age of learning to read.

Raising a Reader, Raising a Writer: How Parents Can Help (brochure), by the National Association for the Education of Young Children and the International Reading Association (1998). A simple set of suggestions for parents to help engage their children in reading and writing. Also, a description of what parents should look for in their children's preschool and school setting that supports raising readers and writers.

REFERENCES

Adams, M. J. (1990). *Beginning to read: Thinking and learning about print.* Cambridge: MIT Press.

August, D., & Hakuta, K. (Eds.). (1997). *Improving schooling for language minority children: A research agenda.* Washington, DC: National Research Council.

Bowman, B. T., Donovan, M. S., & Burns, M. S. (Eds.), *Eager to Learn.* Washington, DC: National Academy Press.

Bruck, M., Treiman, R., Caravolas, M., Genesee, F., & Cassar, M. (1998). Spelling skills of children in whole language and phonics classrooms. *Applied Psycholinguistics, 19,* 669–684.

Burns, M. S., Griffin, P., & Snow, C. (1998). *Starting out right: A guide to promoting children's reading success.* Washington, DC: National Academy Press.

Clay, M. M. (1993). *Reading recovery: A guidebook for teachers in training.* Portsmouth, NH: Heinemann.

Dickinson, D. K., & Snow, C. E. (1987). Interrelationship among pre-reading and oral language skills in kindergartners from two social classes. *Early Childhood Research Quarterly, 2,* 1–25.

Dickinson, D. K., & Tabors, P. (2001). *Beginning literacy with language: Young children learning at home and in school.* Baltimore Brookes Publishing.

Ehri, L. E., & McCormick, S. (1998). Phases of word learning: Implications for delayed and disabled readers. *Reading and writing quarterly, 14,* 135–164.

Fang, Z. (1999). Expanding the vista of emergent writing research: Implications for early childhood educators. *Early Childhood Education Journal, 26,* 179–182.

Fox, B. J., & Saracho, O. N. (1990). Emergent writing: Young children solving the written language puzzle. *Early Child Development and Care, 56,* 81–90.

Gibson, E. (1969). *Principles of perceptual learning and development.* Upper Saddle River, NJ: Prentice Hall.

Goodman, Y. (1986). Children coming to know literacy. In W. H. Teale & E. Sulzby (Eds.), *Emergent literacy: Writing and reading.* Norwood, NJ: Ablex.

Guthrie, J., & Wigfield, A. (1997). *Reading engagement: Motivational, strategic reading through integrated instruction.* Newark, DE: International Reading Association.

Harste, J. E., Woodward, V. A., & Burke, C. L. (1984). Language stories and literacy lessons. Portsmouth, NH: Heinemann.

Hecht, S. A., Burgess, S. R., Torgesen, J. K., Wagner, R. K., Rashotte, C. A. (2000). Explaining social class differences in growth of reading skills from beginning kindergarten through fourth grade: The Phonological awareness, rate of access, and print knowledge. *Reading and Writing: An Interdisciplinary Journal, 12,* 99–127.

International Reading Association. (1999). *Position statement on phonemic awareness.* Newark, DE: Author.

Joyce, B. R. (1999). Reading about reading: Notes from the consumer to the scholars of literacy. *Reading Teacher, 52,* 662–672.

Juel, C. (1988). Learning to read and write: A longitudinal study of 54 children from first through fourth grades. *Journal of Educational Psychology, 80,* 437–447.

Kuby, P., & Aldridge, J. (1997). Direct versus indirect environmental print instruction and early reading ability in kindergarten children. *Reading Psychology, 18,* 91–104.

Maclean, M., Bryant, P., & Bradley, L. (1987). Rhymes, nursery rhymes, and reading in early childhood. *Merrill Palmer Quarterly, 33,* 255–281.

Morrow, L. M. (1997). *Literacy development in the early years: Helping children to read and write.* Boston: Allyn & Bacon.

Neuman, S. B., Copple, C., & Bredekamp, S. (1998). *Learning to read and write: Developmentally appropriate practices for young children.* Washington, DC: National Association for the Education of Young Children.

Neuman, S. B., & Rosko, K. A. (1997). Literacy knowledge in practice: Contexts of participation for young writers and readers. *Reading Research Quarterly, 32,* 10–32.

Orellana, M. F., & Hernandez, A. (1999). Talking the walk: Children reading urban environmental print. *Reading Teacher, 52,* 612–619.

Piaget, J. & Inhelder, B. (1967). *The Child's Concept of Sapce.* New York, NY: W. W. Norton & Co.

Schickendanz, J. A. (1999). *Much more than the ABC's: The early stages of reading and writing.* Washington, DC: NAEYC Press.

Snow, C. E., Burns, M. S., & Griffin, P. (1998). *Preventing reading difficulties in young children.* Washington, DC: National Research Council.

Snow, C. E., & Tabors, P. O. (1993). Language skills that relate to literacy development. In B. Spodek & O. N. Saracho (Eds.), *Language and literacy in early childhood education.* New York: Teachers College Press.

Stahl, S. A., Detpy-Hester, A. M., & Stahl, K. A. D. (1998). Everything you wanted to know about phonics (but were afraid to ask). *Reading Research Quarterly, 33,* 77–101.

Sulzby, E. (1985). Kindergartners as writers and readers. In M. Farr (Ed.), *Advances in Writing Research.* Norwood, NJ: Ablex.

Sulzby, E. (1986). Writing and reading: Signs of oral and written language organization in young children. In W. Teale & E. Sulzby (Eds.), *Emergent Literacy: Writing and Reading.* Norwood, NJ: Ablex.

Tabors, P. O. (1997). *One child, two languages: A guide for preschool educators of children learning English as a second language.* Baltimore: Paul Brookes Publishing.

Tabors, P. O., & Snow, C. E. (2001). Young bilingual children and early literacy development. In S. Newman & D. Dickinson (Eds.), *Handbook of Early Literacy Research.* New York: Guilford Press.

Torgesen, J. K., & Davis, C. (1996). Individual difference variables that predict response to training in phonological awareness. *Journal of Experimental Child Psychology, 63,* 1–21.

Wasik, B. A. (2000). Phonemic awareness and young children. *Childhood Education.*

Wasik, B. A. (2001a). Phonemic awareness and young children. *Childhood Education, 77,* 128–138.

Wasik, B. A. (2001b). Teaching the alphabet to young children. *Young Children, 56,* 34–40.

Whitehurst, G. J., & Lonigan, C. J. (1998). *Child Development, 69,* 848–872.

Yopp, H. K. (1992). Developing phonemic awareness in young children. *Reading Teacher, 45,* 696–703.

CHAPTER 12

Language Arts for Four- and Five-Year-Olds

"*T*oday we are going to visit a grocery store," says Mrs. Bands as she reads the morning message on the blackboard. "What do you think that we might see at the grocery store?" Hands fly up, and Mrs. Bands asks Keith to share his ideas with the class. She holds up two fingers as a signal to remind the other children that they need to listen quietly while Keith is speaking. Keith says, "We'll see some apples and some chicken." Mrs. Bands writes the words "apples" and "chicken" on the blackboard and repeats the words as she writes them. "Tricia, what do you think we will see?" asks Mrs. Bands. "Paper bags," Tricia calls out. "My mom brings home a lot of paper bags when she goes to the grocery store." Mrs. Bands asks two more children to describe what they expect to see at the grocery store and records their responses. The class then rereads the morning message and the words that Mrs. Bands has recorded. The children return to their tables to write shopping lists that they will take on the field trip to the grocery store.*

As these four- and five-year-olds participate in the morning message activity, they are listening to one another, reading the message along with the teacher, expressing their ideas, and placing their ideas in print. In this one activity, the children have engaged in the four key components of the language arts curriculum: speaking, listening, writing, and reading (Seefeldt & Barbour, 1998). The goal of the language arts curriculum is to develop language and literacy skills in young children. It is through these four components that children are provided with opportunities for language and literacy development.

BUILDING LANGUAGE AND LITERACY THROUGH THE LANGUAGE ARTS CURRICULUM

I n Chapter 11, we outlined the developmental precursors necessary for literacy development. We discussed the important role that language development, phonemic awareness, alphabet knowledge, concepts of print, and exposure to reading and writing play in children's literacy development. Children acquire this knowledge by engaging in developmentally appropriate activities that support language and literacy development throughout the curriculum (Bowman, Donovan & Burns, 2001; Bredekamp & Copple, 1997). The purpose of this chapter is to describe how language development, phonemic awareness, alphabet knowledge, concepts of print, and exposure to reading and writing can be taught through developmentally appropriate activities that support the development of the four key components of the language arts curriculum (Neuman, Copple, & Bredekamp, 2000).

THE FOUR COMPONENTS OF THE LANGUAGE ARTS CURRICULUM

Broad goals for the language arts curriculum focus on increasing children's skills in listening, speaking, reading, and writing. It is neither possible nor advisable to totally separate the learning of one skill from the learning of another; however, at times you will focus more on one area of language arts than another. These four broad goals are outlined in the following sections.

Goal 1: Listening

Children will develop the ability to listen in order to make sense of their environment. In order for children to learn, they need to take information in and process it. Listening to and comprehending information is an essential step in acquiring knowledge (Jalongo, 1996). Listening is not a natural, innate ability. Instead, it is learned through the guidance and teaching of parents, teachers, and other people in young children's environment (Kupetz & Twiest, 2000). Strategies such as the hand signal that Mrs. Bands used with her class or environmental cues such as turning the lights off to signal total quiet are helpful in alerting the children that it is time to stop what they are doing and listen.

Teaching children to listen to other children and to adults will increase the opportunities to learn language as well as new ideas. It is also one of the hardest skills to teach young children, who are often very busy initiating activities and expressing themselves and who are not as interested in listening to those around them (Jalongo, 1996).

Goal 2: Speaking

In order to learn language, children need opportunities to talk and be heard (Dickinson & Snow, 1987). Effective adult-child dialogue includes an adult who listens as the child speaks, asks questions that encourages the child to say more, and expands and elaborates on what the child has said. Samantha shows her teacher a picture that she drew. Instead of responding with a typical praise of "That's nice" or "What a good job you did," Mrs. Bands stops what she is doing, kneels down at eye level with Samantha, and says, "Tell me about this picture that you drew." Samantha has the opportunity to describe and explain her drawing.

Children need to learn that the manner in which they speak depends on the situation. Informal speech is appropriate with friends and family, but more precise speech is appropriate for school and other places outside the home. When children want to communicate their ideas, they need to speak in ways that others can understand and hear.

Goal 3: Reading

Although formal reading instruction typically begins in first grade, kindergartners develop many skills that prepare them to learn to read. Children whose daily routines and activities provide them with "reading opportunities" will begin to identify environmental print (West & Egley, 1998). Names on bedroom doors, on cubbies in school, and on backpacks provide multiple and distinct opportunities for children to recognize their names. With repeated exposure to a predictable book, four- and five-year-olds can "read" stories. Mrs. Bands has read *The Three Billy Goats Gruff* to her class multiple times over the last 3 weeks. With their expert knowledge of the book, her class can anticipate when the goats are walking over the bridge and chime in with a chorus of "Trip, Trap, Trip, Trap."

An environment that is rich in books and print helps children begin to discern the meaning of print. What seems like scribbling on a page begins to develop meaning as children begin to understand that print communicates a message (Sulzby, 1992). Children learn to recognize letters and words and eventually become aware of the relationship of sounds to letters and words. For some kindergartners, they effortlessly "crack the code" and begin to identify and sound out words with continued exposure to print. For other kindergartners, reading will take more effort and require more formal instruction in first and second grade.

Goal 4: Writing

Children will learn to write in an increasingly complex and precise manner to communicate their ideas, request things, document their activities, and provide pleasure and amusement. To foster this development, four- and five-year-olds need experiences that encourage them to make marks on paper and write. As described in Chapter 11, children begin writing by scribbling and drawing pictures. As their knowledge of print increases, letters are formed, and collection of nonsense letters come closer to phonetic spellings (Sulzby & Teale, 1985). The first discovery is often their own names, and they become fascinated with the results, as did four-year-old Tommy, who spent an entire afternoon crafting the "T" and "O" in his name when he discovered that "Tommy" was how his name was written.

From these beginnings, children begin to learn the often difficult but exciting task of putting their words and thoughts on paper. They eventually learn that there are different purposes for writing and that the style of writing changes with the purpose.

TRANSLATING GOALS INTO PRACTICE

A variety of activities can support the listening, speaking, reading, and writing goals of the language arts curriculum (Greenberg, 1998). As discussed in Chapter 1, typically the language arts activities are organized around a common theme, topic, and/or project that is at a developmental level that is appropriate for the children. The materials for the language arts curriculum will be selected to support the unit or theme.

BOOK READING

Book reading is among the most important experiences in the language arts curriculum. Through book reading, children expand their vocabularies, learn more complex sentence structures, and are exposed to a world of new information. Book reading offers children opportunities to encounter words, phrases, and sentence structures that are not typically introduced in young children's everyday conversations. Exposure to decontextalized language—which is language and, in particular, vocabulary that is not found in typical conversations—is critical to language development (Dickinson & DiGisi, 1994). While reading the book *Caps for Sale*, Mrs. Bands explains that "caps" is another name for "hat" and that "stacking" means piling many things on top of one another. The words "caps" and "stacking" may not be a part of the typical vocabulary of four- and five-year-olds, but knowledge of these words is essential for understanding the story and will help add important words to their vocabulary.

In order to develop language skills through book reading, the following four critical strategies need to be implemented:

1. *Repeated readings:* Just as Mrs. Bands showed the last page of the book, the children called out, "Read it again, please read it again." "I will read a second time at the end of today as I always do," replied Mrs. Bands. Providing multiple opportunities for children to read the same book is important for language development (MacKey, 1993). Although adults often tire of hearing a book over and over again, young children need this exposure to learn the vocabulary, to comprehend the details of the book, and to make connections between the information in the book and their personal knowledge. Children frequently need to be presented with a new vocabulary word about five to seven times in order for them to make it theirs and be able to use it (Robbins and Ehri, 1994). A rereading of a story does not need to take place immediately after the first reading. Instead, as Mrs. Bands demonstrates, it can be read twice in the same day at different times and also read at different times during the week. It is important to have the second reading of a new book within 2 or 3 days of the first reading in order to provide continuity and help children recall the details and new words in the story. A third and even a fourth reading can take place within a week or month. Old favorites should be revisited so that the children who have memorized the text have a chance to "read" along with the teacher, and others can anticipate the parts of the story that they are familiar with.

2. *Asking questions:* Asking questions during book reading helps children talk about the story, clarify information that they are not sure about, expand on the ideas that are presented in the story, and help them make connections between their own experiences and those presented in the book (Dickinson & Smith, 1994). Mrs. Bands begins the book *Caps for Sale* by showing the children the picture on the cover and asking them what they think the book is about. Asking children to make predictions helps teachers understand the children's expectations about the book and their prior knowledge about information that may be presented in the book. As Mrs. Bands reads through the book, she asks five or six questions that focus on the children's comprehension of the story and that help them make connections between the story and their own experiences. Asking too many questions while reading can distract the children from the meaning of the story (Dickinson & Smith, 1994). When Mrs. Bands finishes reading, she continues to ask the children for their reaction to the story and returns to any part of the story that apparently was not clear for the children. Through questioning, Mrs. Bands helps the children comprehend information about the story.

3. *Extending the story:* On the first day that Mrs. Bands read *The Mitten,* her class made their own mittens and she talked with the children about their mittens as they were constructing them. When she read *The Mitten* the next day for a second time, the children made puppets of the animals that were in the story and learned the names of the animals. At the end of the week, when Mrs. Bands read *The Mitten* for the third time, the children reenacted the story with the puppets they had made. Activities that extend the story provide opportunities to comprehend the story and learn the story-related vocabulary. The activities can take

Extend story reading to other activities.

place in centers or as a whole group activity. In order to build on the language presented in stories, it is important not to end the story when the book is closed. Making the story come alive for the children through reenactments, arts and crafts activities, cooking activities, and science and math activities provides diverse contexts for the children to get the most from a book (Collins, 1999).

4. *Reading in small groups:* As the class is working in centers, Mrs. Bands has her assistant help the children with their projects as she takes a group of four children to the literacy corner to read to them. For four- and five-year-olds, reading books in small groups of three to five children is optimal for developing language and listening skills (Morrow & Smith, 1990). In smaller groups, there are fewer distractions and more opportunities to ask questions, to listen to other children's responses, and to get feedback from the teacher. Using an assistant to work with the class or a small group during independent play once a week can provide the time for small-group reading opportunities. When circumstances do not permit reading in small groups, group management techniques, such as the hand signals that Mrs. Bands used to remind children to listen when others are talking, will facilitate language learning during group book reading.

Types of Books

Exposing four- and five-year-olds to different types of books will teach them that books communicate information in different ways. The five types of books commonly used with kindergartners are storybooks, informational books, concept books, pattern books, and wordless books. Table 12–1 presents a list of classic children's books according to the type that are appropriate for four- and five-year-olds.

TABLE 12–1 **Classic Books**

Book Type	Book Titles and Authors
Storybooks	*The Little Engine That Could* by Watty Piper *The Run Away Bunny* by Margaret Wise Brown *Corduroy* by Don Freeman *Bread and Jam for Frances* by Russell Hoban *Amazing Grace* by Mary Hoffman *The Snowy Day* by Ezra Jack Keats *Swimmy* by Leo Lionni *The Tale of Peter Rabbit* by Beatrix Potter *Curious George* by R. A. Rey *Where the Wild Things Are* by Maurice Sendak *The Cat in the Hat* by Dr. Seuss *Make Way for Ducklings* by Robert McCloskey *Rainbow Fish* by Mark Pfister *Harry the Dirty Dog* by Gene Zion *Stone Soup* by Ann McGovern *If You Give a Mouse A Cookie* by Laura Joffe Numeroff *The Funny Little Woman* by Arlene Mosel *Leo the Late Bloomer* by Robert Kraus
Informational	*A Day at Green Hill Farm* by Sue Nicholson *How a Seed Grows* by Helene J. Jordon *Eyewitness Explorers: Insects* by Steve Parker *Musical Instruments* by Jean Marzollo *My Visit to the Aquarium* by Alike *Vegetables, Vegetables!* by Fay Robinson *Zoo Animals* Published by Dorling Kindersley *France* by Henry Pluckrose *Visiting the Art Museum* by Laurene Krasny Brown and Marc Brown *I'm Going to Be a Vet* by Edith Kunhardt *The Color of Nature* by Bobbie Kalman *Crayons from Start to Finish* by Samuel G. Woods *Ears Are for Hearing* by Paul Showers *Let's Find Out About Toothpaste* by Kathy Barabas *Guess Whose Shadow?* by Stephen R. Swinburn
Concept	*School Bus* by Donald Crews *My Crayons Talk* by Patricia Hubbard *ABC I Like Me!* by Nancy Carlson *Hot, Cold, Shy, Bold* by Pamela Harris *Shapes* by Henry Pluckrose *Is It Red? Is It Yellow? Is It Blue?* by Tana Hoban *Feast for Ten* by Cathryn Falwell *On Market Street* by Arnold Lobel *Hannah's Collections* by Marthe Jocelyn *My Mom and Dad Make Me Laugh* by Nick Sharratt *When This Box Is Full* by Patricia Little *I Spy School* by Jean Marzolla *Me on the Map* by Joan Sweeney *The Icky Bug Alphabet* by Jerry Pallotta

(continued)

TABLE 12–1   **Classic Books—*continued***

Book Type	Book Titles and Authors
Pattern	*Brown Bear, Brown Bear, What Do You See?* by Bill Martin, Jr. *The Very Hungry Caterpillar* by Eric Carle *Better Not Get Wet, Jesse Bear* by Nancy White Carlstrom *Jump, Frog, Jump* by Robert Kalan *The Carrot Seed* by Ruth Krauss *The Wheels on the Bus* by Mary Ann Kovaski *The Ginger Bread Boy* by Paul Galdone *The Little Red Hen* by Lucinda McQueen *May I Bring a Friend?* by Beatrice Schenk De Regniers *Henny Penny* by H. Werner Zimmermann *I Was Walking Down the Road* by Sarah E. Barchas *More Spaghetti, I Say!* by Rita Golden Gelman *If the Dinosaurs Came Back* by Bernard Most
Wordless	*School* by Emily Arnold McCully *The Snowman* by Raymond Briggs *Will You Be My Friend?* by Eric Carle *A Boy, a Dog and a Frog* by Mercer Mayer *Surprise Picnic* by John Goodall *Window* by Jeannie Baker *Anno's U.S.A.* by Anno Mitsumasa *Tuesday* by David Wiesner *Pancakes for Breakfast* by Tomie DePaola *Zoom* by Istvan Banyai *Wind* by Monique Felix *Carl Goes to Day Care* by Alexandra Day *The Grey Lady and the Strawberry Snatcher* by Molly Bank *Magpie Magic* by April Wilson

Storybooks are books that have a beginning, middle, and end; contain a story plot in which a problem arises or an important event occurs; have a resolution to the problem or bring closure to the event; and have characters who are developed throughout the story. Children love the imagination and fantasy in storybooks. Storybooks often bring the pretend world alive by having talking animals, flying people, and wondrous places to travel to. Storybooks invite questioning of children's opinions, their predictions about events, and their comprehension of the story.

Concept books typically present information about colors, shapes, the alphabet, and numbers. Concept books do not tell a story but rather present conceptual information in an engaging, meaningful way, often organized around a specific topic. Mrs. Bands read an alphabet book about food before the class field trip to the grocery store to reinforce the letters of the alphabet. In a concept book, information is presented along with pictures that illustrate the particular concept. The alphabet book on food contained beautiful pictures of an apple for the letter "A" and a banana for the letter "B." Concept books develop language and vocabulary skills while teaching specific concepts. Concept books can be used during math, science, and art activities to reinforce the concepts presented.

Informational books provide factual information about a topic. These books are presented differently to four- and five-year-olds than storybooks and concept books are presented. In reading the informational book on the grocery store, Mrs. Bands reads that vegetables are brought to the grocery store by trucks from local farms. She shows the children pictures of the farm and of trucks driving on the road. She asks the children to explain what they see in the pictures and asks them their opinions of what the facts mean. The informational book becomes a springboard to ask questions, expand vocabulary, and invite various interpretations of the facts presented. Informational books are useful in supporting social science, science, and math themes and projects.

Wordless books contain just pictures without words. Wordless books provide wonderful opportunities for children to create their own stories that match the illustration. Each child has the freedom to be creative and develop his or her own story without the constraints of words. Wordless books encourage the development of language and vocabulary skills, promote the use of spoken language, and encourage pretend reading from young children. Mrs. Bands created a wordless book from the drawings by children of her class. She had the children draw pictures of different parts of their trip to the grocery store. She arranged them according to the sequence of the trip and had the children make up different stories about animals that went to the grocery store. This activity integrated reading, writing, listening, and speaking to help them learn about the grocery store.

Pattern books are typically storybooks that contain words or lines of text that are repeated throughout the book. In *The Three Billy Goats Gruff*, the words "Trip, trap, trip, trap" are repeated throughout the story, describing the sound of the goats' hooves passing over the bridge. Children enjoy the repetition in pattern books and anticipate where in the story the pattern language is found. The children in Mrs. Bands' class have memorized *Chicka Chicka Boom Boom* and call out the lines in unison. This makes the children feel as if they can read because they know the text.

Books in Different Formats

As well as exposing children to different types of books, it is also important to expose them to books in various types of formats. Oversized books (often called Big Books), books on tape, and talking books engage children in the book reading process (Karges-Bone, 1992).

Big Books are oversized books in which the print and illustrations are large enough for children to see as the teacher is reading the book to a group. Big Books come in all five types. Popular children's books, such as *The Three Little Pigs* and *Goldilocks*, as well as pattern books, are frequently found in Big Book form.

Big Books are used to develop children's understanding of concepts about print (Bialystok, Shenfield, & Codd, 2000). Using a Big Book, the teacher can point to the words as she reads from left to right, and the children can follow along. While reading, the teacher can point to each word, and the children can discern many features about the print, such as the fact that the words and not pictures are being read, that individual words have spaces between them, and that words make up sentences. Mrs. Bands reads the pattern book *And The Door Bell Rang* as her class chimed in with the line "And the doorbell rang." The children are so familiar with the book that they anticipate the lines they have memorized. Because they also are able to see the words from the pattern sentence, the children have learned to identify the words "doorbell" and "rang."

Books on tape allow children to follow along with a book as they listen to it. In the reading center in Mrs. Bands' kindergarten, three children sit with headphones as they listen and follow along to a book on tape. Books on tape develop children's listening skills and teach children that print communicates a message in a systematic way.

CIRCLE TIME ACTIVITIES

The activities that take place during circle time are fundamental to the language arts curriculum. During circle time, children have the opportunity to express their own ideas and to listen to those of others. This activity supports the development of oral language and active listening skills that are the foundation of the development of language.

Planning the Day

Mrs. Bands' class gathers in a circle to discuss their plans for the day. Yesterday they had taken a field trip to a plant nursery and had purchased some flowers for their school garden. "We are going to plant our flowers today," says Mrs. Bands. "What do we need to do first?" "Dig some holes." says Alberto. "Yes, but what do we need to dig the holes?" asks Mrs. Bands. "We need shovels," says Kaitlyn. Mrs. Bands begins to write a list on the board of the supplies the children will need to plant their flowers.

During this circle time, children engage in the process of planning the activities for the day (Harris & Fuqua, 2000). They discuss the activities that will take place and the sequence of those activities, and children have the opportunity to ask questions about the activities. "Where will we plant the flowers?" asks Henry. "Around the base of the big oak trees and the side of the school," responds Mrs. Bands. Children also are given opportunities to have input in the planning process. "Can we plant flowers around the tree so we can see them from our window?" asks Rita. "Then we can see them grow." "That's a great idea," says Mrs. Bands.

Writing a morning message on the board or chart paper is one method of introducing the plan for the day. In written form, the children have the opportunity to see in print a message that the teacher reads. The children can add to the message, and the teacher can write their responses, turning children's spoken words into print right before their eyes.

Circle time used for planning the day prepares children for the day, creates opportunities for children to ask questions or to provide reactions to the day's plan, and allows the children to hear others' opinions, comments, or concerns about what the day will bring.

Sharing Work

Circle time can also be used as a time when children share the work that they have been doing during centers or other activities. In the construction center, Justin had made an elaborate plant store similar to the one the class visited during their field trip. During circle time, Mrs. Bands invited Justin and two other classmates who were playing in that area to describe to the class how they built the store and what they were doing in it. The other children were encouraged to ask Justin and his other classmates questions about their store. Justin explained that he made a lot of aisles in his store for all the plants and how he needed hoses to water the plants. During this exchange, the children had the opportunity to talk about the work that they had accomplished and to listen to their classmates' reactions.

Sharing News

Circle time can be a time for sharing news (Spangler, 1997). News can range from children's personal stories to information about the children's community and the world. Children need opportunities to share what is happening in their lives. Sarah could not wait to share her news about her new baby brother. Jack's dog was sick last night. Bridget just got a new pair of sneakers. Fran has peanut butter crackers for lunch. Children love to talk, and adults need to make the time to listen. All this information is newsworthy to the children and special to each child. Creating a time for children to share important things in their lives allows them to have that information validated by a significant adult.

Sharing community news also puts the children in touch with the world around them. Mrs. Bands started the circle time with a newspaper picture of a construction site. "We are going to have a new library by spring," says Mrs. Bands. "Here is a picture of the people building it." Sharing news in the community that is developmentally appropriate brings the world into the children's classroom. A baby elephant born at the zoo, a balloon show coming to town, the opening of a new grocery store, or a new child in the third grade all provide information about the community of which the children are a part. Allowing the children to hear about community news builds their curiosity about the world outside their classroom.

Group Meeting

Circle time can be used as a forum for a class meeting if there is something specific that the children need to discuss. Perhaps the children are given the opportunity to vote for their choice of a class activity or their choice of the next theme that they will work on. During circle time, children can express his/her opinions and preferences. The class can hear each child's reason for their selection, and the group can vote on their choices. This forum provides the opportunity for children to learn how to work in a group and how to make compromises. Most important, children can express their ideas and actively listen to the ideas of others.

Reviewing the Day

Circle time is often done at the end of the day and provides the opportunity for children to review and reflect on the activities that they engaged in. Mrs. Bands asked her children to retell how they planted the flowers. She asked them to think of their favorite part of planting and asked them to describe the bottom of the plants before they buried them underground. After children have an experience, it is important to have them think about what they have just done and express their ideas and opinions about the activity.

After the trip to the plant nursery, Mrs. Bands was delighted to find that her children experienced a variety of things during the trip. In reviewing the trip, Jake said he enjoyed listening to the water fountain in the store, Kyle really enjoyed all the colors of the plants, and Ashley felt that the best part was the hoses that were used to water the plants. Without the circle time as a review, Mrs. Bands may have sent her children home without allowing them to share their unique interpretations of the trip. Language and active listening skills are being reinforced as the children continue to talk.

CENTER ACTIVITIES

Center activities play a significant part in developing speaking, listening, reading, and writing skills in four- and five-year-olds (Ferguson, 1999). Working in small groups during center time, children have the opportunity to interact with one another in a more personal way. They can talk, share ideas, and actively listen to one another.

Mrs. Bands has several centers in her classroom, including an art center, a construction center, a reading/listening center, and a writing center. Before the class went on the field trip to the grocery store, Mrs. Bands filled the reading/listening center with books about food, shopping, and how food gets from the farm to the supermarket. The children were able to look through the books and listen to books on tape. In the writing center, the children made shopping lists and wrote about what they expected to see at the grocery store and what their favorite foods were. On their return from the field trip, the children wrote their reactions to the field trip and wrote thank-you notes for the employees who guided the children through the store.

To facilitate reading, writing, speaking, and listening throughout the classroom, center activities do the following:

1. *Facilitate interaction:* During center time, the teacher can circulate to the various activities and interact with the children. One-to-one conversations can take place during this time. Teachers can ask children about what they are working on, why they decided to do what they are doing, and their opinions about their work. This will encourage oral language and listening skills. This is especially important for students for whom English is not their first language. One-to-one interactions will help improve their spoken language, build their vocabulary, and increase their listening comprehension skills.

2. *Provide individualized activities:* Center activities can be individualized so that children can work at their own pace and develop their skills at a rate that is appropriate for their own development. In the reading and writing center, Sandy and Kasey are writing letters to their moms. Sandy uses pictures to tell her mom

Center work allows children to work at their own level.

that she estimated the weight of different toys today at school. Kasey writes her mom about a similar experience, yet she uses a combination of letters and pictures to communicate her message. Both five-year-olds are at different stages in their writing but can work side by side during center time, on a writing project.

3. *Allow one-to-one contact with the teacher:* Center time also provides needed opportunities for one-to-one contact with the teacher. In whole group settings, it is difficult for the teacher to talk with and actively listen to one child without being aware of the other children. However, during center time, teachers can circulate around to different centers and talk with children individually (Hope & Cumming, 1998). This experience increases the possibility of children having meaningful conversations with the teachers. Through this, vocabulary is developed, listening skills are strengthened, and verbal skills are modeled and reinforced.

POETRY, RHYMES, AND SONGS

Mrs. Bands' class is walking back from the playground, singing, "The ants go marching one by one." The class discovered an anthill by the jungle gym and watched the ants scurry in and out of their hole. Although they had learned this song months ago, with Mrs. Bands leading, they were able to sing the entire song. Integrating poetry, rhymes, and song throughout the classroom activity is an essential component of the language arts curriculum. Teaching children poems, rhymes, and songs fosters important skills that are key to language and literacy development (Adams, Foorman, Lundberg, & Beeler, 1997). Teaching poetry, rhymes, and songs helps develop the following:

1. *Phonemic awareness:* As discussed in Chapter 11, phonemic awareness is the ability to manipulate sounds in words. This ability is an important precursor to learning to read. As children learn rhymes and poetry, they begin to play with language and make up their own rhymes. Because Mary just got a dog, she was singing her own version of "Mary Had a Little Lamb": "Mary had a little dog whose fur was brown as a log, and everything the dog was fed he ate just like a hog." Mary learned that some words sound the same as others and that she can create her own rhymes to fit her own experiences. Teachers should encourage children to make up poems, songs, and rhymes to learn about language and the sounds in language. This is especially important for children for whom English is not their first language. Learning songs and rhymes that have words that sound alike helps children develop the ability to discriminate sounds in words.

2. *Memory skills:* Sally came home and proudly recited the "Incy, Wincy Spider" to her mom and dad. This eight-line poem is a big task for a five-year-old to remember, but after hearing it multiple times in school, Sally was able to repeat the poem all by herself. Learning poems and rhymes helps children develop memory skills. It helps them retain a large chunk of information, which is not often required of young children. Using the finger plays along with the poem helps as a memory cue for the words. Sally knew the finger play actions before she could remember each line of the poem. Raising her arm in the air helped her remember the line "Out came the sun."

3. *Active listening:* Learning poems, rhymes, and songs help develop active listening skills. In order for children to learn a song with many words and lines, they need to attend to individual words in the song. Although it is very common for four- and five-year-olds to use words in a song or poem that sound like the real word but that change the meaning of the poem, children still accurately learn many words in a poem of rhyme. These active listening strategies generalize to other aspects of the curriculum.

4. *Fun with language:* The room is often filled with laughter and positive energy when children are singing or reciting silly poems. These verbal activities are often accompanied by motor activity, either finger plays or gross motor activities, such as dancing or jumping. Through these activities, children experience playing with language, which can be fun. After singing the song "No More Monkeys Jumping on the Bed," Carol changed the rhyme to "No more monkeys jumping on my head." She continued to vary the poem using other words that rhymed with "bed." She and her friend were laughing at the silliness of their poems. The rhythmic pattern of the language in poetry, rhymes, and songs is very pleasing and inviting to young children.

Selecting Poetry, Rhymes, and Songs

Here are suggested guidelines that teachers of young children may follow in selecting poetry, rhymes, and songs for four- and five-year-olds (Wasik, 2001a).

1. *Length:* For young children, it is best to select poetry, rhymes, and songs that are not too long, especially for work that you would like the children to recall. If these are too long, children will have difficulty remembering the lines and will become frustrated by the experience, and even when poetry or rhymes are read for enjoyment without intended for the children to commit them to memory, children will not comprehend the information and will lose interest.

2. *Repetition:* Choose rhymes and poems that include repetition of words or key phrases (Yopp, 1992). "Old MacDonald Had a Farm" is easy to learn because a key phrase is repeated throughout, and children can change a few words to make a new verse. Children enjoy the repetition, which facilitates easy mastery of the poem or rhyme.

3. *Topic:* Select poetry and rhymes that are related to the class theme. Mrs. Bands' class recited "Patty Cake" during their unit on the grocery store, which included a trip to the bakery. Using the same tune, Mrs. Bands changed the word "baker man" to "fireman" and taught the children "Patty cake, Patty cake, fireman, put out a fire as fast as you can" when the class was learning about fire safety and community helpers. Old favorites can be adapted to fit a current theme.

The rule of thumb should be to keep the piece simple, theme-related, and fun. Learners of English as a second language will benefit from learning poetry and rhymes because of the variety of new words that they will learn and the exposure to rhythms and sounds in the language.

Back in the classroom, children talk about and act out their experiences.

Poetry, Rhymes, and Songs in the Curriculum

Poetry, rhymes, and songs can be used in many parts of the kindergarten curriculum. Mrs. Bands always starts her children's day with a song, poem, or rhyme. This is a part of her daily routine. In addition to a specific time set aside for these activities, poetry, rhymes, and songs are woven throughout the day. Songs are often used to signal transitions from one activity to another. For example, the song "Clean Up, Everybody Do Their Share" is used to signal children to end the current activity and clean up. During movement and music activities, children dance and move to songs and poems. As the children sit to hear a book, Mrs. Bands uses the rhyme "crisscross applesauce" as a cue for everyone to sit quietly and listen to the book. In these various contexts, poetry, songs, and rhymes are integrated throughout the kindergarten day.

WRITING

Writing is a critical part of the language arts curriculum, but it is often the activity that gets the least attention. There are many ways in which writing can be integrated into the kindergarten language arts curriculum (Fang, 1999). As discussed in Chapter 11, writing for four- and five-year-olds can take many forms, and children will vary in their ability to express themselves in written form, ranging from scribbling and drawing pictures to some approximation of letters and words. The most important thing is to provide children opportunities to write and express themselves. Writing is intimately connected to reading, and opportunities to write will facilitate the development of emergent literacy skills.

Writing Throughout the Curriculum

Written work is abundant in Mrs. Bands' classroom. Words and expressions from the interactive morning message are on the blackboard. In the writer's corner, the children's written work is prominently displayed. Throughout the room, objects are labeled, and there are posters and objects with writing on them. In each child's cubby, there is a writing journal, which is used everyday. The focus is on expressing oneself in print. Mrs. Bands uses several activities to encourage and support writing in her classroom:

1. *Language experience:* Mrs. Bands wants her children to write about the experiences they have in the classroom. This will encourage them to think about their experiences as well as to begin to learn the relationship between print and reading. When the children returned from the playground and saw an anthill, Mrs. Bands had the children write about this experience. Some children drew pictures of what they saw, some drew pictures about what they speculated the ant farm looked like underground, and others wrote stories about ants going on a picnic. After the children wrote about their experience, Mrs. Bands asked three children to read what they had written about. The children then "read" and talked about what they had written. One student used the beginning letters of words followed by a scribble to depict her story. These children are learn-

ing that print is something you make and then read. This is the beginning of emergent writing.

2. *Shared writing:* In shared writing, the teacher writes the story or message as the children compose (Bajtelsmit & Naab, 1994). In doing this, the teacher is modeling the writing process, showing how the spoken word is translated into print. After the teacher read *Dr. DeSoto* to the children, the class composed a story about a trip to the dentist. As the children took turns, Mrs. Bands wrote down each child's line of the story. After the story was complete, she read it to the class.

3. *Journaling:* When the children in Mrs. Bands' class enter the classroom in the morning, they hang up their coats and backpacks in their cubby, take out their journals and begin writing. Children are encouraged to write about anything they want in their journals. They can write about what they did the night before, what they want to do in school during the day, or what they wish for or pretend about. Journal writing often is a private activity and not shared with the class. The teacher can ask children individually if they want to read something from their journal.

4. *Center writing:* To encourage writing, a writing corner is set up as one of the centers in the kindergarten classroom. Children are encouraged to write about topics related to the current theme. In the writing center, there are pictures and questions related to the theme that serve as story starters to help stimulate children's ideas about things to write about. In addition to a specific writing center, opportunities to write are provided in other centers. In the dramatic play center, a restaurant is set up with pads and pencils for children to take orders. In the construction center, the children have built a city and labeled the streets and stores. Integrating writing activities across the curriculum makes writing a natural part of the kindergarten curriculum.

DEVELOPING LETTER KNOWLEDGE

Learning letters is a milestone of the kindergarten curriculum (Wasik, 2001c). Through repeated and meaningful exposure to literacy events, children become aware of letters and understand that letters make up words. Learning letters in kindergarten creates a foundation for beginning reading in first grade (Schickedanz, 1999).

Young children learn best when they are constructing meaning from their environment and not being drilled with rote, meaningless information (Wasik, 2001c). There are several approaches to teaching the alphabet to kindergartners:

1. *Letter in a theme:* Teaching the alphabet through the theme approach is one way to instruct children in letter knowledge (Reutzel, 1992). In teaching a theme, the teacher selects letters that are likely to be encountered when teaching that theme. For example, in the grocery store theme, Mrs. Bands chose to teach the letter "A." She selected words that had a high probability of being encountered in the grocery store. Words such as "apple," "asparagus," "aisles," and "apron" were some words that she focused on to present the letter "A." Mrs. Bands then

introduced the letter "A" as the letter that these words begin with. On the field trip, she let the children search through the store and find other words that began with "A." Other activities during the grocery theme included attending to the letter "A." When Mrs. Bands read the alphabet book on fruits and vegetables, she highlighted the letter "A." Depending on the length of a theme, a letter is presented weekly. This approach requires that the teacher plan what themes he/she will do throughout the year and have a general plan of the letters that will be presented in each theme. Throughout each theme, letters that have already been presented are revisited to keep children reminded of the old letters as well as the new ones.

2. *Letter in names:* There is nothing more meaningful and personal to a child than his or her name. Teaching the alphabet using children's names is one approach of providing meaningful context for letters. Selecting a beginning letter of a child's name and giving the class repeated exposure to the name will facilitate letter learning. One of the drawbacks to using the letters in names is that not all 26 letters of the alphabet are likely to appear as the beginning letters in children's names. Names can be used as a way to introduce letters and then transition to another method to ensure that children are exposed to all the letters.

3. *Letter of the week:* Another common approach to teaching the alphabet to four- and five-year-olds is through the letter of the week. Teachers select a letter that they want to focus on and spend that week highlighting objects, names, and activities that begin with that letter. Children often bring in an object that begins with the letter of the week. One drawback with letter of the week is that there is not a context for learning the letter. Children learn best when there are connections between pieces of information that they are presented with. A letter of the week that is presented in isolation from other activities becomes devoid of meaning to the children. Because letters are very abstract to young children, it is important to present them in a context that is familiar or meaningful to them. In doing this, children can integrate an abstract symbol such as a letter, into meaningful information.

Integrating Letter Learning Throughout the Curriculum

Mrs. Bands is teaching the letter "D" as part of her theme on plants and growing. She has selected the words "dirt," "digging," and "dandelion," and the children added "daisies," "David" (a boy in the class who liked plants), and "drought." These words are focused on during the direct teaching of the letter "D." During the direct instruction, Mrs. Bands will model how the letter "D" is written in both upper- and lowercase, demonstrate what the letter "D" sounds like in the context of the words presented, and ask the children to generate other words beginning with the letter "D." Mrs. Bands will then talk about the letter "D" as opportunities present themselves throughout the day. The music teacher, Mr. Daniels, came to teach the children a new song, and Mrs. Bands was quick to ask the children what Mr. Daniels' name began with. Fred eagerly added that Mr. Daniels' drums also began with the letter "D." Mrs. Bands presented the letter and then looked for opportunities throughout the classroom experiences to reinforce knowledge of that letter. Through these multiple experiences, kindergartners will have many exposures to the letters of the alphabet.

IN SUMMARY

The language arts curriculum is an important aspect of children's language and literacy experiences. The language arts curriculum develops listening, speaking, reading, and writing skills in young children. These are critical components of an effective language arts curriculum for kindergartners. The activities that support the development of these abilities occur during book reading, circle time, center activities, writing, and letter learning. Integrating these activities across the kindergarten curriculum provides opportunities for young children to construct meaning from these experiences and develop a solid foundation in language and literacy skills.

EXTEND YOUR IDEAS

1. During a circle time activity, observe how much time you spend talking and how much time you spend listening to the children. Do you talk more than you listen? Do you provide opportunities for the children to speak in more than a one-word response?

2. Select five different types of books—for example, a concept book, a wordless book, a storybook, a pattern book, and an informational book—that focus on a similar theme. Plan how the books will be used in the week's activities. How are the different books used in different ways?

3. Find a community news item that is relevant to four- and five-year-olds. Discuss the news with the children. Help the children relate the news item to their experiences in their lives.

4. Select a poem or a rhyme for a class that is related to the current theme. Teach the children the poem or rhyme. After the children have learned the poem or rhyme, have them make up their own using the same tune. Have them play with the various rhyming patterns and rhyming words.

5. Develop a writing activity connected to the class theme. See how the children's writing varies depending on their developmental abilities. Have the children read what they write. Observe whether there is a relationship between what the child has written and what the child has read.

RESOURCES

Phonemic Awareness in Young Children: A Classroom Curriculum, by M. J. Adams, B. R. Foorman, I. Lundberg, and T. Beeler (Baltimore: Paul Brookes Publisher, 1997).

Early Childhood Language Arts: Meeting Diverse Literacy Needs Through Collaboration With Families and Professionals, by M. R. Jalongo (New York: Allyn & Bacon, 1999).

The Arnold Lobel Book of Mother Goose, by A. Lobel (New York: Random House, 1986).

The 20th Century Children's Poetry Treasury, by J. Prelutsky (New York: Knopf, 1999).

http://www.edpsych.com. This website has information regarding language arts in early childhood.

REFERENCES

Adams, M. J., Foorman, B. R., Lundberg, I., & Beeler, T. (1997). Phonemic awareness and young children: A classroom curriculum. Baltimore: Paul Brookes Publishers.

Bajtelsmit, L., & Naab, H. (1994). Partner writers: A shared reading and writing experience. *The Reading Teacher, 48,* 91–93.

Bialystok, E., Shenfield, T., & Codd, J. (2000). Language, scripts, and the environment: Factors in developing concepts of print. *Developmental Psychology, 36,* 66–76.

Bowman, B. T., Donovan, M. S., & Burns, M. S. (Eds.). (2001). Eager to learn: Educating our preschoolers. Washington, DC: National Academy Press.

Bredekamp, S., & Copple, C. (Ed.). (1997). Developmentally appropriate practice in early childhood programs. Washington, D.C.: National Association for the Education of Young Children.

Collins, F. (1999). The use of traditional storytelling in education to the learning of literacy skills. *Early Child Development and Care, 152,* 77–108.

Dickinson, D. K., & DiGisi, L. L. (1994). The many rewards of the literacy-rich classroom. *Educational Leadership, 55,* 23–26.

Dickinson, D. K., & Smith, M. W. (1994). Long-term effects of preschool teachers' book reading on low-income children's vocabulary and story comprehension. *Reading Research Quarterly, 29,* 104–122.

Dickinson, D. K., & Snow, C. (1987). Interrelationship among pre-reading and oral language skills in kindergartners from two social classes. *Early Childhood Research Quarterly, 2,* 1–25.

Fang, Z. (1999). Expanding the vista of emergent writing research: Implications for early childhood. *Early Childhood Education Journal, 26,* 179–182.

Ferguson, C. J. (1999). Building literacy skills with child-centered sociodramatic play centers. *Dimensions of Early Childhood, 27,* 23–29.

Greenberg, P. (1998). Some thoughts about phonics, feelings, Don Quixote, diversity and democracy: Teaching young children to read and write. *Young Children, 53,* 72–83.

Harris, T. T., & Fuqua, J. D. (2000). What goes around comes around: Building a community of learners through circle times. *Young Children, 55,* 44–47.

Hope, S., & Cumming, J. (1998). Language and laughter in the kitchen. *Primary Source Review, 53,* 22–23.

Jalongo, M. R. (1996). Teaching young children to become better listeners. *Young Children, 51,* 21–26.

Karges-Bone, L. (1992). Bring on the big books (in the classroom). *Reading Teacher, 45,* 743–744.

Kupetz, B. N., & Twiest, M. N. (2000). Nature, literature, and young children: A natural combination. *Young Children, 55,* 59–63.

Lietz, B. N., & Twiest, M. M. (2000). Nature, see also literature, and young children: A natural combination. *Young Children, 55*(1), 64–70.

Mackey, M. (1993). Many spaces: Some limitations of single readings. *Children's Literature in Education, 24,* 147–163.

Morrow, L. M., & Smith, J. K. (1990). The effects of group size on interactive storybook reading. *Reading Research Quarterly, 25,* 213–231.

Neuman, S. B., Copple, C., Bredekamp, S. (2000). Learning to read and write: Developmentally appropriate practices for young children. Newark, DE: International Reading Association Press.

Reutzel, D. (1992). Breaking the letter-a-week tradition: Conveying the alphabetic principle to young children. *Childhood Education, 69,* 20–23.

Robbins, C., & Ehri, L. E. (1994). Reading storybooks to kindergartners helps them learn vocabulary words. *Journal of Educational Psychology, 86,* 54–64.

Schickedanz, J. A. (1999). *Much more than the ABC's: The early stages of reading and writing.* Washington, DC: National Association for the Education of Young Children.

Seefeldt, C., & Barbour, N. (1998). *Early childhood education: An introduction* (4th ed.). Upper Saddle River, NJ: Merrill/Prentice Hall.

Spangler, C. B. (1997). The sharing circle: A child-centered curriculum. *Young Children, 52,* 74–78.

Sulzby, E. (1992). Transitions from emergent to conventional writing. *Language Arts, 69,* 290–297.

Sulzby, E., & Teale, W. H. (1985). Writing development in early childhood. *Educational Horizons, 64,* 8–12.

Wasik, B. A. (2001a). Phonemic awareness and young children. *International Journal of Childhood Education.*

Wasik, B. A. (2001b). Phonemic awareness and young children: Research into practice. *Childhood Education, 77,* 128–133.

Wasik, B. A. (2001c). Teaching the alphabet to young children. *Young Children, 56*(1), 34–39.

West, L. S., & Egley, E. H. (1998). Children get more than a hamburger: Using labels and logos to enhance literacy. *Dimensions of Early Childhood, 26,* 43–46.

Yopp, H. K. (1992). Developing phonemic awareness in young children. *Reading Teacher, 45,* 696–703.

CHAPTER 13 Integrated Mathematics in the Kindergarten

*J*ulia pours the brownie mix into a bowl. "Now you add one of the eggs," Mrs. Leaf says to Nikka. Nikka cracks the egg into the bowl and picks out some of the shells. "Jack, you can add the other egg. Remember we need two eggs." After the eggs are mixed in the bowl, Mrs. Leaf guides Mason in measuring a cup of oil. "Add the cup of oil into the mix," directs Mrs. Leaf. "Now we need to stir it about 50 times. How long do you think that is? Let's all count as everyone gets a chance to stir. When we finish, we need to put the pan in the oven and set our timer so we don't let the brownies overcook."

In this baking activity, there is a rich, exciting math lesson developing with Mrs. Leaf's four- and five-year-olds. The children are counting, estimating, measuring, and following directions. Four- and five-year-olds are interested in these activities and have the cognitive abilities to understand these mathematical concepts.

Unfortunately, mathematics is one of the most important yet least emphasized activities in the kindergarten classroom (Patton & Kokoski, 1996). Often teachers of young children express their own discomfort and lack of familiarity with mathematical concepts. Because of this, they are less willing to spend curriculum time on math. However, mathematical thinking and reasoning skills have their roots in early concepts such as identifying relationships and patterns in objects and events and developing a sense of number. With a good understanding of mathematical concepts, teachers can effectively integrate math activities throughout the curriculum.

In this chapter, we will address the essential mathematical concepts that young children must develop as a solid foundation in their mathematical thinking. This chapter will first address the cognitive skills that four- and five-year-olds need to develop to allow them to understand certain math concepts. Second, essential components to teaching mathematics to young children are presented. Finally, the goals for mathematics learning will be presented according to the Principles and Standards for School Mathematics (National Council of Teachers of Mathematics [NCTM], 2000). With each goal, activities that are appropriate for four- and five-year-olds will be detailed that support the goal.

FOUR- AND FIVE-YEAR-OLDS' THINKING AND MATHEMATICS

As we discussed in Chapter 3, four- and five-year-olds' thinking and reasoning are changing and developing at rapid rates. These changes in cognition allow young children to understand mathematical concepts in new ways. During this period, children are beginning to do the following:

1. **Think symbolically:** They are beginning to understand that words such as "Mary" and "Sam" represent a person. Similarly, they are beginning to understand that abstract things such as numbers can represent the quantity of objects (Unglaub, 1997).

2. **Understand conservation of number:** Conservation is the ability to understand that materials and objects stay the same regardless of changes in form or arrangement in space. For example, when a child understands that three sticks placed close together are the same number of sticks as three sticks placed far apart, they understand conservation of number. Four-year-olds are not capable

of understanding conservation. For five-year-olds, conservation of number is developing and is generally solidified by the time children turn six years of age. Conservation is an important ability that allows children to understand more complex concepts in mathematics (Sophian, 1995).

3. Think semilogically: Children's thinking and reasoning at this age is called *semilogical* because their logical reasoning is limited. Four- and five-year-olds are unable to keep in mind more than one relationship at a time. They have difficulty making comparisons and seeing relationships (White, Alexander, & Daugherty, 1998). In addition, they are unable to use reversible thought processes that would allow them to think with the same logic as an older child or adult.

These cognitive constraints limit the amount of mathematical understanding young children can have. However, experiences and opportunities to learn provide a context for young children to develop the precursors they need for more complex mathematical thinking.

ESSENTIAL COMPONENTS OF A MATH CURRICULUM FOR FOUR- AND FIVE-YEAR-OLDS

According to the *Principles and Standards for School Mathematics* (NCTM, 2000), the foundation for children's mathematical development is established in the early years. Mathematics builds on the curiosity and enthusiasm of children and grows naturally from their experiences. In order for young children to learn age-appropriate math concepts, they must (1) develop mathematical language, (2) have interactive opportunities for math experiences, and (3) be motivated to be interested in math.

Developing Mathematical Language

"This circle is bigger than that one," reports a five-year-old when he is asked to look at the two circles that he drew and tell the class something about them. In Ms. Valle's kindergarten class, the children are encouraged to learn the language of mathematics. Children's talk and informal conversations about their activities can lead to the development of language that can be used to describe mathematical concepts and procedures (Towse & Saxton, 1997). As children learn the names of shapes, such as circles, squares, and triangles, they are learning the language of mathematics. Similarly, as children learn to accurately use the words "smaller than," "bigger than," and "different from," they are learning words to describe mathematical concepts. Learning words that help describe patterns, the size and shape of objects, and the relationships of objects to one another helps children develop the language of math.

Children's literature can reinforce the development of mathematical language (Liedtke, 1997). Counting books, such as *Ten Black Dots* (Crews, 1986) and *Feast for Ten* (Falwell, 1993), are a good way to reinforce math concepts through reading. Books about sorting, such as *Hannah's Collection* (Jocelyn, 2000) and *The Button Box*

(Reid, 1990), and books about shapes, such as *So Many Circles, So Many Squares* (Hoban, 1998) and *The Shape of Things* (Dodds, 1996), are examples of literature that can be related to math.

Some direct instruction of mathematical vocabulary has been recommended to help children understand certain words (Munroe & Panchyshyn, 1996). Because children do not typically use mathematical vocabulary spontaneously, they can be reminded that they want "half" of a sandwich and "one quarter" of an apple, that the window is a "rectangle," and that a yield sign is a "triangle."

Interactive Opportunities for Math Experience

In one corner of the room, two children are sorting buttons into similar colors. In the construction center, a small group of children is laying out all the blocks to see how long the row is. Three children are weighing different objects using the scale at the sand table. Children need a variety of materials to manipulate and the opportunities to sort, classify, count, weigh, measure, stack, and explore if they are to construct mathematical knowledge. In order to have opportunities to learn math, children need (1) firsthand experiences related to math, (2) interaction with other children and adults concerning these experiences, and (3) time to reflect on the experiences.

Firsthand Experiences.   Children's firsthand experiences with materials related to math serve a number of purposes (Pratt, 1995). First, using manipulatives forces children to think about and react to concrete objects in their environment. The child who counts the number of Legos that will fit into his footprint or the child who graphs the number of children who like chocolate are not only thinking about a problem but also actively solving it. Activities that require children to think, seek relationships, make patterns, count, and sort help children work through the activity mentally and physically.

Providing children opportunities to work with materials with open-ended objectives that have no specific preset goals offers children the chance to explore their own questions and generate a variety of answers. These experiences help children think about their world in alternative ways and help them understand that there are multiple ways to solve problems. Generating multiple solutions to problems is an essential strategy in mathematics.

Interaction with Others.   Children construct knowledge by interacting with people (Inhelder & Piaget, 1969; Vygotsky, 1978). Through interaction with peers, children's ideas about the way things are bump head-on into other people's ideas about the world. It is through this bumping together of differing ideas that children are able to question their own views of the world and make adjustments to their own thinking. In Mrs. Thompson's class, four children are trying to figure out how to arrange the blocks of varying shapes so that they will have enough blocks to build a bridge over the pretend lake. One child tries to use the smaller blocks because he says that they are lighter and will not fall down as easily. Another child shows how the larger block is a better choice because it is length, not weight, that is important. Through trial and error and encouraging one another to "try this and try that," a bridge is carefully constructed. Children learn from one another.

Group projects are a good way to encourage peer exchange and feedback. When children are working on solving a common problem, the situation encourages children to share their ideas and strategies (Ward, 1995). Working together making pancakes or creating a hideout from a discarded computer box, children will have to count, measure, and compare as they exchange ideas, correct one another, and adjust their thinking to take into account other children.

Interactions with and feedback from teachers is also critical to developing mathematical thinking in four- and five-year-olds. Through formal instruction, teachers can teach children concepts such as "bigger than," "smaller than," "more than," and "less than." By providing feedback, teachers can also correct misconceptions that children may have about mathematical principles. Mrs. Thompson asked one of the children building the bridge, "Do you think that the longer blocks would be better?" as the child was stringing the small blocks together. As the child reached for a long block, he said, "I'll give it a try." This questioning provides a context for children to think about the strategies that they are using and to consider alternative strategies.

Teachers can focus children's attention or thinking by demonstrating a skill or procedure, making a statement, or asking a question. For example, "You put all those buttons together. Why did you do that? Why do you think they belong together?" Teachers might ask children to try something another way: "What would happen if we separated all the buttons with 2 holes and all the buttons with 4 holes?" "Can you do it another way?" As the teacher observes the children as they play and work, she can try to make connections and extend their thinking to mathematical concepts.

Children can focus their attention on a specific skill.

Time for Reflection.   To reason, to solve problems, and to see mathematical connections, children need time to think about their actions on the world (Franke & Carey, 1997). This is not a natural activity for four- and five-year-olds. Therefore, circumstances need to be created in the classroom that allow for the reflection to occur.

Teachers need to create opportunities that allow children to reflect on their thinking. After an activity, teachers can ask, "Why did you put all the yellow chips in one pile and all the red ones in another?", "How many muffins do we need to make for everyone to have one to eat?", and "We have four center activities; how many children can be at each center?" These questions allow children to think about math concepts in everyday activities that they engage in. With repeated exposure to these kinds of inquiry, children will begin to view the world through a mathematical lens.

Motivating Interest in Math

Four- and five-year-olds can learn to love to think and reason mathematically if they learn to enjoy math. One of the goals of the kindergarten experience is to instill in children a love of math (May, 1995). However, this attitude must begin with the teacher. Teachers of young children must be comfortable with math concepts and develop a firm understanding of how to weave math throughout daily activities. Also, teachers must positively reinforce children's perceptions of themselves as learners of math. Explicitly telling children that they are good in counting, sorting, or math will help shape their perception of themselves as mathematical thinkers.

In order for teachers to present mathematical concepts effectively to young children, they must understand what four- and five-year-olds are capable of learning. Typically, teachers of young children err in not challenging children with age-appropriate math. There is a misconception that math is difficult and that it should be reserved for older children. However, it is important to know that the activities used to present math concepts are designed for young children and are effective in teaching math (Clements, Battista, Sarama, & Swaminathan, 1997). A teacher can present abstract concepts, such as "more" and "less," by graphing preferences to chocolate and vanilla ice cream or the number of children wearing sneakers and shoes. Activities that are appropriate for the children's age and interest can motivate them to love math.

MATH STANDARDS FOR FOUR- AND FIVE-YEAR-OLDS

The *Principles and Standards for School Mathematics*, which was developed by a group of educators from the National Council of Teachers of Mathematics (NCTM, 2000), describe the expectations for math for four- and five-year-olds. In the following section, the concepts that four- and five-year-olds can understand regarding number, geometry, measuring, and probability and graphing are outlined. Activities that support the learning of these concepts are also presented.

Number

One of the most important mathematical concepts learned by four- and five-year-olds is the development of number sense. A sense of number is more than just counting. It involves developing a sense of quantity and an understanding of one-to-one correspondence (Hartnett & Gelman, 1998). As number sense develops, children begin to recognize gross interpretations of quantity, such as "more" and "less." Janis has more crayons than Phillip. Mrs. Wiest has more children than chairs in the room.

As children's sense of number develops, they become increasingly interested in counting. This counting becomes the foundation for children's early work with numbers (NCTM, 2000). Like the counting segment on *Sesame Street*, four- and five-year-olds love to count for the sake of counting. They will count the stairs they climb, the treats they eat, and the petals on a flower.

Most four-year-olds are learning the names for numbers and can often rattle off one, two, three, four, or five without an understanding of the relationship of quantity to number. Often the numbers are called out like a string of words without the appropriate meaning connected with them. This occurs because, although four-year-olds have an intrinsic interest in numbers and counting, they lack an understanding of the one-to-one relationship between number and object. Four-year-olds do not entirely grasp the concept that the term "one" represents the concept of one object and that the term "two" represents the quantity of two objects and so on. Repeated exposure to counting will help young children learn the names for numbers and the sequence that numbers follow. Counting the number of children in a center, the number of children present in the class, and the number of napkins passed out at snack time will reinforce counting.

With growth and experience, four-year-olds initially develop the concept of "one" and "more than one" (Unglaub, 1997). As children's sense of number develops, four-year-olds begin to comprehend that the word "one" indicates a single object and that "more than one" is associated with the remaining numbers—two, three, four, five, and so on. Although counting continues to be a frequent activity, children are developing an increased awareness of "more" and "less" and "one" and "more than one."

The concept of number and one-to-one number correspondence becomes more solidified for five-year-olds. Children make more of an effort to assign a number value to an object that they are counting. Counting activities can be woven into children's daily activities. Children count the number of children who want juice for a snack, the number of children allowed in a center at one time, the number of beads needed to make a necklace, and the number of children who like the color red.

Learning the names that correspond to numbers is also part of learning how to count (Caufield, 2000). Numbers are a part of children's daily experiences. People will ask children how old they are, the numbers on the buses they take, the numbers on their classroom doors, and the numbers on their houses. Four- and five-year-olds are learning that the number "one" is written as "1" and that it means a quantity of "one." Activities such as writing children's ages on their birthday, reading counting books that show numbers associated with the quantity of items, and writing their height and weight help children learn the names of numbers and the symbols that are associated with them. Five-year-olds are developing a better understanding of numbers and number names (Sophian, 1995). They want to count and record the number of chocolate chips on their ice cream and are interested in writing numbers and learning what numbers mean.

Algebra

According to the NCTM standards (NCTM, 2000), young children's first encounter with algebra begins with sorting, classifying, comparing, and ordering objects by size, number, and other properties. Also, recognizing, describing, and extending patterns contribute to the children's understanding of classification.

Classification

Classification—putting things together that are alike or that belong together—is one of the necessary processes for developing a concept of number. In order for four- and five-year-olds to classify or sort objects, they must develop an understanding of "belongingness," "likeness," "sameness," and "different" (Ginsburg & Seo, 1999). Mathematics programs for young children need to focus on the acquisition of these concepts and verbal labels for them (Milko, 1995). Classroom activities that support the development of children's ability to classify and sort objects into same and different categories reinforce the development of these concepts.

Children's encounters with algebra begin with sorting and classifying.

Sorting and classifying can be a part of everyday activities. Four- and five-year-olds learn classifying through the following:

◆ Sorting the toys in the classroom into appropriate categories, placing all the blocks in one cubby, all the puzzles in another cubby, and all the arts and crafts materials on another shelf.

◆ Providing children with manipulatives of various shapes and sizes and guiding them to sort them into groups that are the same and different. Ask the children to tell you why they grouped the objects in the way that they did.

◆ Providing children with collections of things, such as buttons, seashells, beads, or rocks. Ask the children to sort them into groups and describe the rationale for their decisions.

◆ Asking children to sort themselves into groups on the basis of their likes and dislikes, things that they are wearing, or the color of their hair. For example, have the children identify who likes pizza better than hotdogs. Group the children accordingly.

◆ Using common objects in the classroom, such as a box of blocks, colored chips, or plastic food from the housekeeping center, have the children sort the objects into groups of same and different.

Four- and five-year-olds typically do not use superordinate categories to sort and classify objects (Gelman, 1998). They will group a dog, a cat, and a mouse together on the basis of the color of the fur or the fact that all have two eyes. Four- and five-year-olds select the attributes that they choose to group things by and can often change classification strategies halfway through the process. Angel was sorting beads on the basis of color and then decided to sort on the basis of the size of the bead. Five-year-olds develop a better sense of consistent categories and can follow through from beginning to end.

Comparing.   Comparing is the process by which children establish a relation between two objects on the basis of some specific attribute. Four- and five-year-olds frequently make comparisons, especially when the comparisons involve them personally. It is not uncommon to hear four- and five-year-olds say, "I want the biggest piece of cake," "She got more than me," "I want the new cup," and "He got to use the toy the littlest."

Four- and five-year-olds are learning to observe the world and are becoming aware of the relative size of objects (Olson & Olson, 1997). They are learning the concepts and the labels for "biggest," "smallest," "tallest," "shortest," "more," and "less." Shelia made a tower out of Legos and announced to the class that hers was the tallest in the room. Tyrone bangs the drum and proudly claims that he is making the loudest noise. At that moment, the bell rings, and the teacher asks, "Is that bell louder than your drum?" Children are learning to recognize similarities and differences while making comparisons.

The following activities can guide four- and five-year-olds in making comparisons:

◆ Have children get into pairs and make comparisons to see who is the tallest, who is the shortest, who has the longest hair, and who has the biggest feet. Have the children lie on the floor and trace their bodies and hang them on the wall.

◆ Keeping children in partners, have them run across the playground to see who is faster.
◆ Have two children swing on the swing set and ask the children to observe who is swinging the highest and who is moving the fastest.
◆ Using the water table, have the children fill up containers and the ones that keep more water to the ones that keep less.

Literature provides another way of reinforcing the use of comparisons. Books such as *The Three Little Bears, The Three Billy Goats Gruff,* and *When the Door Bell Rang* highlight comparisons that are made among characters and objects.

Ordering. Ordering is a higher level of comparing. It involves comparing more than two things or more than two sets and involves placing things in a sequence from first to last. The ability to seriate, or order, often follows children's development of conservation and classification (Southard & Pasnak, 1997). This is a difficult concept for four- and five-year-olds. They are able to follow a pattern of ordering objects when a model is present. However, without a model, four- and five-year-olds make comparisons on the basis of the most proximal objects in a series. For example, in ordering sticks, they may order two sticks, one larger and one smaller. The next stick added to the sequence could be a smaller stick because they have switched the unit of comparison from bigger to smaller.

For four- and five-year-olds, ordering is a concept that can be practiced in classroom activities. As the children line up to transition to the next activity, they can order themselves in a line from the tallest to the smallest child. The blocks in the cabinet can be stacked from the biggest to the smallest. The books can be arranged from the thickest to the thinnest. These experiences expose young children to the concepts and vocabulary of ordering.

Patterns. Identifying and creating patterns is related to classification and sorting. Children begin to see the same and different attributes of pictures and objects (James, 2000). Four- and five-year-olds love to make and recognize patterns in their environment. Allan marched in from the rain, watching the footprints that his sneakers were making, and said, "Look at the cool pattern I made!" Children search for similarities in their environment. Discovering patterns in a snowflake, in drips of paint, or in the design on a container of applesauce is fun and challenging for four- and five-year-olds.

Activities that allow children to construct patterns from beads and blocks will support the development of this skill. Also, matching activities, which allow children to copy a pattern, help children develop a sense of sequence and relationships. The following activities can support children's recognition and construction of patterns:

◆ Have pairs of children alternate stamping a paper so that they form a repeated pattern.
◆ Have the children string beads, making a pattern. Have their partners match their pattern.
◆ Use the calendar to create patterns to mark off the days of the week.
◆ Identify repeated patterns in familiar and new songs.

Identifying and creating patterns is related to sorting and classifying.

The ability to recognize patterns will help children develop skills that can be used in sorting, classifying, identifying shapes, and making graphs.

Geometry

Building concepts of geometry in young children begins with identifying shapes and exploring the construction and taking apart of common figures such as squares, circles, rectangles, and triangles (Hannibal, 1999). In addition, learning both the concepts and the language to express location such as under, on top of, left, and right sets the rudimentary foundation of understanding geometry.

While four- and five-year-olds are playing with blocks, doing a puzzle, or playing a board game, they are learning the principles of geometry. Hannah is sitting on the floor constructing a large puzzle, and she asks the teachers, "What piece would fit into this spot?" The teacher replies, "What does that shape look like?" Hannah responds by saying that it looks like her baby brother's head. "Yes, it does," says the teacher, "it looks like an oval piece."

Create situations in the classroom that can reinforce children's learning of shapes. Provide children with experiences in their immediate environment that allow them to identify shapes and figures. What shape is the kite? How many squares can fit into that place mat? What shape blocks would you need to fit through the narrow space?

Making children aware of geometric forms in their natural environment allows them to make associations between familiar objects and unfamiliar words. The top of the teacher's desk is a rectangle, the welcome flag at their classroom door is a hexagon, and the pretty pink purse in the dress-up corner is a triangle. Using geoboards and tangram pieces provides children with opportunities to construct geometric forms and to learn the appropriate names for them (Clements, Swaminathan, Hannibal, & Sarama, 1999).

When teachers use terms that communicate direction in space, children will become more aware of these terms and learn to use them appropriately. "Get the block from under the table," "Leave the paint next to the easel," "Put the book on top of the table," and "Put the fabric over the doll" are examples of commands that indicate the location of objects in space. Games such as "Simon Says" and "Looby Loo" reinforce terms such as "up/down," "right/left," and "top/bottom." Practice using these terms in everyday activities to reinforce children's knowledge of these words.

Measurement

Four- and five-year-olds' interest and ability to use measurement develops from experiences with classifying, comparing, and ordering. As children compare the length of two teddy bears, weigh a cup of milk, and see that a red cup holds as much water as two blue cups, they are learning about the concept of measurement (Outhred & Mitchelmore, 2000).

Four- and five-year-olds typically do not use standard units to measure, such as a tape measure or a ruler. Instead, they use arbitrary units, such as the number of footsteps, the length of an arm, blocks, or paper clips, to measure. In discussing measurement, four- and five-year-olds will use an analogy to describe the size of an object, such as "We made a fort that was as big as my dog" and "Johnny was about 10 footsteps away from me." Four- and five-year-olds need experiences in measuring objects in order to conceptualize the size of familiar things around them.

Measurement of weight is also a concept that four- and five-year-olds are capable of learning and are extremely interested in. At the water table, Freddy is using a plastic scale to weigh the water toys along with some of the rocks and seashells from the tide pool that his class constructed. "Watch, just one rock and all these shells, and the rock still pulls the scale way down." Four- and five-year-olds still have difficulty with conservation of size and weight and will not understand that one object is heavier than four or five objects.

In order to have hands-on experiences with measurement, children can do the following:

◆ Measure their body length using blocks or string
◆ Measure the growth of an amaryllis plant in the winter
◆ Measure the distance between each activity table or the length of their gloves using pipe cleaners
◆ Weigh their snacks to see whose weighs the most
◆ Weigh the objects that children bring in for show-and-tell to see whose is the lightest and whose is the heaviest

As four- and five-year-olds have opportunities for hands-on experiences to measure, weigh, and compare the size of objects, they are learning concepts of measurement. Through these experiences, four- and five-year-olds develop a solid foundation in the concepts of measurement that will help them use more standard units of measure, such as rulers and scales, as they enter primary school.

Data Analysis and Probability

Experimenting with measurement, along with classifying and sorting, provides young children with tools to understand probability and data analysis (Hinnant, 1999). For four- and five-year-olds, this means posing questions, gathering information about themselves and their surroundings, and representing this information pictorially. Four- and five-year-olds can be introduced to graphing and learn how graphs allow them to compare quantities of objects or preferences (Whitin, 1997).

The children in Mr. Evans' class are deciding on which stuffed animal they want as a class mascot. The choices are a turtle, a bear, and a monkey. On the bulletin board, he has posted pictures of each of the animals. One by one, Mr. Evans asks the children what their choice is for the mascot. Each child places a round circle with his/her name on it on a line above the mascot of his/her choice. After all the children's circles are on the board, Mr. Evans leads the group in counting the number of circles in each row. As the children could clearly see, the turtle won hands down.

Providing opportunities for children to use graphs to represent comparisons, preferences, and the number of objects in a category helps children understand concepts such as "more," "less," and "equal." With four- and five-year-olds, it is important to keep graphing simple and related to the children's experiences. By using circles, Mr. Evans was able to have the children see that 9 out of the 15 children selected the turtle. However, children did not need to have an understanding of number to see that one row had *more* circles in it than the others. Graphing reinforces sorting, classifying, and comparing using pictures, which young children can relate to.

Graphing can be integrated into various activities. As the children take off their boots, have them sort them by color and graph the number of each different color boots. At snack time, graph children's selection for milk, juice, and water. Have children collect data on the growth of a plant or grass seed. Once a week, have the children measure their plant with strips of paper and chart the plant's growth. Have children vote on their preference of peanut butter and jelly, pizza, or hotdogs for lunch. Experiences that allow children to gather data and represent the data using concrete objects, pictures, or graphs will support children's understanding of fundamental math concepts.

Although graphing and charting data is fun, one of the most important purposes of collecting data is to answer questions when answers are not immediately obvious. Four- and five-year-olds need guidance in asking questions and figuring out ways to answer the questions. Ted asked Mr. Evans how many different kinds of magnets they had in the science corner. Mr. Evans asked Ted to try to figure this out by sorting all the same magnets into different piles. When Ted finished, Mr. Evans asked Ted which pile looked like it had more in it. Ted correctly said that it was the one with all the round magnets. Mr. Evans then helped Ted graph the number of magnets in each pile. Ted began with a simple question and, with the guidance of Mr. Evans, was able to expand his simple query into a mathematical question and found a solution.

Problem Solving.   According to the NCTM standards (2000), problem solving is a hallmark mathematical activity and a significant means of developing mathematical knowledge. For four- and five-year-olds, problem solving is a very natural activity because so much in the world is new to them and they are constantly exhibiting curiosity, intelligence, and flexibility in their thinking as they face new situations.

Four- and five year-olds are filled with questions. How much food should I give to the rabbit? How can I make a train out these boxes? How can I get this puzzle piece in the open space? Children need opportunities to explore their environment and have the freedom to ask questions.

Teachers are an important part of the problem-solving process (Myren, 1996). Teachers can stimulate children's curiosity and make it possible for them to solve problems in active ways. Teachers have to be willing to let children's questions guide them into activities or projects that are not always planned. Seeing all the boots were lined up in the hallway, Daton asked who had the biggest feet in the class. Mr. Evans could have said that that was a good question and then told Daton that he could solve that by looking at the boots. Instead, because the children were interested, he guided them through the problem-solving process. First, he asked the children how they could figure this out. Tommy said that they could look at one another's feet. Daton said that they could line up the boots and find out whose were bigger. Mr. Evans suggested that they line up the boots and try to see whose are bigger and whose are smaller. The class worked together solving this problem. Mr. Evans encouraged the children to ask questions and think about ways to develop solutions to their problems.

Integrating Math Throughout the Curriculum

In most four- and five-year-old classrooms, time is made in the schedule for mathematics. Typically, this time is used as an opportunity for teachers to explicitly explain and demonstrate concepts such as sorting, classifying, and identifying shapes. However, math concepts can be reinforced throughout the day through most activities that take place in the classroom.

In order for this to occur, teachers of young children need to think mathematically. In reading a story, they can count the number of characters on a page. Cooking activities are minilaboratories for reinforcing a variety of math concepts. Making a batch of cookies involves measuring, comparing, sorting, and counting. In a finger play activity, there are opportunities to count and hear patterns in language. Lining up to go to the washroom, children come to understand "first" and "last" and "front" and "back." Children see patterns in their flower beds at school. Teachers need to take advantage of the opportunities that present themselves and find teachable moments to reinforce math concepts.

Children need opportunities to see that math can be a part of everyday life. We count the number of napkins that we need for snack time and figure out how long we have to play outside before we need to leave for home. Keeping math isolated from natural experiences will reinforce that math is separate from other learning experiences. Math can be made to be an integral part of all learning. Children need to be provided with opportunities to count, sort, and classify in a variety of contexts. This will support children's development of mathematical thinking and reasoning.

IN SUMMARY

Mathematics plays an important part in the kindergarten curriculum. Four- and five-year-olds are developing cognitive skills that allow them to think and reason about numbers and quantities. According to the National Council of Teachers of Mathematics (2000), the foundation for knowledge of mathematics must begin in the early years. Young children must develop mathematical language, have opportunities for interactive mathematical experiences, and be motivated to learn about math.

An effective early childhood curriculum needs to teach young children using developmentally appropriate activities to introduce specific concepts regarding number, geometry, measuring, probability, and graphing. Young children need to have opportunities to develop a sense of number, which includes more than just counting. They need to develop a sense of quantity and one-to-one correspondence. Four- and five-year-olds need to have opportunities to interact with activities that support the fundamental concepts of algebra that include classifying, sorting, comparing and contrasting, ordering of objects, and identifying patterns. Fundamentals of geometry are also an important part of the kindergarten math curriculum, including identifying shapes and learning to communicate direction in space.

Measurement is also an important math skill for four- and five-year-olds to learn. Children learn these concepts by measuring the length and weight of objects in the world that surrounds them. Typically, four- and five-year-olds do not use standard units in measuring and instead are learning concepts such as "bigger or smaller than," "longer or shorter than," and "heavier or lighter than." Kindergartners are collecting information from their environment and representing that data through pictures. Children are beginning to understand that information can be expressed in number and amounts such as the number of children who like chocolate and the amount of rain that fell during each day of the week.

Providing experiences that allow four- and five-year-olds to think about their world in terms of numbers, quantity, and categories will help them develop essential early math skills. Integrating mathematics throughout the curriculum will help young children develop a solid foundation in mathematical thinking.

EXTEND YOUR IDEAS

1. Have four- and five-year-olds keep a growth journal. Have them weigh and measure themselves at three points throughout the year. Have them trace their hands and feet at the beginning and the end of the year and compare the differences.

2. Select books that can be used for a math lesson, such as *When the Doorbell Rings*. Read the book to your class and design a math activity that supports the concepts presented in the book. Have the children tell their own stories that include math concepts.

3. Have the children keep a math journal. In the journal they can write about things that they count, measure, weigh, and sort.

4. Plan five math activities related to the current theme in the classroom. Have the activities include the following: sorting, measuring, classifying, and counting.

5. Have the children sort the toys in the dramatic play area according to categories that they suggest. Note how they classify the objects. Discuss with the children the underlying logic upon which they based their reasoning.

6. Plan a walking trip of the school in which the children identify various shapes that are in common objects such as squares, rectangles, ovals, circles, and triangles. Have the children draw some object when they return to the classroom.

7. Observe in a kindergarten classroom and record the math activities in a day. Design activities that could have been incorporated into the theme and would be integrated into the other classroom activities.

REFERENCES

Caufield, R. (2000). Number matters: Born to count. *Early Childhood Education Journal, 28,* 63–65.

Clements, D. H., Battista, M. T., Sarama, J., & Swaminathan, S. (1997). Development of children's spatial thinking in a unit on geometric motions and area. *Elementary School Journal, 98* (2), 171–186.

Clements, D. H., Swaminathan, S., Hannibal, M. A., & Sarama, J. (1999). Young children's concept of shape. *Journal for Research in Mathematics Education, 30,* 192–212.

Crews, D. (1986). Ten black dots. New York, NY: William Morrow & Company.

Dodds, D. A. (1996). The shape of things. Cambridge, MA: Candlewick Press.

Falwell, C. (1993). Feast for ten. New York, NY: Clarion Books.

Franke, M. L., & Carey, D. A. (1997). Young children's perceptions of mathematics in problem-solving experiments. *Journal for Research in Mathematics Education, 28,* 8–25.

Gelman, S. A. (1998). Categories in young children's thinking: Research and review. *Young Children, 53,* 20–26.

Ginsburg, H. P., & Seo, K. H. (1999). Mathematics in children's thinking. *Mathematical Thinking and Learning, 1* (2), 113–129.

Hannibal, M. A. (1999). Young children's developing understanding of geometric shapes. *Teaching Children Mathematics, 5,* 353–357.

Hartnett, P., & Gelman, R. (1998). Early understanding of numbers: Path or barriers to the construction of new understanding. *Learning and Instruction, 8,* 341–374.

Hinnant, H. A. (1999). Growing gardens and mathematics: More books and math for young children. *Young Children, 54,* 23–26.

Hoban, T. (1998). So many circles, so many squares. New York, NY: Greenwillow Press.

Inhelder, B., & Piaget, J. (1969). *The psychology of the child.* New York: Basic Books.

James, A. R. (2000). When I listen to music. *Young Children, 55,* 36–37.

Jocelyn, M. (2000). Hannah's collections. Toronto, Ontario: Tundra Books.

Liedtke, W. (1997). Fostering the development of mathematical literacy in early childhood. *Canadian Children, 22,* 13–18.

May, L. (1995). Motivating activities: Teaching math. *Teaching PreK–8, 26,* 26–27.

Milko, S. J. (1995). Developing young children's classification and logical thinking skills. *Childhood Education, 72,* 24–28.

Munroe, E. E. & Panchyshyn, R. (1996). Vocabulary considerations for teaching mathematics. *Childhood Education, 72,* 80–83.

Myren, C. L. (1996). Encouraging young children to solve problems independently. *Teaching Children Mathematics, 3,* 72–76.

National Council of Teachers of Mathematics (2000). Curriculum and evaluation standards for school mathematics. Reston, VA: Author.

Olson, J., & Olson, M. (1997). Classification and logical reasoning. *Teaching Children Mathematics, 4,* 28–29.

Outhred, L. N., & Mitchelmore, M. C. (2000). Young children's intuitive understanding of rectangular area measurement. *Journal for Research in Mathematics Education, 31,* 144–167.

Patton, M. M., & Kokoski, T. M. (1996). How good is your early childhood science, mathematics, and technology program? Strategies for extending your curriculum. *Young Children, 51,* 38–44.

Pratt, D. (1995). Young children's active and passive graphing. *Journal of Computer-Assisted Learning, 11,* 157–169.

Reid, M. (1990). The Button Box. New York, NY: E. P. Dutton Publishers.

Sophian, C. (1995). Representation and reasoning in early numerical development: Counting, conservation, and comparison between sets. *Child Development, 66,* 559–577.

Sophian, C., Wood, A. M., & Vong, K. I. (1995). Making numbers count: The development of early numerical inferences. *Developmental Psychology, 31* (2), 263–273.

Southard, M., & Pasnak, R. (1997). Effects of maturation on preoperational seriation. *Child Study Journal, 27,* 255–268.

Towse, J. N., & Saxton, M. (1997). Linguistic influences on children's number concepts: Methodological and theoretical considerations. *Journal of Experimental Child Psychology, 66,* 362–375.

Unglaub, K. W. (1997). What counts in learning to count? *Young Children, 52,* 48–50.

Vygotsky, L. S. (1978). *Mind in society: The development of higher psychological processes.* Cambridge, MA: Harvard University Press.

Ward, C. D. (1995). Meaningful mathematics with young children. *Dimensions of Early Childhood, 23,* 7–11.

White, L. S., Alexander, P. A., & Daugherty, M. (1998). The relationship between young children's analogical reasoning and mathematical learning. *Mathematical Cognition, 4,* 103–123.

Whitin, D. J. (1997). Collecting data with young children. *Young Children, 52,* 28–32.

CHAPTER 14 Children Study Their World: The Life, Physical, and Earth Sciences

"*L*ook, *there's a spider climbing up the wall,*" Sabrina exclaimed just as Ms. Benesh, who was leading a lesson on numeracy, had asked the children to find three red things in the classroom. "Oh," said one of the children, "it's the Itsy Bitsy Spider." "No, it's Ms. Muffet's spider," said another. "It's climbing, climbing higher and higher," others chimed in. By now no child was counting three of anything and all eyes were focused on the rather large, furry, spider climbing up the wall.

Responding to the children's interests, Ms. Benesh, stopped talking about numerals and asked the children, a few at a time, to get their clipboards, or a pad of paper and marker from the writing area so that they could sketch the spider. As they sketched, she began the process of scientific inquiry by asking questions: "How many legs does the spider have?" The children engaged in counting, not to three but eventually to eight. "How does it move its legs—all at once or one at a time?" "Look at its body parts—how many body parts does it have? What parts seem furry? Which are smooth?"

When the spider settled down in a corner of the ceiling and started to spin a web, the teacher asked, "How can we find out what kind of spider is making its home in our room?" The children said, "We know, we know. Let's look in a book." "I found it," said one child, bringing a book of insects to the group. To their surprise, spiders were nowhere to be found in the book about insects. This raised a great deal of puzzlement on the part of the children and additional questions.

The life, physical, and earth sciences are not a once-a-week or even a once-a-day occurrence (Landry & Forman, 1999; Rakow & Bell, 1998). They take place continually as children wonder about their world and all that is in it. Like Ms. Benesh, teachers use every opportunity to promote the skills and methods of scientific inquiry and at the same time the scientific concepts that will enable children to do the following:

◆ Learn and understand their world
◆ Be open to divergent ways of thinking and knowing
◆ Develop the skills involved in thinking and problem solving
◆ Take the long leap into new ideas and more complex ways of thinking

The National Science Education Standards (National Academy Press [NAP], 1996) and the National Council for the Social Studies (NCSS, 1998) both advocate introducing students to scientific inquiry early in their schooling. They do so not to create life, physical, or earth scientists but to enable children to gain scientific inquiry skills as well as knowledge and understanding of their physical and biological worlds. The NCSS states that the "skills that are appropriate for young children to learn include, but are not limited to, research skills, such as collecting, organizing, and interpreting data; and thinking skills such as hypothesizing, comparing, drawing conclusions and inferences" (NCSS, 1998, p. 2).

Similarly, the National Academy Press calls for the multifaceted activity of scientific inquiry that "involves making observations; posing questions; examining books and other sources of information to see what is already known . . . planning investigations; using tools to gather, analyze, and interpret data; proposing answers . . . and communicating the results" (NAP, 1996, p. 23).

SCIENTIFIC INQUIRY SKILLS

 o be able to think and act in ways associated with scientific inquiry, children will learn to do the following:

◆ Ask questions
◆ Plan investigations
◆ Conduct investigations using observations, appropriate tools, and techniques to gather data
◆ Organize their thoughts, thinking logically about relationships between evidence and explanations
◆ Reflect on and make generalizations about their findings, considering alternative explanations
◆ Communicate their ideas to others (NAP, 1996)

Asking Questions

Anyone who has worked with kindergarten children knows that four- and five-year-olds are at their peak question-asking age. Their "Whys?" and "Hows?" are endless. Many times, though, children are not really interested in an answer. They simply use questions to keep the conversation going or to gain attention. Teachers want to build on children's natural questioning by encouraging them to ask questions in order to try to understand reality. "What kind of spider is it?" asked Ms. Benesh, focusing the children's observations and stimulating their questioning.

A measure of psychological safety is necessary in order to question. It is difficult to question when you feel insecure or think your ideas and questions will be ridiculed. Children in Ms. Benesh's kindergarten clearly knew that they were respected, and they felt safe to question: "Why is it climbing?" "Will it bite?" "Let's write our questions on a chart," responded Ms. Benesh, "that way we won't forget any of them."

Planning Investigations

Kindergarten children are not very skillful at making plans. Limited by their cognitive immaturity, four- and five-year-olds have problems determining what is important to focus on and what is not. Nor are they skillful at remembering or making associations, taking other perspectives in solving problems, or anticipating long-range consequences when making decisions. This, coupled with their lack of background knowledge and experience, negates children's ability to make solid, rational plans.

Despite this fact, or perhaps because of it, children are involved in planning investigations of their world. Four-year-olds will be involved in on-the-spot, spontaneous planning. Individual four-year-olds or small groups may be asked to think about what they will do next, how they could find an answer to their question, or what they might need to solve a problem they are facing. "Is the spider an insect?

How can we find out?" Five-year-olds are ready for more formal planning. They may brainstorm about what they want to study and how they will go about their study.

Conducting Investigations

Young children learn about their world and themselves in many ways. They observe and use tools to collect information and data. Learning to observe is essential in the scientific process. By encouraging children to use all their senses, you can strengthen their observation skills. Field trips are especially useful in fostering observation skills. Whether a trip is within the school building, school yard, or immediate community, children have opportunities to gather information through the senses.

Observation.   Observation is a process that continues throughout the day. Ms. Benesh used the spider on the wall as an opportunity to help children locate information by observing. Look for ways to challenge children as they observe. Questions such as "What else do you see? Is it larger than . . .? Smaller than . . .? How does it feel?" and such statements as "Look at this part," "Find another one just like it," "It's green just like . . .," and "Look at the dots on it" help children collect information through close observation of the environment.

Other information can be located in references and resource materials. Locating information through the library and media does not take the place of direct observation but is used in addition to it. When children ask, "Where does the garbage go after it's in the truck?", "Why did the orange tree die?", or "How does the telephone work?", you can reply, "I don't know, but let's find out." In this way, children can use prints, photographs, pamphlets, magazines, newspapers, maps, and other reference materials to collect information.

People who are experts in different areas of the life, physical, and earth sciences are another resource for children's learning. Children can visit veterinarians, scientists, or stores and shops and observe community helpers at work. Or these experts can visit the classroom, bringing with them the tools they use or examples of their work.

Organizing and Interpreting Information

Once children have collected information, they must organize it. Using the notes they collected, the records they kept, and the photographs of themselves at work in the field, children organize their findings in charts, sketches, tables, graphs, pictures , or other forms of record. In the process they will classify, compare and contrast, summarize, and interpret the information, ideas, and questions that arise from their observations and fieldwork.

Graphs, one way of presenting information in summary form, can be used by young children. Graphing—portraying information in pictorial form—is usually introduced to children in the fourth grade. However, when kindergarten children graph their own experiences, they appear to grasp readily the relationships and information the graphs illustrate. "Amy has the most brothers in her family; see—she has more boys on our family graph than anybody else," pointed out

Cannala, age four, to the visitor, demonstrating that, although she was only four years old, she could interpret pictures in the form of a graph and gather useful information.

When children actually use a graph as Cannala did, you know they understand that information can be obtained from pictorial representation. To increase children's ability to use graphs, you might ask them to show which has the most, the least, more than, less than, or fewer than and encourage them to discuss the representations of the graph.

Reflecting, Generalizing, and Reaching Conclusions

Having collected, compared, classified, and contrasted information, children need time to think and reflect, draw conclusions, and make generalizations, connecting two ideas or two or more concepts. The process of generalizing, or connecting one idea with another, cannot be taught but can be learned only through experiences. The child who says, "Mud and paint are the same, they both feel slippery," could not have done so without experiencing both paint and mud. The child who states the generalization that everyone has a home could not have done so without first observing the homes of rabbits, birds, and classmates. Both children could have collected information from various media and then reflected on, organized, and analyzed this information (Seefeldt & Galper, 2002). Teachers can help by doing the following:

◆ Asking children to stop working on a problem or project—to pull away and think again about what they want to accomplish, what they have done so far to achieve this goal, and what they still have to do.
◆ Helping children organize their ideas. Either group or individual activities enable children to do so. They may dictate or write a story, create a book or chart, or write a poem. Journal writing, keeping a diary, or writing "My History in Kindergarten" are other ways for children to organize their ideas.

Communicating with Others

An investigation is not finished until children can communicate their ideas and findings to others. The act of communication helps children clarify and rethink their ideas. In the process, they search for symbols and ways to make their ideas clear to others as well. You might ask children to communicate their findings, ideas, and conclusions to others. Children might also do the following:

◆ Describe and discuss how they completed their project, found a solution to some problem, or put on a play
◆ Report to the class, either by speaking, writing, or dictating to the teacher, who then reports to the others
◆ Draw, paint, or model something that describes their findings
◆ Act out a skit, play, or story, telling all about the topic
◆ Find ways through movement, song, and dance to convey their feelings and ideas

CONTENT OF THE LIFE, PHYSICAL, AND EARTH SCIENCES

Developing the skills and attitudes of scientific inquiry is considered critical. Regardless, children must have something to think about and study if they are to develop scientific inquiry skills and gain knowledge and understanding of the world in which they live (Rakow & Bell, 1998; Ross, 2000).

The content of the life, physical, and earth sciences is truly overwhelming. Teachers must make decisions about what content to include in the already crowded kindergarten curriculum. They begin by consulting national standards, **state or local scope and sequence charts,** and other curriculum guides. These identify hundreds of concepts key to the fields and describe how they can best be introduced to young children.

It is not feasible to introduce kindergarten children to the multitude of concepts listed in the standards or other guides. When faced with the vastness of scientific content, it is helpful to remember that kindergarten is just the beginning of children's scientific learning. The concepts children develop while in kindergarten will be embryonic and incomplete and may be inaccurate. Still, they will form the necessary foundation for later and more sophisticated scientific learning.

Some teachers select content on the basis of two guidelines. First, because they know that children gain skills in scientific inquiry and learn best through firsthand experiences, they choose content that children can experience for themselves, in their here-and-now world (Cartwright, 2000; Dewey, 1944). The other criterion is children's interests. As Ms. Benesh demonstrated, children will learn concepts more readily, like counting, when they are interested in the content.

Children become acquainted with the variety of life.

The science standards outline what students should know, understand, and be able to do over the course of K–12 education. The standards for physical sciences include the following:

1. The study of the properties of objects and materials in their world
2. Understanding that these are made of many things
3. Properties can be changed

Standards for the life sciences that can be included in the kindergarten are as follows:

1. Knowledge and understanding that the earth is filled with a variety of organisms
2. Organisms can survive only in environments that meet their basic needs

The earth sciences standards include the concepts of the following:

1. The earth is the place we live
2. The atmosphere (the sky) surrounds the earth, and the earth and sky change

The Life Sciences

The National Academy Press claims that the study of the life sciences should be designed to answer children's questions by introducing them to the key concepts that the earth is filled with a variety of organisms, each of which has basic needs and different life cycles. As in Ms. Benesh's kindergarten, children's sense of wonder with living things, their life cycles, and their habitats dictate which content from the life sciences will be a part of the kindergarten curriculum (Seefeldt & Barbour, 1998).

The earth is filled with a variety of organisms, each with its own basic needs. Take other trips in and around the school to identify all the things that live in the children's environment. You might focus children's observations on plants by asking them how many different plants are growing in the cracks covering their playyard. Back in the classroom, count the plants and categorize them by type. Which are the three most prevalent plants found? Consult reference books to identify the names of the plants. Repeat the trip during different seasons of the year to find out which plants grow in different seasons.

Children observe plant life in their environment.

In a five-year-old kindergarten, each child can make his or her own terrarium. Large, clear plastic food jars can be obtained from the cafeteria or a local restaurant. Those lidded, plastic containers that cookies and other baked goods come in are just as handy and will do as well. Make a chart for children to follow as they build their terrarium. They will fill the bottom with gravel for drainage, add a piece or two of charcoal to prevent spoilage, and cover with planting soil.

Each child creates the terrarium, choosing two small green plants, two pieces of moss, two rocks, and two ferns from a variety of plants. Then, as the plants grow, measure them (Hinnant, 1999). Which grew the tallest? Which was the first to blossom? Which was the first to make new shoots? Which stayed the same?

Look for animal life on the playyard or in the community. A variety of animal and insect life is found under rocks, stones, or logs. Do a trial run first, however. If you find scorpions, black widow spiders, or other poisonous insects or other animals that live under rocks or in logs, you should choose another activity to study the variety of life in the children's environment.

Dig a small square of playyard dirt or ask children to bring a plastic bag full of dirt from their own backyard. In the classroom, spill a small amount of one sample of dirt onto a piece of paper. Look at it with magnifying glasses. What do the children see? Heat the dirt by placing a light over it. The heat of the light will make any insects in the dirt move to a cooler place. You might identify earthworms, insect larvae and pupae, woodlice, earthworms, spiders, centipedes, or egg cases of insects in addition to grains of sand in the soil, plants, leaves, stems, and roots.

Giving each child a clipboard and a marker, go on an insect hunt. Divide the group into sketchers and photographers. The sketchers will draw insects they see, and the photographers will take their picture. Switch halfway though the trip.

Organize your findings using an overhead projector to count and categorize the number and type of insects you saw. Consult reference books to find out the names of the insects, their habitat, and their other functions.

Connect home and school by asking parents to become involved in children's hunt for insect and animal life. Write parents, telling them about your insect/animal hunts at school and asking them to continue this work in their home or when they are on trips.

Organisms can survive only in environments that meet their needs. The world has many different environments, and distinct environments support the life of different types of organisms.

To teach children this concept, extend the insect hunt to another neighborhood in your city or area. E-mail another kindergarten class, asking them to conduct an insect hunt and to e-mail their findings back to you. Go further afield and contact a kindergarten in another region to join you in your insect hunt. Now children can answer questions about how insects are alike and different in various regions of the earth and why.

Caring for living things in the kindergarten is one way for children to gain concepts that distinct environments support the life of different types of organisms. Before introducing living things in the classroom, teachers, aides, and children must make a commitment to providing the optimal living environment for whatever animal they choose to keep in their classroom. If the animals or insects were collected on a science walk, they should be released to their natural habitat once they have been observed.

Insect farms fascinate children. An ant farm is reasonable to include in the classroom. You can find ants almost anywhere. Dig a shovel full of ants and dirt, placing them into a large, clear plastic jar and covering the outside with dark construction paper. A secure lid is necessary, or place the jar in a pan of water, which will inhibit the ants from going outside the jar. Very small bits of food and an occasional drop or two of water are enough to feed them. After a week or so, remove the paper from the outside of the jar. Children can sketch and record the tunnels they observe. In one kindergarten the children found that the ants cared for aphids, milking them for honey.

A class terrarium can be established. A leaky aquarium, with a gravel bottom, a few bits of charcoal and earth, a branch or two, some living plants, and a pan of water, makes a fine home for lizards, chameleons, worms, praying mantises, snails, or frogs. The nature of the habitat will change depending on which animal or animals the terrarium will house.

A truly balanced aquarium requires little care or changing. Snails and other scavenger fish will clean debris, and plants supply the necessary oxygen. Feeding fish living insects is enough of an introduction to the life chain for five-year-olds. If you do not wish to do so, show children how to feed the fish very small amounts of food. Children can record the amount and date of feeding.

Using the Scientific Method.   Throughout, focus on the processes of the scientific method. Encourage children to use all their senses as they observe the life around them and different habitats. Consult reference books, use videos and other media to extend and expand children's firsthand experiences, and provide time for children to reflect, organize, and communicate their findings and ideas (Sloan, 1999).

Plan ways that children can organize their findings. Ask children to reflect on their experiences with materials. Categorize and classify things children have observed by size, shape, color, texture, or what the object is made of or by type of plant, animal, or insect life and where these live. Have them sketch the objects and write about them.

Children observe and use other scientific skills.

The Physical Sciences

Kindergarten children are introduced to the ideas that objects have many properties: size, weight, shape, color, temperature, and the ability to react with other substances. These can be measured using tools such as rulers, balances, and thermometers.

Building with blocks, handling objects, splashing in water, and playing in sand, children experience the properties of the objects in their world. In the kindergarten, the goal now is to focus children's observations on the physical properties of their world, name these, describe what they are made of, and examine, experiment with, and reflect on these objects.

To encourage children to focus on the properties of materials, you could make science tool kits. These are made of shoulder bags or backpacks and are perfect for children to take along on walking field trips or to use in their room, the school, or the playyard. With a science tool kit, children are turned into scientists who have all the equipment necessary with which to study the physical properties of their world (Holt, 1977).

Fill the science kits with the following:

- A magnifying glass or two wrapped in soft cloth
- Thermometers (one with a string for hanging) and also wrapped
- Tape measures or arbitrary measures such as wooden dowels, yarn, or ribbons
- Plastic bags and twist-close wires
- Transparent plastic collecting jars and boxes
- Mirrors
- A flashlight
- Tape
- A small garden trowel and a couple of sturdy spoons for digging
- Clipboards or pads of paper, pencils, crayons, and markers

You might plan different types of field trips to teach children how to use their science kits.

On a trip through the school building , ask children to look for different colors, shapes, and sizes that they notice within the building or even within a room of the building. Perhaps they can sketch a triangle window on their paper and compare it to a sketch of a rectangular window.

Stop to measure things that interest children. You might start by asking them to measure the door, the hall, windows, or a counter. Children could measure using their feet or hands, the tape measure, or wooden dowels. As they measure the things in their school, ask them to describe the height, width, and depth of these. Which is the longest thing they found? The shortest, tallest, and widest? Teach children the vocabulary of tall, thin, wide, narrow, shiny, low, bright, or tiny instead of the usual big or small.

Extend children's ability to observe by taking a trip through the building to discover different textures in the building or outside the school. Ask them to feel the textures and why different things feel rough or smooth. Use the magnifying glasses so that children can actually see why different surfaces are rough or smooth.

Take large pieces of newsprint and blunt, chunky crayons with the paper removed to make "rub-overs" of the textures they find. Placing the paper over the texture of a tree trunk, sidewalk, screen grating, or concrete block, children rub over the paper with the side of their crayon, actually feeling the differences between rough and smooth, and observe the texture appearing on the paper. Back in the classroom, children could discuss the textures they noted, observe other textures in the room with their hands and eyes, and try to incorporate roughness and smoothness in their drawings and paintings.

Five-year-olds can classify textures as rough or smooth. Have them cut different shapes from their rub-overs to paste under the category of rough or smooth. Name and count the things that were rough or smooth.

Back in the classroom, children can build their school with boxes or hollow blocks and draw or write about the things they saw in their school. They do not have to focus only on the physical materials of the school but, depending on their interests and your goals, can expand their observations to include the following:

◆ Who works in the school, what are their roles are, and where do they live?
◆ How many machines in the school office are used to communicate with others?
◆ How many rooms are in the school? How many are for children, furnaces, water heaters, and other school equipment and how many are for adults?
◆ How and why was the school given its name?

Go on other trips to identify the properties of the things in their world. You could take a return trip to the fire station. The first trip would have been to see the fire station, fire fighters, and so on, and the purpose of the return trip would be to examine the physical properties of the fire truck and other things. Children can feel the smoothness of the truck and the roughness of the tires and record the different shapes and sizes at the fire station. What is round? What is square? Which is the longest ladder on the truck? Back in the classroom they could make a group book called "At the Fire Station," paint or construct fire trucks, or make a collage and drawing of the fire station.

Children begin to understand that the things in their world are made of many things. "What is it made of?" is another question to ask children while on field trips in and around the school. With clipboards in hand, have children mark all the things they find made of wood, metal, concrete, plastic, or other building material. Start with their own room, then expand to the school building. A homework assignment could be to find and categorize the building materials in their home or neighborhood.

Ask children to be a scientist and find out what a milk carton is made of. Scrape the wax off the carton. Open it up and lay it flat to discover that the carton is made of heavy cardboard covered with wax. What are other things made of? Look at children's toys. What are they made of? What are children's shoes made of? How many children have shoes that are made of several materials, not just one? Have children draw their shoes or make a graph of how many materials are found in one pair of shoes. Make a chart of what shoes are made of and read the poem "Choosing Shoes" by Ffrida Wolfe:

Choosing Shoes
New shoes, new shoes,
Red and pink and blue shoes,
Tell me, what would you chose

If they let us buy?
Buckle shoes, bow shoes,
Pretty pointy toe shoes,
Strappy cappy low shoes;
Let's have some to try.
Bright shoes, white shoes,
Dandy dance by night shoes,
Perhaps a little tight shoes;
Like some, so would I.

Write a class poem of shoes that children would like to buy and what and how they are made.

When objects are checked for safety, five-year-olds can take apart discarded telephones, clocks, or watches and classify the materials they find inside. You might provide them with toys that no longer work, such as trucks, cars, or even dolls. Again, all need to be safety checked, and ask them to find out what materials were used to make these. Make sure that they record what they find inside, sketching or writing about their research.

Graphs can be made to organize the textures, shapes, sizes, and materials children have observed. A "Texture Book" scrapbook could hold samples of rub-overs, or a "Shapes in Our School" book that includes children's drawings and stories of the shapes they found in their school could be made. A sorting activity would be useful

CHILDREN STUDY THEIR WORLD

To help children collect information about the physical properties and things in their world, teachers can do the following:

◆ Give each child a clipboard, paper, and marker. On a trip to a home supply store to purchase plants, give children a paper marked into fours. Label the quarters "Plants," "Tools," "Plant Food," and "Other Things," and include pictures of these. Children can draw the things they see during their trip in these squares. Using clipboards, have children take notes about what they saw and why. When the photos are developed, they can be mounted in scrapbooks or on charts or just left on a table for children to sort through and talk about.

◆ Take along pieces of yarn to circle places on the playyard for children to observe.

◆ Have children make viewing tubes (empty cardboard rolls that they have decorated) to look through to spot birds, insects, special leaves, or blossoms.

◆ Make collecting bins to take on a trip so that children can categorize leaves, seed pods, or rocks as they find them in the field.

◆ Use hula hoops to place on the ground and ask groups to observe and record everything they see within their hoop.

◆ Extend children's ability to look by providing them with inexpensive cameras. You can solicit donations from local businesses or ask your school to keep a supply of inexpensive cameras and film available for all classes. Remember that it is not necessary for each child to have his or her own camera because children can take turns. Show them how to look through the camera and frame what they are taking.

◆ Take photographs of the children observing and collecting information to use back in the classroom. Digital cameras permit duplication of photographs for books or to be given to individual children and their families.

for children to categorize the building materials found in their school and home. See the box on the bottom of page 270 for ideas on how children can study their world.

Materials exist in different states: solid, liquid, and gas. Some materials can be changed from one state to another by heating or cooling.

The concept that materials change is central to all the physical sciences. This important idea is also highly abstract and includes the concept of the atomic structure of matter and the conservation of energy. These complex and abstract ideas have their foundation in children's observations and reflection on their experiences with change while in kindergarten (Marxen, 1995).

Cooking is one way for children to observe, record, and reflect on how matter changes. Beat some egg whites. Separate the whites of a couple of eggs from the yolks, add a pinch of salt, and beat them with a whisk, with children taking turns talking about how the egg whites change and why. When stiffly whipped, add a bit of sugar and mix again. Have children take turns dropping a spoonful of the mixture on a greased baking tray and bake for 2 hours at 200 degrees. Have children make a sketch of their experience, recording how the egg whites changed. Ask them to think about how motion and heat changed the whites.

Using the method of one-cup cooking (Johnson & Plemons, 1984) puts children in charge. With one-step cooking, children follow a recipe chart and prepare their own individual portion of a food. This gives them practice in reading and following a recipe, making their own decisions, and experiencing the consequences of those decisions. Begin with something simple, like stuffing celery or making lemonade or instant pudding.

Integrate language experiences into the study of change (Seefeldt & Galper, 2000; Trepanier-Street, 2000). Eat blueberries when you read *Blueberries for Sal* (McCloskey, 1976), prepare bread with marmalade or butter and vote on which is best after reading *The King's Breakfast* (Milne, 1961), or make curds and whey to try along with "Little Miss Muffet" (Barclay, Benelli, & Schoon, 1999).

Water is a perfect media with which to study physical change (Planje, 1997). With cooling, it turns into ice; with heat, into steam. On a hot day, get a block of ice and put it on the playyard. You will not have to do much prompting to use the block of ice as a learning tool. Children's fascination will permit you to focus their observations on what will happen, how small the ice will become, how long it will take, and what will happen to the water that is left.

Dissolving things is another way for children to observe how matter changes. It is a bit messy, but all you need is a pitcher of water that children can handle, small clear plastic cups, and a tray of baby jars filled with a variety of materials and wooden spoons. You might place sand, instant coffee, gravel, salt, sugar, bits of paper or cloth, and other things in the jars. Children are directed to pour a bit of water into a plastic cup and add a small spoonful of a material, observe what happens, and record their observations. The class then categorizes the materials into what did and did not dissolve.

The Earth Sciences

The purpose of the earth sciences in the kindergarten is for children to effectively understand the properties of their earth, the sky, and changes in the earth and sky

(NAP, 1996). Through firsthand study of content from the social sciences, children will gain embryonic concepts of (1) the earth as the place they live, (2) the sky, and (3) changes in the earth and sky. Even though children's initial ideas of these concepts will be inaccurate, incomplete, and vague, they will form the necessary foundation for the development of fully formed concepts and ways of thinking later in life (Kilmer & Hofman, 1995; Seefeldt, 2001).

The Earth Is the Place We Live.   Children are fascinated with the earth. They dig in it, explore the nature of water, let sand sift through their fingers, and ask questions. From these initial sensory and exploratory experiences in their home and school, children learn that the earth is the place they live, that the earth is covered with different surfaces and landforms, and that humans and nature change the earth.

The earth is covered with land and water and is a part of the solar system. The physical characteristics—landforms, water bodies, climate, soils, natural vegetation, and animal life—and the human ideas and actions that have shaped their character are included in the concept of place.

The playyard, nearby vacant lot, park, or children's backyards are convenient laboratories for the study of the earth. Taking along your science kits, take field trips to collect rocks, observe plant life and where it grows, and become aware that soil varies from place to place in its color, texture, and reaction to water (Fromboluti & Seefeldt, 1999).

As you walk along, point out and name the surfaces covering the earth. "How does this gravel feel under your feet? "This is concrete—how does it feel? How do you think it got here?"

Are there surfaces that are slippery or difficult to walk or ride on? Ask children why they think this is so. Take turns walking or running on different surfaces and stopping on a given signal. On the playyard, children could experiment with riding their tricycles on the blacktop, grass, or a gravel or sandy area. Talk with them about the differences in the soft, slick, smooth, and hard surfaces of the playyard and what these mean to their safety when walking or riding wheeled toys.

As you study the earth, ask children to name, count, and record the different surfaces, either made by humans or nature, that you find. Take photos of children exploring their earth and construct a poster "Surfaces on Our Earth."

On another day, walk a little farther from the school. Ask the children to note the different types of soil they see. You could divide the children into groups of three or four with an adult volunteer. Give each group an assignment card with directions and a space for recording findings.

Assign small groups of children to do the following:

◆ Find out what color the soil is where plants are growing
◆ Note the color of soil where no plants are growing
◆ Collect soil samples in small plastic bags for examination once back in the room
◆ Look for footprints in the soil, in the sand, or on the sidewalk surface
◆ Record what different types of soil feel like

Back in the classroom, discuss, compare, and contrast soils. Order the soils by color from darkest to lightest or by texture from sandy or loamy to rocky or dense. Collect a variety of soils. Experiment with the soil. This will be messy, so cover the table with plastic or paper. Arrange for children to "test" different soils by placing different soils in a cup of water and observing what happens to the soil:

◆ How long does it take for the soil to settle on the bottom?
◆ Which soils change color?
◆ Which soils change the color of the water?

Give each child a small clipboard, a marker, and paper to record his or her findings. The goal is to have children play with soil and water and to find out how different soils feel and behave in water, not necessarily to make profound hypotheses. Still, you will want to talk with children about their experiments.

If you are not able to find a variety of soils near your school, ask parents to let their children fill a plastic sandwich bag with soil from their yard or somewhere in their neighborhood, noting what was growing or living in the soil. Or you could go farther away from the school by working with a school in another area of the county or city, asking them to send you samples of soil or drawings of plants and animals living in the soil to compare with the soil near you.

Identify the bodies of water or other landforms in the area that could be used as a part of your geographic laboratory. Make a list of the things you see and words that can be used to describe these. Are there rivers, lakes, ponds, hills, or mountains that children observe in their daily lives? You could involve parents by asking them to take their children to see these landforms, name them, and talk with them about what makes these places special.

If it is possible, take the children to see a prominent landform in your area. If you live near a desert, the mural could be titled "In Our Large, Large Desert" or, near a mountain, "In the Beautiful Mountain," and so on. If it is not possible for children to experience spaces that make their neighborhood and community special, you could view videos, movies, or photographs and read books about these places together.

Try to personalize these vicarious experiences. You might do the following:

◆ Talk about and show pictures of places children were born, have lived, or will be moving to. Their parents may be able to share photographs or videos of these places.
◆ When you eat oranges, apples, pineapples, blueberries, or other foods, find out where they were grown. Show children the place on a map and pictures of apple or orange orchards. Find out what foods are raised in the place you live.
◆ Sing songs about different places. Children enjoy learning "This Land Is Your Land" or the opening phrases of "America, the Beautiful."

The Sky. Because children cannot touch the sky or the things in it, learning experiences with the sky are based on observing the sky, the effects of the earth's rotation around the sun, and the moon, clouds, and stars.

Caution: Looking directly at the sun can damage children's eyes. Ask children to focus only on the clouds and the blue sky and not to look directly at the sun.

Take children outside to observe the sky. The only way children can gain concepts about the sky is for them to be able to observe it and the effects of the earth's rotation. Start by reading Christina Rossetti's "Clouds." The poem begins, "White clouds, white clouds, on a blue hill." Or you might choose to read Tomie De Paola's *The Cloud Book*, Eric Carle's *Little Cloud*, or Charles G. Shaw's *It Looked Like Spilt Milk* (Seefeldt & Galper, 2000).

After you read the poem or story outside, lie on the grass and look up. Ask children what they see. Ask them what words they would use to describe the clouds they see. Back in the classroom, ask children to draw and write about what they saw in the clouds.

Ask children to talk about what they saw in the sky. Ask what colors they saw. What else is blue? How does the blue of the sky compare to blue clothing, the blue on a butterfly's wings, or blue eyes? Have art materials ready so that children can represent their ideas about clouds and sky and reflect on their experiences. White and blue construction paper and different shades of white and blue paints, brushes, and markers could be added to the usual array of art materials. Children can write their own stories to accompany their paintings and drawings or dictate it to you.

The Sky Changes.   Observing the sky over time, children will be able to identify changes in the sky and clouds. Observing clouds, teach children to predict what the weather will be like. See the Types of Clouds box for a description of different types of clouds.

On a day when the sky is filled with cumulus clouds, go outside to watch the clouds go by again. This day, name the clouds. Tell children that cumulus clouds are called cauliflower clouds because some people think they are shaped liked cauliflower. Ask the children what they think the clouds look like. Tell children that sometimes cumulus clouds bring rain. Have children predict whether the cumulus clouds they see will bring a storm or rain. Make a chart to record children's predictions.

When nimbus clouds are in the sky, repeat the experience, first observing the clouds and then predicting whether they will bring storms and rain.

Start a chart of clouds. Ask children to keep track of the clouds each day for a week. Have children draw a picture of what they see and then make a check if it rained.

The sky changes from day to night. Have children make a "Day Book." Ask each child to think of the things they do during the day and draw a picture of their favorite daytime activity. Encourage them to write about the activity or dictate the story of the activity to you. Punch holes in the drawings and place between two construction paper covers. The title of the book is "Our Day Book," by the Kindergarten. Read Tomie De Paola's *The Wind and the Sun*, a fanciful tale of the sun and wind, or Jennifer Armstrong's "Sunshine, Moonshine," a poem of the sun and moon shining down on a boy spending his day at sea.

Observing changes in the night sky necessitates involving parents by asking them to look at the

TYPES OF CLOUDS

Cumulus clouds are cauliflower shaped. They often develop into clouds that bring thunderstorms.

Cirrus clouds are high, thin, and wispy. They look like tufts of hair. They are so high that the water they contain is frozen into ice crystals.

Stratus clouds are flat, gray clouds.

Nimbus clouds are dark and threatening.

night sky with their children and asking children to draw what they see in the night sky. Have them chart the changes in the moon. Sometimes the moon is round as a ball, and other times it looks like a half a ball or just a sliver of melon. You might send home some paper and a small box of markers so that parents and children can draw the shape of the moon and where they see it in the night sky once a week or so. Have them send the drawings of the night sky to school so that you can talk about what you have observed and learned about the night sky.

Use the pictures the children drew of the night sky with their parents to start discussions and study of the night sky. When children bring their drawings of the shape of the moon, mount these on a poster board and talk about how the shape of the moon changes. You can tell children that the changes of the moon are related to the rotation of the earth around the sun. Show them pictures of the moon in an encyclopedia or other reference book, but do not try to show them a model of the earth, sun, moon, and stars. These initial experiences will enable them to better understand this model when they are 11 or 12 years old and able to think abstractly.

The Earth Changes.   As children develop skills of observing the objects and properties of their world, they will notice that just as the sky changes, so does the earth. Some of the changes are the result of the earth's rotation on its axis around the sun; others are slow processes, such as erosion and weathering; and some are due to rapid processes such as landslides, earthquakes, and other natural phenomena. Still other changes to the earth are made by humans.

Weather conditions change the earth. The *National Science Education Standards* (NAP, 1996) advocate observing these changes, describing them by measurable quantities, such as temperature, wind direction and speed, and precipitation. Ask children to keep a class weather journal to discover weather changes over the year. They could take turns drawing a daily weather picture based on what they see out of a window or at recess (NAP, 1996). At the end of a month, the drawings could be analyzed and the number of rainy, sunny, and windy days recorded.

You might begin studying how weather changes the earth right on your own playyard or neighborhood. On a walking field trip, note any changes that have occurred because of weather conditions. It may be that a heavy rain caused the sand to float out of the box onto the cement or left rivulets of mud on the playyard. Or during a drought, children can note the hardness of the earth; the dry, powdery nature of the ground; or even cracks in the earth.

One class decided to make changes in their playyard. As a group they brainstormed about the things they wanted on their dream playyard. An architect met with them and went over their plans, helping them make choices about what would and would not be feasible and how much the changes would cost. The kindergarten took their plans to the principal and the PTA and planned ways to finance the changes they wanted. Together they created a hill to climb and roll down, an area for digging, and places for trees.

How humans make changes in the earth on a larger scale is studied in many kindergartens. The Center for Young Children at the University of Maryland took advantage of the construction of a new recreation center across the street from the center. Throughout the construction, children observed, recorded, and made predictions. They wondered about the large mounds of earth that were created to dig the foundation of the building. To answer their questions, they interviewed truck drivers and the building supervisor.

As the building took shape, they were invited on a walk-through. With hard hats and consulting blueprints, the children tried to visualize the swimming pool and other parts of the building that were just beginning to be built. The project ended at the dedication of the building, with displays of children's drawings, graphs, and stories from the beginning to the end of the construction.

Watching a tree change on the playyard provided another kindergarten with a year's activity revolving around the concept of change. Even in tropical climates, trees change—they bud, blossom, and bear fruit. One kindergarten observed an apple tree outside the classroom for an entire year. In the fall, the children collected, counted, and sorted the leaves. They gathered apples, cut them open, saw the seed star, ate them for a snack, made applesauce, and dipped them in honey to wish one another a happy new year in celebration of Rosh Hashanna. In the spring, they recorded the first green leaves, the day of the first buds and blossoms, and the first beginnings of fruit.

EVALUATING AND ASSESSING CHILDREN'S SCIENTIFIC LEARNING

The science standards portray science as a rich, varied, all-encompassing field (NAP, 1996). Because science includes the ability to use the processes of scientific inquiry as well as to know and understand scientific facts, concepts, principles, laws, and theories, assessment and evaluation of children's scientific learning will also be multidimensional and complex. No one single method will be sufficient to determine children's growth in inquiry skills or scientific concepts. Further, because scientific inquiry and learning take place each day on a continual basis, the evaluation process is ongoing as well. It will include both spontaneous and informal observations of children, more structured observations and individual interviews, and collections of children's work.

Observe children on walking field trips. What do they attend to as you walk along? How involved are they in measuring objects in their environment or in finding out what they are made of? How many materials can they name? Note growth in children's abilities to do the following:

◆ Ask questions
◆ Plan investigations
◆ Conduct investigations using observations, appropriate tools, and techniques to gather data
◆ Organize their thoughts, thinking logically about relationships between evidence and explanations

- ◆ Reflect on and make generalizations about their findings, considering alternative explanations
- ◆ Communicate their ideas to others (NAP, 1996)

To further evaluate children's growth in using scientific inquiry, observe when and how children use their science tool kits. Note when they are used, where, and how children used them. Are they doing more than just playing with the tools and taking the leap into putting two or more ideas together to form generalizations?

Specific concepts, facts, and information can be assessed through the use of photographs taken of the children on field trips or in the playyard. Show individual children the photographs, asking them to tell you about what they are doing and learning. Additionally, can they identify:

- ◆ the names of the different surfaces of the earth in the school yard and neighborhood?
- ◆ the names of plants and animals pictured in the photographs?
- ◆ different landforms pictured?

Another way to evaluate children's concepts of the life, physical, and earth sciences is through structured interviews. You will have to design questions that address the specific content you have studied. The idea is not to check whether children have memorized certain items of information but rather to probe "for students' understanding, reasoning, and the utilization of knowledge" (NAP, 1996, p. 82):

- ◆ Ask children to tell you everything they know about . . . (the earth or sky, how they change, or another topic).
- ◆ Ask children to go deeper and ask "why" they think as they do. Record what children say.
- ◆ Ask children what they think they would like to learn or know about a topic: "What else would you like to learn about spiders?"

Interviewing children before and after an experience permits you to draw conclusions about their learning. You can judge their learning by counting the number of things they said, the accuracy of their statements, and the complexity of their ideas before and after the experience.

Collecting samples of children's drawings, writing, data collection, graphs, and other products to include in their portfolios gives you the opportunity to assess how well children are able to communicate their findings and ideas in pictorial or written form.

Communicate the conclusions of your assessment and evaluation to parents and other school personnel. Convincing and compelling evidence of children's scientific learning is the result of multidimensional assessment and evaluation based on observations, interviews, and collecting and analyzing work samples.

IN SUMMARY

Science in the kindergarten is doing and thinking, and making the two come together. In the kindergarten, science is an everyday occurrence. Teachers carefully plan to enable children to gain both scientific inquiry skills and scientific concepts from the life, physical, and earth sciences. The *National Science Education Standards* and the National Council for the Social Studies both suggest that the skills of scientific inquiry be developed during the early years of life. Therefore, kindergartens are places where children are encouraged and taught how to ask questions, plan and conduct investigations, organize their thoughts and findings, reflect on and make generalizations, and communicate their ideas to others.

Content from the life, physical, and earth sciences gives children something to study. From the multitude of scientific concepts listed in the standards, teachers select those that children can learn through firsthand experiences and are of high interest to children.

In the physical sciences these might include studying the properties of the materials in their environment and understanding that these objects are made of many things and that properties can change. The life sciences include the concepts that the earth is filled with a variety of organisms, which can survive only in environments that meet their basic needs. In the earth sciences, children study the nature of the earth and sky and the changes in both.

EXTEND YOUR IDEAS

1. Observe children interacting on the playyard. Record the times they refer to concepts from the life, physical, or earth sciences. How accurate and complete are their ideas of science? Discuss in class how you, as a teacher, would extend and clarify their ideas.

2. Obtain a copy of the *National Science Education Standards* from National Academy Press, 2101 Constitution Ave. NW, Box 285, Washington, DC 20055 (800-624-6424), or from the Web at *http://www.nas.edu*. Which content and concepts, from the multitude concepts and inquiry skills, should children learn by the time they leave fourth grade, which would you select to teach in your kindergarten? Why?

3. Upgrade your own understanding of scientific concepts by taking a science course, visiting a science museum, or reading books about the life, physical, and earth sciences.

4. Make a sample science tool kit to use with children. Include tools that would be useful in your area. You might include an insect cage, containers for seed pods, rocks, or different types of soil. If you can, give the tool kit to a group of children and observe and record how they use the kit.

RESOURCES

Contacting the National Science Foundation and the American Association for the Advancement of Science will put you in touch with a multitude of resources.

American Association for the Advancement of Science
1200 New York Ave NW
Washington, DC 20005
292-326-6400
http://www.aas.org

National Science Foundation
4201 Wilson Blvd.
Arlington, VA 22280
703-306-1234
http://www.nsf.gov

REFERENCES

Barclay, K., Benelli, C., & Schoon, S. (1999). Making the connection: Science and literacy. *Childhood Education, 75,* 146–152.

Cartwright, S. (2000). Education is experience: The rest is only information. *Young Children, 55*(4), 14–16.

Dewey, J. (1944). *Democracy and education.* New York: The Free Press.

Fromboluti, C. S., & Seefeldt, C. (1999). *Early childhood: Where learning begins: Geography.* Washington, DC: U.S. Department of Education.

Hinnant, H. A. (1999). Growing gardens and mathematicians: More books and math for young children. *Young Children, 54,* 23–26.

Holt, B. G. (1977). *Science with young children.* Washington, DC: National Association for the Education of Young Children.

Johnson, B., & Plemons, B. (1984). *One-cup cooking.* Mt. Rainier, MD: Gryphon House.

Kilmer, S., & Hofman, H. (1995). Transforming science curriculum. In S. Bredekamp & T. Rosegrant (Eds.), *Reaching potentials: Transforming early childhood curriculum and assessment* (Vol. 2) (pp. 43–64). Washington, DC: National Association for the Education of Young Children.

Landry, C. E., & Forman, G. E. (1999). Research on early science education. In C. Seefeldt (Ed.), *The early childhood curriculum: Current findings in theory and practice* (3rd ed., pp. 133–158). New York: Teachers College Press.

Marxen, C. E. (1995). Push, pull, toss, tilt, swing: Physics for young children. *Childhood Education, 71,* 212–217.

McCloskey, R. (1976). *Blueberries for Sal.* New York: Viking.

Milne, A. A. (1961). The King's breakfast. In A. A. Milne, *When we were very young,* (p. 57). London: Dutton.

National Academy Press. (1996). *National science education standards.* Washington, DC: Author.

National Council for the Social Studies. (1998). *Curriculum standards for social studies: Expectations of excellence.* Washington, DC: Author.

Planje, A. (1997). Playing with water in primary ways. *Young Children, 52*(2), 33–41.

Rakow, S. J., & Bell, M. J. (1998). Science and young children: The message from the National Science Education Standards. *Childhood Education, 74,* 164–167.

Ross, M. E. (2000). Science their way. *Young Children, 55*(2), 6–14.

Seefeldt, C. (2001). *Social studies for the preschool/primary child* (6th ed.). Upper Saddle River, NJ: Merrill/Prentice Hall.

Seefeldt, C., & Barbour, N. (1998). *Early childhood education: An introduction* (4th ed.). Upper Saddle River, NJ: Merrill/Prentice Hall.

Seefeldt, C., & Galper, A. (2000). *Active experiences for active children: Social Studies.* Upper Saddle River, NJ: Merrill/Prentice Hall.

Seefeldt, C., & Galper, A. (2002). *Active experiences for active children: Science.* Upper Saddle River, NJ: Merrill/Prentice Hall.

Sloan, M. W. (1999). All kinds of projects for your classroom. *Young Children, 54,* 71–72.

Trepanier-Street, M. (2000). Multiple forms of representation in long-term projects. *Childhood Education, 77,* 18–22.

INDEX